International Political Economy Series

The global political economy is in flux as a series of cumulative crises impacts its organization and governance. The IPE series has tracked its development in both analysis and structure over the last three decades. It has always had a concentration on the global South. Now the South increasingly challenges the North as the centre of development, also reflected in a growing number of submissions and publications on indebted Eurozone economies in Southern Europe. An indispensable resource for scholars and researchers, the series examines a variety of capitalisms and connections by focusing on emerging economies, companies and sectors, debates and policies. It informs diverse policy communities as the established trans-Atlantic North declines and 'the rest', especially the BRICS, rise.

More information about this series at
http://www.palgrave.com/gp/series/13996

Chithra Purushothaman

Emerging Powers, Development Cooperation and South-South Relations

palgrave
macmillan

Chithra Purushothaman
Carleton University
Ottawa, Canada

ISSN 2662-2483 ISSN 2662-2491 (electronic)
International Political Economy Series
ISBN 978-3-030-51536-2 ISBN 978-3-030-51537-9 (eBook)
https://doi.org/10.1007/978-3-030-51537-9

This Palgrave Macmillan imprint is published by the registered company Springer Nature Switzerland AG
The registered company address is: Gewerbestrasse 11, 6330 Cham, Switzerland

Acknowledgements

This book was born out of my Ph.D. thesis submitted to Jawaharlal Nehru University (JNU), New Delhi. I express my sincere gratitude to my supervisor Prof. Jayati Srivastava for her guidance, encouragement and constant support during and after my Ph.D. I am grateful to Prof. Rajesh Rajagopalan, Prof. CSR Murthy and Prof. Varun Sahni, for their guidance. The Junior and Senior fellowships from the University Grants Commission (UGC) helped fund my Ph.D. research in JNU.

My field visit to Brazil in March-April 2015 was made possible by the financial support from Indian Council of Social Science Research (ICSSR) and Jawaharlal Nehru University Field Research Fund. I am thankful to all the interviewees including government officials, policymakers and academia in Brazil and India for sharing their experiences and thoughts with me that have contributed in enriching my thesis. I particularly thank my Portuguese teacher and friend Ms. Georgia Quartin for hosting me in Brasilia.

In New Delhi, the Institute for Defence Studies and Analyses (IDSA), where I worked for two years (2017–2019), has helped me expand my research on emerging powers. I am especially grateful to my IDSA colleagues, Rajeesh Kumar and A. Vinod Kumar, for their constant encouragement to revise my thesis into a book. I would take this opportunity to thank IDSA library staff Mr. Pitambar Datt, Ms. Bhawna Mungali and Ms. Hitakshi for all their support with research materials and books.

I am grateful to Palgrave Macmillan for showing interest in this book and to my editor Timothy Shaw and his team—Anca Pusca and Katelyn Zingg—whose feedbacks did much to improve this book. The anonymous reviews organised by the publisher helped finessing the shape and form of the book.

It is my husband Rahul Nair's wholehearted support, love and his belief in my dreams that made this book possible. I dedicate this book to my parents, amma (Radhamony N. K.) and achan (P. Purushothaman), and my maternal grandparents, achachan (Konnan N. K.) and ammamma (Karthiyayani V. T.), for their selfless love and support.

Contents

Abbreviations

AAA	Accra Agenda for Action
ABC	Brazilian Cooperation Agency
ACTO	Amazon Cooperation Treaty Organization
ADB	Asian Development Bank
ADF	African Development Fund
ADR	Aid to Disaster Relief
AFD	French Development Agency
AIIB	Asian Infrastructure Investment Bank
APCTT	Asian and Pacific Centre for Transfer of Technology
ASEAN	Association of Southeast Asian Nations
AU	African Union
BAPA	Buenos Aires Plan of Action
BMZ	German Federal Ministry of Economic Development and Cooperation
BNDES	Brazilian Development Bank
BRI	Belt and Road Initiative
CAGR	Compound Annual Growth Rate
CARICOM	Caribbean Community
CELAC	Community of Latin American and Caribbean States
CEPAL	Economic Commission for Latin America
China Exim Bank	China Export-Import Bank
CIDCA	China International Development Cooperation Agency
CNPq	National Council for Scientific and Technological Development
COBRADI	Brazilian Cooperation for International Development
COMESA	Common Market of Eastern and Southern Africa

Conare	National Committee for Refugees
CPC	Communist Party of China
CPEC	China Pakistan Economic Corridor
CPR	Centre for Policy Research
CVRD	Companhia Vale de Rio Doce
DAC	Development Assistance Committee
DAG	Development Assistance Group
DCF	Development Cooperation Forum
DCOPT	Division of International Technical Cooperation
DEA	Department of Economic Affairs
DFID	Department for International Development
DPA	Development Partnership Administration
DPRK	Democratic People's Republic of Korea
EBRD	European Bank for Reconstruction and Development
ECD	Economic and Coordination Division
ECOSOC	Economic and Social Council
ECW	Economic Cooperation Wing
EMBRAPA	Brazilian Agricultural Research Corporation
EPC	Engineering Procurement Construction
EU	European Union
EXIM Bank	Export-Import Bank of India
FA	Financial Aid
FAO	Food and Agriculture Organization of the UN
FC	Federal Constitution
FDI	Foreign Direct Investment
Fiocruz	Oswaldo Cruz Foundation
FOCAC	Forum on China-Africa Cooperation
G-20	Group of Twenty
G-77	Group of 77 Countries
GDP	Gross Domestic Product
GNI	Gross National Income
GOI	Government of India
GTI-CHI	Inter-ministerial Working Group on International Humanitarian Cooperation
HIPC	Highly Indebted Poor Countries
HRF	Haiti Reconstruction Fund
IAFS	The India-Africa Forum Summit
IAM	Indian Aid Mission
IASO	Ibero-American States Organization
IATI	International Aid Transparency Initiative
IBRD	International Bank for Reconstruction and Development
ICGEB	International Center for Genetic Engineering and Biotechnology

ICM	Indian Cooperation Mission
ICRISAT	International Crops Research Institute for the Semi-Arid Tropics
IDA	International Development Association
IDB	Inter-American Development Bank
IDC	Indian Development Cooperation
IDCR	The Indian Development Cooperation Research
IDEAS	Indian Development and Economic Assistance Scheme
IDI	India Development Initiative
IFIs	International Financial Institutions
IICA	Inter-American Institute for Cooperation in Agriculture
IIDCA	India International Development Cooperation Agency
ILO	International Labour Organization
IMF	International Monetary Fund
IOC	Indian Oil Corporation
IOR-ARC	Indian Ocean Rim Association for Regional Cooperation
IOs	International Organisations
IPE	International Political Economy
IPEA	Institute for Applied Economic Research
ITEC	Indian Technical and Economic Cooperation
ITP	Investment and Technology Promotion Division
JC	Joint Commission
JICA	Japan International Cooperation Agency
LDCs	Least Developed Countries
LOCs	Lines of Credit
MCT	Ministry of Science and Technology
MCTI	Ministry of Science, Technology and Innovation
MD	Ministry of Defense
MDGs	Millennium Development Goals
MEA	Ministry of External Affairs
MEC	Ministry of Education
MERCOSUR	Southern Common Market
MINUSTAH	United Nations Stabilisation Mission in Haiti
MoCI	Ministry of Commerce and Industry
MoF	Ministry of Finance
MOFCOM	Ministry of Commerce
MoU	Memorandum of Understanding
MP	Ministry of Planning, Budget and Management
MRE	Ministry of External Relations
MS	Ministry of Health
NAM	Non-Aligned Movement
NDB	New Development Bank
NGOs	Non-Governmental Organisations

NIDC	National Industrial Development Cooperation
NIEO	New International Economic Order
OA	Official Aid
OAS	Organisation of American States
OBOR	One Belt and One Road
OCHA	Coordinator of Humanitarian Affairs
ODA	Official Development Assistance
OECD	Organisation for Economic Cooperation and Development
OEEC	Organisation for European Economic Cooperation
ONGC	Oil and Natural Gas Corporation
OPEC	Organisation of the Petroleum Exporting Countries
PALOPs	Portuguese-Speaking African Countries
PMNRF	Prime Minister's National Relief Fund
PPP	Purchasing Power Parity
PR	Presidency of the Republic
PRC	People's Republic of China
ProSavana	Mozambique Tropical Savannah Agricultural Development Project
PRSPs	Poverty Reduction Strategy Papers
RCB	Regional Centre for Biotechnology
SADC	Southern African Development Community
SAIS-CARI	School of Advanced International Studies-China Africa Research Initiative
SAPs	Structural Adjustment Programmes
SCAAP	Special Commonwealth Assistance for Africa Programme
SCO	Shanghai Cooperation Organization
SDGs	Sustainable Development Goals
SENAI	National Service for Industrial Training
SEPLAN	Secretariat for Planning
SMEs	Small and Medium Enterprises
SSC	South-South Cooperation
SSCAF	South-South Cooperation Assistance Fund
SSDC	South-South Development Cooperation
STC	Scientific and Technological Cooperation
SUBIN	Sub-Secretariat for International Technical and Economic Cooperation
SVP	Special Volunteers Programme
TA	Technical Aid
TCDC	Technical Cooperation among Developing Countries
TCS	Technical Cooperation Scheme
UERJ	State University of Rio de Janeiro
UFRJ	Federal University of Rio de Janeiro
UK	United Kingdom

UN	United Nations
UNASUR	Union of South American Nations
UnB	University of Brasilia
UNCTAD	United Nations Conference on Trade and Development
UNDEF	United Nations Democracy Fund
UNDP	United Nations Development Programme
UNESCAP	United Nations Economic and Social Commission for Asia and the Pacific
UNESCO	United Nations Educational, Scientific and Cultural Organization
UNFAO	United Nations Food and Agriculture Organization
UNFPA	United Nations Population Fund
UNIDO	UN Industrial Development Organization
UNSC	United Nations Security Council
US	United States
USAID	United States Agency for International Development
USP	University of Sao Paulo
USSR	Union of Soviet Socialist Republics
WB	World Bank
WFP	World Food Program
WTO	World Trade Organization

List of Figures

List of Tables

CHAPTER 1

Introduction: Emerging Powers as Development Assistance Providers in International Aid Architecture

The contemporary form of foreign aid emerged in response to a dramatically changing global political and economic milieu since the end of the Second World War (1939–1945). The war-torn Europe was on the verge of collapse and there was an urgent need for economic reconstruction of the European countries for their recovery from the catastrophe. This led to the introduction of the Marshall Plan[1] by the US in 1948. While the key concerns that guided the US to give foreign aid to Western Europe were the containment of Communism, getting access to natural resources and raw materials, and gaining a prominent role in the global trade and investment system, altruistic claims of the US helped them mobilise support from a wide spectrum of political opinion both at home and abroad (Tarp 2006, 26). The motives behind the US aid could therefore be characterised as multifaceted.

After the success of the Marshall Plan, the attention of the industrialised developed countries turned to the developing countries, many of which became independent in the decade of 1960s. The aid policy during this period was framed in the context of Cold War. Later, the provision of development assistance to poorer countries came to be considered as a taken-for-granted function played by all major Western democracies

[1] From 1948 to 1951, under the Marshall Plan, the Western Europe received $13 billion in aid from the US (De Long and Eichengreen 1991, 2).

C. Purushothaman, *Emerging Powers, Development Cooperation and South-South Relations*, International Political Economy Series,
https://doi.org/10.1007/978-3-030-51537-9_1

(Alesina and Dollar 2000). With the Marshall Plan began the legacy of the foreign aid programmes and aid transfers from the developed to the less-developed countries. Eventually, the North to South flows of money and resources came to be understood as an established feature of the international political economy (IPE), and the international aid architecture became a new theatre of power play between countries.

The idea of international aid architecture being exclusively a North to South flow of resources is being challenged by those countries of the Global South that are providing development assistance to other developing countries. Some of these countries despite being recipients of Western aid have been providing development assistance to their peers for more than six decades. This dual role of a recipient and a donor is played by many countries in the Global South including, China, India and Brazil. Even though their development assistance volume and scale are much smaller than the traditional donors, they have been involved in development assistance for as long as the developed countries. What is new is that these countries have increased their development assistance budgets and scope, thereby receiving much greater attention from both the Western donors and also from the recipient countries which have got more choice when it comes to donors. These developing countries are repositioning themselves from recipients to that of "providers" of development assistance, thereby endorsing and further strengthening South-South Cooperation (SSC). Even though the emerging powers are making a mark in international development through their changing roles and identities, some of them prefer not to join the traditional donors club of the Organisation for Economic Cooperation and Development (OECD)–Development Assistance Committee (DAC) and continue to maintain their Third World/ Southern identities. This book analyse the role of emerging powers as development assistance providers, their growing assistance to the Global South, their changing identities and motivations, and its overall impact on international politics.

Emerging Powers in Global Power Transition

It is the continuous struggle for power that defines international politics. The relation between countries is driven by their struggle for power in the international system (Liska 1960; Baldwin 1966; Morgenthau 1962). The nature of competition among states is continuously changing in the wake of increasing economic competition between them, thereby changing it from competition for control over territory to competition for market shares in the world economy (Strange 1995, 55). In the present scenario of economic globalisation, the chances of major wars are more or less diminishing and the possession of nuclear weapons has made wars much more dangerous and costly affair. The use of military force has, therefore, become less enticing and the use of economic instruments has become more alluring to countries seeking power shift in the international system. Strange (1995) finds growing prominence of industrial and trade policy over defence and foreign policy.

With the rising prominence of emerging powers in the international system, there are growing concerns on the changing contours of power, which seems to be shifting in favour of the emerging economies. The power structures in international politics are in constant flux, where emerging economies are gaining more traction, especially in terms of economic power which they want to translate into political influence. This power shift was increasingly evident with the high economic growth achieved by the Asian economies in the twenty-first century, especially China and India. This power transfer is taking place not just from the North to South but also from the West to East (Hoge 2004; Layne 2012). Depending on their interests and based on the issues, emerging powers are trying to create changes in the international system, which could in turn help them rise in the emerging world order. As the case may be, they are also trying to maximise their gains by taking up different roles that can cater to their aspirations and interests. The emerging powers are making their presence felt in areas that were traditionally considered as the domain of the developed countries of the Global North.

Foreign aid is an important economic instrument through which the emerging powers are trying to wield influence in international politics. Here, they are not directly challenging the international aid architecture created by the traditional donors; instead, they are slowly making inroads into the system. With the developed countries in the world increasingly looking inward and cutting down on their aid commitments, the void left by them is being filled by the emerging powers that are bringing in new dimensions and scope into foreign aid architecture. Even though some of these countries have a strong disagreement over OECD's definition and principles on foreign aid, they are not keen to reform the international aid architecture created and maintained by the great powers. Instead, they are trying to make their aid look like independent but complementary to the existing foreign aid architecture. Hence, challenging the existing system is not in their immediate interest.

As Randall Schweller (2011, 287) puts it, current system is in a state of "time's entropy" in which "the old architecture is becoming creakier and more resistant to change. New rules and arrangements will be simply piled on top of old ones". Hence, it is not great power conflict or a great power concert that would change the international order, but a time's entropy (Schweller 2011). The emerging powers choose not to be the direct challengers of the existing system, unless challenged by a great power in its core area of interest. Though their efforts are focussed on creating greater economic and political clout, they aim to achieve it through economic instruments that can assist them in the process of power transition in a hierarchical international system. The experience of the emerging powers as recipients of aid has made them realise that foreign aid helps to buy influence and is a useful tool in delivering policy outcomes from the recipients (Liska 1960). This understanding has helped the emerging powers in creating their own aid programmes for the Global South, based on the principles of SSC. Susan Strange argues that an effective way to change the current hegemonic order is to bring together "Latin American, Asians and Africans who share some of the same interests and concerns for the future" (Strange 1995, 71). By expanding their aid to the developing countries in the Global South, the emerging powers are trying to lead these countries. While several motivations drive emerging powers' assistance to the Global South, one important factor driving their assistance is their realisation of the power of aid to change the global distribution of wealth (Strange 1995). Hence, the emerging powers are looking forward to power transitions at both systemic and state levels through their foreign aid to the Global South.

Emerging Powers and Development Partnerships

Various terminologies have been used by the traditional donors to denote developing countries of the Global South who give development assistance, including non-DAC donors,[2] non-traditional donors,[3] emerging

[2] Non-DAC donors denote those countries which give foreign aid but are not a part of the OECD-DAC (Sato et. al 2010, 1).

[3] These are countries that are not a part of traditional donors' club of the OECD, but are still involved in giving foreign aid (Kragelund 2010, 18).

donors,[4] new donors[5] and re-emerging donors.[6] However, these countries themselves do not agree with these terminologies and have officially declared their discomfort at being called as donors, which they consider a Western construct. Most of these countries consider themselves as development partners in the growth story of other developing countries. Furthermore, these countries have been also called emerging powers, Southern powers, rising powers, regional powers or middle powers by various scholars (Hurrell 2006, 9; Quadir 2013; Sahni 2012; Jordaan 2003; Nel 2010; Mthembu 2018). According to Varun Sahni (2012), a rising power is a significant systemic player today and their actions would have an effect on the system. On the other hand, emerging power is one that has shown its willingness and capability to play a systemic role but does not have the system-shaping capabilities at present. These emerging powers could also be the middle powers in the system (Sahni 2012). In this manner, China is rising, and India and Brazil are rather emerging. However, the terminology "emerging power" is used in this book for Brazil, China and India, despite the three countries being in different stages of development, where China is far ahead of Brazil and India, and India stands in between China and Brazil. The following section will focus on the concept of emerging powers.

Emerging Powers in International Politics

Even though there are several definitions of what an emerging power is, there exists no commonly accepted definition. The expression "emerging country"[7] comes from the field of economics and even finance. The term

[4] The countries who are new to the field of foreign aid giving are also being called emerging donors. However, it is important to note that developing countries like China and India have been involved in development cooperation, since the 1950 s, as long as the traditional donors.

[5] The countries that have recently made their forays into international aid architecture are also termed new donors by some scholars (Manning 2006, 374; Dreher et al. 2015, 3).

[6] The re-emerging donors are those countries who have been giving foreign aid for long but their volume was almost negligible, which has changed in recent times, and have started to be noted by other countries because of their increased volume, geographical spread and scope of their foreign aid (Mawdsley 2012).

[7] Jaffrelot (2008, 1) notes that emerging country label has been given to certain developing countries by some financial organisations such as the International Monetary Fund

"emerging market economies", which is in use since the 1980s, refers to "rapidly growing economies that offer investment opportunities for companies in developed countries" (Jaffrelot 2008, 1). With the growing economic weight of some developing countries in the world economy, the term emerging power came to be used primarily to denote their "economic take-off" (Jaffrelot 2008, 1, 2).

Gabas and Losch (2008) observe that these developing countries were those "underdeveloped category" of countries, which emerged after the Second World War that was later renamed as Third World countries and then rechristened as the Global South (Gabas and Losch 2008, 15).

Andrew Hurrell (2006) argues that the emerging powers are countries that could be considered as "pivotal states in international relations" (Hurrell 2006, 9). These countries aim to manoeuvre a greater role and influence, in both their own region and the outside world (Hurrell 2006, 9; 2008, 4). It is through their increasing economic capabilities that they hope to change the economic and political setting of the twenty-first century (Hart and Jones 2010, 65). However, the concept of emerging powers presupposes common traits.

Chenoy (2010) lays out the characteristics of an emerging power, including

> high growth rates; influence on international economics through purchase of bonds, impact on trade, foreign exchange and competitiveness; stable political systems and demographic depth. They are also found to be high military spenders with huge standing armies. (Chenoy 2010, 2)

These countries, through their increasing military spending and nuclear capabilities, aim to enhance their regional and international influence (Chenoy 2010). They are also increasingly found to have strategic partnerships with other developing countries. The group of Brazil, Russia, India, China and South Africa (BRICS) and the group of India, Brazil and South Africa (IBSA) are examples of the emerging powers' groupings that these countries think would enhance their status internationally. Furthermore, these emerging powers are also an inevitable part of global governance institutions. The expansion of G-8 into G-20 is a significant

(IMF) or the World Bank (WB). However, the list of emerging countries is in constant flux and countries can be included or excluded from the list depending on the IMF criteria.

reminder of the West's acceptance of the emerging powers as important actors in international politics.

Schirm (2006) affirms that the emerging powers' geographic size, high population, economic and military capacities have helped them play a greater role in international politics. Countries like China, India and Brazil have a dominant position in terms of "power over resources", including demographic depth, huge territory, high gross domestic product (GDP) and good military strength (Schirm 2006, 2).

Emphasising the weight of economic power in the era of globalisation, Mistry (2004) asserts that "economic power is as significant as military might in determining a country's world standing" (Mistry 2004, 66). The emerging powers have been able to maintain a high economic growth and this has favoured them tremendously in consolidating their national power, which has put them in an advantageous position in the international front (Mistry 2004). Some of the emerging powers are also nuclear powers, like India and China with a huge military spending.

Apart from high growth rates and growing integration into the world economy, emerging powers have a stabilised institutional apparatus and some form of capitalism, despite the differences in the nature of their trajectories (Jaffrelot 2008, 3). The institutional stability helps these emerging powers in sustaining the high economic growth enjoyed by them in the past several years (Jaffrelot 2008, 3). Relying on the increased economic clout and demographic dividends, emerging powers have exhibited their renewed political ambitions for a greater role in international politics (Jaffrelot 2008, 4). Furthermore, these countries have increasingly shown their readiness, capacity and willingness to be leaders in their regions as well as internationally (Schirm 2006, 2).

Currently, the emerging powers play a prominent role in managing climate change to nuclear proliferation which makes them inevitable partners in all institutions of global governance (Hurrell 2010, 12). Furthermore, these countries themselves are quite vocal about their demands for an equitable international political and economic system. Emerging powers like India, Brazil and South Africa have been pushing for changes at various international institutions dominated by the Western countries, most important of which has been a permanent seat for them in a reformed United Nations Security Council (UNSC). These emerging economies have initiated their own financial institutions like the Asian Infrastructure Investment Bank (AIIB) and the BRICS New Development Bank (NDB). The increased development assistance from these emerging powers like Brazil, China and India increasingly shows their readiness to take a global role and their willingness to take more responsibilities in the international system.

All these emerging economies, including Brazil, China and India, have "power over resources" and have enjoyed a high economic growth in the twenty-first century. Even though these countries have institutional stability and economic growth, all of them have crippling domestic issues like severe poverty and high income inequality. Despite pressing issues at home, these countries are playing an increasingly important role in the international system. Andrew Hurrell (2010) claims that "both the international political system and the structures of global capitalism can be said to be in a state of flux and uncertainty" (Hurrell 2010, 1). He asserts that the "power shift" of the twenty-first century has focussed on the emerging powers (Hurrell 2010, 1). Emerging powers, like Brazil, China and India, through their relentless efforts, have been trying to bring changes into the power calculus that existed both regionally and internationally.

In this book, emerging powers have been considered in the context of development cooperation. These countries have been giving development assistance for approximately six decades. However, the volume of the development assistance from these countries was considerably low when compared to traditional donors' aid. Despite the low volume and scope of their development assistance, these countries are carving out a niche of their own in the international aid architecture. They are not following the rules created by the developed countries and are trying to make their own rules and regulations for their development assistance based on horizontal cooperation, mutual benefit, non-interference, equality and no-conditionalities. They are not status-quoist powers in the international aid architecture as they have brought fresh ideas and imperatives into the development cooperation framework which has made even the traditional donors look at them in a new light. Undoubtedly, there are changes in the international aid architecture which has been the result of emerging powers' efforts to bring their own ideas and struggles.

Over the past two decades, the volume and scope of emerging powers' development cooperation have visibly increased, which has brought them in the limelight. Though the emerging powers have been involved in development cooperation for over six decades, their development cooperation is still in nascent stages when compared to the OECD aid. However, their presence and visibility have increased considerably in the twenty-first century with the increasing volume, scope and geographical reach, additional resources, and specific expertise, which makes it crucial to study their development cooperation.

Emerging Powers as Development Assistance Providers

Emerging powers are not a homogeneous group. There are differences and similarities among them as there are with the OECD-DAC. Most of the emerging powers like China, India, Brazil and South Africa are not a part of the OECD-DAC. However, some of the emerging powers like Turkey, Mexico and Saudi Arabia are all part of the OECD.[8] This makes the scenario completely ambiguous with some countries eager to join the rich donors' club of the OECD and some totally against the idea of getting into the developed country club. Therefore, it differs from one country to the other whether they consider OECD rules and standards as relevant to their foreign aid policy. Countries like China and India have not shown any interest in joining the OECD-DAC and have been quite vocal about their position.

The Western narrative has dubbed the emerging powers who provide development cooperation as "emerging donors". Many emerging powers that have been categorised as emerging donors have been giving aid since the 1950s which is when many of the traditional donors also started their aid programme. Hence, their development assistance programme is nothing new, even though the volume of their assistance and the geographic spread has increased considerably in recent years. Therefore, it would be unfair to call them "emerging donors". These countries have officially conveyed their disapproval for these terms introduced by the traditional donors and the Western scholars. They do not consider their development cooperation with the Global South as foreign aid and have clarified that they believe in horizontal cooperation and equality among the provider and the beneficiary countries. Their preferred term is "development cooperation partners" which emphasises horizontality unlike the hierarchical donor-recipient relationship of the traditional donors. For that reason, in this book while discussing emerging powers and their SSC, instead of the term "donor", "development assistance provider" has been used; "development partner/beneficiary" has been used in place of

[8] These countries belong to the OECD but are not part of DAC.

"recipient"; and "development cooperation partnership" has replaced the hierarchical donor-recipient relationship. However, when the traditional donors and their foreign aid are analysed or compared, the terms that have been in use traditionally by OECD-DAC is used.

Changing Roles, Identities and Motives of the Emerging Powers

The motivations driving emerging powers' development cooperation activities and their changing identity from a recipient to a development assistance provider are important to understand the changing role of emerging powers in international politics.

While the advocates of aid argue that foreign aid is quite effective and should be expanded, the critics of aid claim that aid has been largely ineffective and should be reduced. Even though aid was supposed to promote growth and poverty reduction abroad, in reality, it has been used for a variety of purposes (Lancaster 2007). Hence, the way the actors shape the reality of aid in a given context is quite crucial, be it the traditional donors or the emerging powers (Hilhorst and Jansen 2010, 1122). Like any country that provides development cooperation, emerging powers are also seen in both positive and negative light.

Motivations guiding the emerging powers for providing development assistance have been plentiful. Traditional donors blame them for pursuing their own commercial and political interests by using development cooperation as a means to promote exports and securing access to natural resources and raw materials in partner countries. Woods (2008) explains that through their development assistance, the emerging powers hope to fulfil their "quest for energy security, enlarged trading opportunities and new economic partnerships" (Woods 2008, 1205). Further, the traditional donors blame the emerging powers for granting aid to corrupt and undemocratic regimes, which they consider would undermine their efforts to grant aid according to the merit of their recipients. The emerging powers are also criticised by the Western donors for supporting African dictators. For example, China and India are accused of providing aid to all African states, including the "rogue states" like Sudan (Kragelund 2010, 19). The emerging powers are also accused of not sufficiently focussing on poverty-alleviation programmes through their development cooperation.

There are certain reasons for both success and failure of emerging power leadership and why some of them fail to reach their goals. One of the reasons for the lack of their success is the resistance from the powerful countries of the West, especially the US. The traditional donors claim that the emerging powers' development cooperation has been harmful to the recipient country in the long term because they encourage poor policies like absence of conditionalities; extending support to even rogue states; lowering standards especially environmental standards and good governance; and increasing debt burdens by giving too many loans to their "partner" countries (Woods 2008, 2). The traditional donors have also made efforts to counter the influence of the emerging powers by giving more aid to countries in their region, which is reminiscent of the Cold War realities. For example, Australia and New Zealand are trying to keep off Chinese influence on the Pacific islands by trying to compensate with more aid, the share of which has shrunk. In the wake of growing Chinese competition, both Australia and New Zealand are trying to work on their aid programmes so as not to lose partners. However, emerging powers' development assistance has become more appealing to recipient countries mainly because of the failures of the traditional donors to increase aid, reduce the strict conditionalities imposed on the recipients, enhance alignment and coordination, and reform the traditional aid architecture (Woods 2008, 2).

The industrialised developed countries of the North feel challenged by the emerging countries' call for changing the existing power structures. However, these countries have been supportive of the emerging countries playing the role "as regional stabilizers and strategic partners in their regions" (Schirm 2006, 3). The neo-Marxists and neo-Gramscians often argue that the emerging powers would "build a bulwark against neoliberal imperialism" (Harris 2005, 7). According to them, both the set of countries would try to stop each other from gaining power—emerging powers would battle against the developed countries' hegemonic project, and the Global North would try to ensure that the emerging powers would never attain power position in the international system.

Another factor that is pulling back the emerging powers from successfully pursuing their goals has been the lack of support from their neighbouring countries. In order to perform successfully, any leadership has to be accepted by followers (Schirm 2006). The appreciation and support of neighbours become important to enhance their regional and global power projections. Schirm (2006) avers that emerging countries should "offer material as well as political-ideational incentives to potential followers which are perceived as superior to the option of not following or of following other 'leaders'" (Schirm 2006, 5). The major trends in allocation of development assistance from emerging powers suggest that most of the emerging powers provide more development cooperation to their neighbouring countries, including India and Brazil. Even though geographical proximity is a major indicator of the direction of development assistance flows, it cannot be considered as the single-most determinant. Undoubtedly, factors like language, historical links, cultural similarities, search for markets, opportunities for increasing trade and strengthening political and economic relations do play an increasingly prominent role (Kragelund 2010). However, aid to neighbouring countries need not produce desired results if several countries compete in the same region to buy loyalty. For example, in South Asia, both India and China are vying for influence, which has led to countries like Nepal play one against the other.

Furthermore, the next crucial aspect for increasing emerging powers' influence is whether they are able to commit themselves to regional and international organisations, which can help bring more credibility and legitimacy into their actions. By adhering to multilateral setting, emerging powers can project themselves as role models in political, economic and security matters in order to be accepted by others, not just their immediate neighbours but also the traditional donors.

Today, development cooperation has become an integral part of the economic diplomacy efforts of the Global South. The emerging powers are using development cooperation as a tool for economic statecraft. Even though China has a no-conditionalities-attached policy for its development assistance, it has been using geopolitical and project-specific conditionality in order to bring desired results. By putting pressure on its partner countries to drop their diplomatic recognition to Taiwan, several countries were forced to choose China over Taiwan for which they received economic, political and diplomatic support in return. For example, China opposed U.N. sanctions against Sudan for human rights violations in Darfur (O'Keefe 2007, 8).

Behaviourally, emerging powers are more likely to opt for reformist and not radical global change and exhibit a strong regional orientation favouring regional integration. However, they also seek to construct identities distinct from those of the weak states in their region (Jordaan 2003). However, they also form coalitions with the other powerful countries of the Global South to become new power centres. For instance, BRICS and

IBSA have become important players in the international system with the economic powerhouses of the Global South coming together to form a bloc (Gu et al. 2016, Bergamaschi and Tickner 2017). These countries are perceived to become "agents of change" (Nel 2010, 952). The establishment of the New BRICS Development Bank could be considered as an effort on the part of these emerging powers to bring alternatives to institutions like the World Bank and IMF, established by the developed countries of the Global North (Gu et al. 2016).

Even though emerging powers' development assistance is much less in comparison with the aid given by the OECD-DAC, their development assistance has gained momentum in the Global South. Noticeably, certain tenets of emerging powers' development cooperation are appealing to other developing countries. This includes their high economic growth and own policy experiences which are relevant to their development process; the technology and expertise provided by these countries prove to be a good match for the level of economic, political and institutional development of their partners; absence of aid conditionality and the political neutrality derived from its colonial history. Above all, their own experience as a recipient of foreign aid makes them better equipped to understand the needs and demands of their recipients (ODI 2010, 2). These countries continue to receive aid from certain traditional donors which makes them recipients and donors simultaneously. For example, India and China play dual role as donor and recipient at the same time.

Furthermore, the emerging powers have always shown their readiness and commitment to strengthen and deepen SSC as a means of transforming the Third World after several decades of decimation by "poorly phased, externally induced programmes of structural adjustment and trade liberalization, fluctuating aid flows, and unfulfilled promises of technology transfer" (Nel 2010, 958). Small countries in particular are already finding that bilateral South-South development cooperation from the emerging powers could be of great significance for them as it brings extra financial resources to their economy. Also, the experiences of emerging powers as recipients of traditional aid would make them more considerate to the recipient need and therefore, are seen to provide better targeted aid.

New sources of assistance or cooperation that are outside the established OECD-DAC fold is offering not only new opportunities but also greater political leverage for aid recipients (Chaturvedi et al. 2012). However, their benefits would depend on how they are using this increased choice of development assistance providers. With the emerging powers gaining more visibility and ensuring their presence in the international aid framework, there are visible changes in the way foreign aid has been envisaged by the players, both the donors and the recipients. The traditional donors' exclusive competence in the international aid architecture has been declining with the emerging powers' development assistance programme.

The struggle for recognition between the North and the South has been a reality. Nel (2010) makes a case that this struggle is not only on the part of the developing countries "to be recognised as full and equal partners in the society of states, but also as states with specific developmental needs" (Nel 2010, 952). He interprets the goals of these emerging powers in terms of the notions of redistribution and recognition. He argues that the major regional powers of the Global South are much more integrationist in their outlook to the international political economy.

Hart and Jones (2010) put forth three important factors that might explain emerging power's global influence, comprising their ties with the weak and fragile states, disunity among the Western powers during negotiations and emerging powers' unity at multilateral platforms. Emerging powers are often in a position to exert much greater economic leverage over many weak and fragile states than the Western powers, especially through trade and investment linkages. Hence, there are deep, bilateral economic and political ties these states have with certain "fragile" or "rogue" states. Also, the Western disunity has given the emerging powers an edge in the multilateral negotiations as they are bargaining against a fractious, undisciplined and often internally competing set of Western actors with somewhat divergent goals. Furthermore, these states can often wield influence disproportionate to their individual economic size or formal voting power within some multilateral institutions, especially at the UN. At the UN, these emerging powers wield a certain amount of influence over decisions through their capacity to mobilise regional blocs (Hart and Jones 2010, 74).

Emerging powers like Brazil, China and India do pose certain challenges for the development assistance regime set up by the traditional donors. One of the key features of their development assistance is respect for the sovereignty of their partner countries, which has gained them much advantage over traditional donors. For example, Brazil uses the term "development cooperation" instead of development assistance or foreign aid and considers respect for sovereignty and non-interference as most important tenet of its development cooperation. China also emphasises sovereignty, equality and mutual respect. Likewise, Indian development assistance is centred on respect for sovereignty, non-interference in domestic affairs of partner countries, equality, peaceful coexistence and mutual benefit. By "quietly" offering alternatives to the recipients, emerging powers are bringing "competitive pressures into the existing system thereby weakening the bargaining position of Western donors" (Woods 2008, 17).

The current structure of international aid framework cannot be concluded as the North-South hierarchical donor-recipient configuration. Today, it also constitutes SSC, which is based on horizontal partnership, equality, mutual benefit and win-win situation for both partners. The principles of SSC brought a fresh perspective into the aid architecture which is based on partnership and solidarity of the Global South. The emerging powers' own colonial past and experience as a recipient of traditional aid make them better understand the concerns and challenges faced by other developing countries in similar stages of development. The foundation of SSC in development is built on friendship, solidarity and mutual goodwill. The emerging powers have consciously distanced themselves from the policies of the traditional donors and have always emphasised their identity as one among the Global South.

What distinguishes countries like Brazil, China or India is not their richness or poverty but the "desire of the country for power" (Griffin and Enos 1970, 314). The main objective of this book is to examine the increasing role of emerging powers as development assistance providers, their motivations and agendas, and the scope and reach of their development assistance programmes. The comparative study of the three major emerging powers, Brazil, China and India, would help us to understand how these states have carved out a niche of their own in international aid architecture, how they use development assistance as an instrument of economic statecraft, and in what ways are they similar and where all do they differ from each other.

Rationale and Scope of the Book

This book focusses on the changing roles of Brazil, China and India from being principal recipients to development assistance providers, the motives and orientations behind their development cooperation programme; their development cooperation policies, strategies and agendas. It will also assess how emerging powers use development cooperation as an instrument of economic statecraft and how their development cooperation is different from the traditional donor's aid. Brazil, China and India act as a lens for building a general understanding of the emerging powers as development assistance providers, their nature, volume, scope, motives and markedly their changing identities. The study locates the overall impact of the changing role of these countries in international politics.

A comparative study of the three emerging powers, Brazil, China and India as development assistance providers, delves into the convergences and divergences of their development cooperation policies and agendas. At the same time, these emerging powers' development cooperation is compared to the traditional donors' aid to understand what new ideas and strategies do the emerging powers bring to the table. Furthermore, the emerging powers not being a homogenous entity, their similarities and differences have been brought out through an in-depth analysis of each provider and then compared. The ambit of this study is the changing bilateral aid architecture and how the emerging powers are positioning themselves in a system dominated by the developed donor country club, the OECD-DAC.

Brazil, China and India make strong cases for comparative study keeping in view their similarities and dissimilarities. As developing countries, Brazil, China and India act in similar ways in many crucial issues and areas. Their structural positioning in international relations also shows proximity. These states are unusually large for their extended neighbourhood, i.e. Brazil in Latin America, China in East Asia and India in South Asia. Thus, their resulting regional roles and responsibilities are similarly huge. All three of them are rapidly developing countries, huge in size and population; all three are regional powers and are aiming for a powerful global role. Poverty is one of the central challenges faced by these countries. They have been recipients of aid for considerably long period but have been giving some amount of aid to select countries as part of SSC. Besides, they have been able to reach an admirable overall economic growth. Now, they are trying to establish their position in the international development landscape, which was largely dominated by the economically developed countries.

Their development cooperation policies also show certain common tenets; that is, they do not belong to the OECD- DAC, impose less conditionalities and try to wield influence and resources from their fellow developing countries and aspires for the leadership role of the developing countries of the Global South. They also qualify as the three largest emerging powers that are also development assistance providers. Along with similarities, they have several dissimilarities. While Brazil's development cooperation is more focussed on multilateral and trilateral cooperation with maximum assistance going to Latin American countries followed by the Portuguese-speaking countries in Africa, we can conclude that Brazil's priority is to have historical, geographic, cultural and linguistic proximity; China is keen on its policy goals and orientations and play both hard and soft powers whenever necessary to increase its trade and investments; and India is more of a user of soft power and diplomatic mileage in order to strengthen regional solidarity, trade and investment opportunities and search for new markets. Thus, they divert at several crucial policy areas including definition of development cooperation, geographical scope, modalities and agendas behind their development cooperation.

Data Sources

Lack of transparency is one of the major limitations of the emerging powers' development assistance. All the three countries, Brazil, China and India, are criticised for lack of transparency in their development cooperation. Even though Brazil and China have reports and White Papers on development cooperation published by the government, the data is considered to be neither comprehensive nor accurate. However, for the purpose of analysis, the government data has been used despite the discrepancies. For India, there are no separate government projections or reports on development cooperation available. Data has been culled out from the Annual Reports of the Ministry of External Affairs (MEA), MEA Outcome Budgets, Export-Import Bank (EXIM Bank) Reports and Economic Survey.

With the lack of regular dissemination of official data and no accountability mechanisms in place, it becomes truly difficult to capture the precise financial flows from these countries under development assistance heading. This problem is further worsened with no clarity in definition of their development assistance, the existence of numerous institutions responsible for their development assistance and different modalities. This has been found true for most of the emerging powers including India, Brazil and China.

Brazil

In the case of Brazil, the primary source of data is the two Brazilian Cooperation for International Development/ Cooperação Brasileira para o Desenvolvimento Internacional (Cobradi) Reports, Brazilian Cooperation for International Development, 2005–2009, and Brazilian Cooperation for International Development, 2010, published in 2010 and 2014, respectively. These reports are published by the Instituto de Pesquisa Econômica Aplicada/Institute for Applied Economic Research (IPEA).[9] The available data is only till 2010 and no new Cobradi reports have been published since 2014.

As per the IPEA reports, the Cobradi totalled R$1.6 billion (USD923 million) in 2010. Of this, R$1.3 billion (USD752 million), which accounts 81.4% of the total, was allotted for multilateral cooperation and R$302 million (USD171 million) (i.e. 18.6% of the total amount allocated) for bilateral cooperation. Regarding the geographical spread of Cobradi, Latin America and the Caribbean get the maximum assistance amounting to R$192 million (USD111 million) followed by Africa which received R$65 million (USD37 million) (IPEA 2014).

In the interviews[10] conducted with the officials at Agência Brasileira de Cooperação/Brazilian Cooperation Agency (ABC) and IPEA, they made it clear that the real volume of Cobradi could be much higher than government projections. Even though the government projections are approximately USD 923 million, the actual volume could go much higher than these projections if all the institutions involved in development cooperation are brought together and the actual amounts were revealed. Several institutions involved in Brazilian development cooperation have not been brought under the radar while calculating development cooperation including federated states and the municipalities.

Even though the efforts made by IPEA in coordinating more than 100 agencies involved in development cooperation are commendable, noticeably, this data might not be comprehensive in predicting the real amounts given by each agency. Also, ABC is not the single institution managing and coordinating Brazilian development cooperation, most of

[9] IPEA is a public foundation that offers technical and institutional support to the Federal government of Brazil.

[10] Interviews with the officials of the ABC, IPEA and the Ministry of External Relations (MRE) were conducted in Brasilia during March 2015 by the author.

the ministries can directly deal with the partner country and decide on the projects and volume of development assistance to be given.

Despite the creation of the ABC, the centralised coordination of Brazilian development cooperation remained a distant dream. The actors involved in Cobradi also include the non-traditional state actors like federal agencies[11] and subnational entities[12]; non-state actors; and private sector businesses (Milani 2014, 5).[13] These actors do not work under the authority of the Presidency of the Republic of Brazil. They could advance their own agendas, different from that of the Federal government's agendas, which could affect the authority of the state as the real centre of power in executing the development cooperation policy (Milani 2014, 5). The plurality of actors and agendas makes it a herculean task to manage, quantify and access accurate data on Brazilian development cooperation. This also makes it hard for the ABC and the IPEA to calculate the volume of Cobradi, and hence make the volume quoted in the Cobradi report problematic and inaccurate by a huge margin.

Decentralisation of the Brazilian development cooperation was further encouraged and legitimised by the federal government in 2012 through the Decentralised Programme for South-South Technical Cooperation (Planalto 2016a).[14] This further led to proliferation of agendas and actors in the field of Brazilian foreign policy in general and its development policy sector in particular. The debate on building centralised institutional structures for Cobradi was further diluted with this move and Itamaraty[15] further lost its monopoly over its development cooperation programme. With the federated states and municipalities playing a greater role internationally, it has become common that most governmental agencies have their own budget for their endeavours abroad (Milani 2014, 11).

[11] Like the Brazilian Agricultural Research Corporation (Embrapa) and the Oswaldo Cruz Foundation (Fiocruz) that are affiliated to the Ministry of Agriculture and the Ministry of Health, respectively.

[12] This includes federated states and municipalities.

[13] Prof. Carlos Milani, during an interview with him on 3 April 2015, explained this issue in detail. Similar views were expressed by interviewees like Prof. Alcides Costa Vaz of University of Brasilia (UnB) and Mr. Marcio Correa of ABC.

[14] The main objective of this programme was to encourage Brazilian states and municipalities to develop international technical cooperation projects with their counterparts in other developing countries (Planalto 2016b).

[15] Brazil's Ministry of External Relations is called Itamaraty.

Furthermore, the Federal government outlines its development cooperation as based only on grants and anything that doesn't reach 100% grants will fail to get included as the Cobradi. This means that all the loans, credits and donations, and investments by Brazil gets removed from Cobradi. All this has led to much lower figures of Cobradi than what it should have actually been.

China

In the case of China, the major sources of data are the two White Papers on Foreign Aid published in 2011 and 2014, respectively. These White Papers only give the data for the years 2009–2012. China does not publish data regularly and there are several gaps in the White Papers. Even though the White Papers give an overall volume of Chinese development assistance, this is not a comprehensive report of country-wise data and project details. Hence, the lack of micro-analysis results in data incompatibility for comparisons with other countries. Several field studies conducted in the recipient countries totally invalidate the data given in the White Paper. Although various secondary sources of data are available, they do not give a comprehensive figure as how much China is giving as development cooperation, as they are based on case studies or sector-based investigations. Even though the data from these secondary sources has also been used in this study, the main source of data remains the White Papers. The creation of Chinese International Development Cooperation Agency (CIDCA) in 2018 is supposed to bring more coherence into the development cooperation efforts of China.

India

The Development Partnership Administration (DPA) was set up in 2012 under the Ministry of External Affairs (MEA) as the agency entrusted with the responsibility to coordinate India's development cooperation. Apart from the MEA, there are two other government institutions that are involved in India's development assistance, Ministry of Finance (MoF) and the Ministry of Commerce and Industry (MoCI).

MEA has the coordinating role and enjoys a greater decision-making power over others despite the fact that other ministries are equally important players in India's development cooperation. Department of Economic Affairs (DEA) in the MoF is in charge of coordinating bilateral cooperation with other developing countries. MoCI also plays a role in Indian development cooperation, especially with the increasing interweaving of trade and India's development cooperation flows. The Indian Export-Import Bank (EXIM)[16] also plays an important role in financing projects and sanctioning loans. EXIM Bank handles India's Line of Credit (LOC), which is a major component of Indian development cooperation (IDC). LOCs that are tied to Indian goods and services have been instrumental in supporting India's small and medium enterprises (SMEs).

Further, the Indian embassies and consulates have been entrusted with the duty of periodic assessment of the projects on the ground so that IDC is utilised properly. The presence of a varied number of institutions and the lack of dissemination of data from each of these organisations publicly make it difficult to calculate the volume of development assistance from India.

Since the emerging powers like Brazil, China and India do not belong to the OECD or any other donors' club which demands transparency, they are not obliged to disseminate data systematically and accurately. Several other factors further complicate the data challenge. The lack of a common and clearly stated definition for development cooperation makes the comparing of data rather difficult. Conceptualisation of development cooperation has been different for these countries and all three of them have different definitions and ideas of what constitutes their development assistance. Furthermore, the diversity in each country's development cooperation modalities and the multiplicity of institutions involved in development cooperation make the data comparisons largely inaccurate and non-comparable. Another major hurdle in data comparisons is the absence of systematic availability of data which makes it impossible to track the patterns of development cooperation for any specific time period. With technical and institutional problems in data reporting looming large, comparing any two emerging powers' development cooperation becomes difficult. Because of the unavailability of data,

[16] EXIM Bank is India's apex financial institution that has the responsibility to promote and facilitate India's international trade around the world (EXIM Bank 2015, 21).

and the inaccuracy and discrepancies in the available data, the volume of development assistance from these three countries will not be compared in this book.

Structure of the Book

Though the emerging powers lack the political and military might of the developed countries, they are seen to be making a mark on the economic realm. They have shown their capacity to influence international economics and development finance. The increasing prominence of the emerging economies of the Global South has given a boost to the idea of SSC. Apart from trade and investments, these countries have come to use development assistance as an instrument to facilitate their economic ties with countries of the Global South. These countries wield a greater economic and political influence in their respective regions, and countries like China and India have been expanding their footprints from their region to other far-off lands (Modi 2011, Mthembu 2018).

Even though China, India and Brazil could be labelled as the largest development assistance providers from the Global South, other developing countries like South Africa, Indonesia and Mexico are also playing an increasingly important role in providing development assistance to other developing countries (Kragelund 2010, VI). Some of these countries like Mexico, South Korea and Turkey have shown a keen interest in the Western development financing that led them to join the OECD. However, countries like China, India or South Africa have always distanced themselves from the Western donors' club and their mechanisms for development finance to the lesser developed countries. These countries have also tried to develop their own unique system for development cooperation that suits their ideologies and interests.

The emerging powers' development cooperation has some common features that have been seen in a favourable light by other developing countries. This includes lack of conditionalities; emphasis on equal partnership between the provider and receiver; use of local technology and expertise that suits the economic and institutional development stage of their beneficiaries; and their own experience as a recipient of foreign aid which gives them a greater understanding of the needs of their partners and the limitations of the OECD aid. Collectively, they give emerging donors some comparative advantages in development assistance, as suggested by the increasing demand for their cooperation from the developing countries (ODI 2010, 2).

Emerging powers have become important players in the international aid architecture, making changes in the way foreign aid is traditionally conceptualised and implemented by the traditional donors. Many developing countries find emerging powers' development cooperation attractive, which has made the international aid system increasingly competitive (Woods 2008). This has given the recipients more choice and a greater say on their incoming development assistance flows-with the emerging powers' assistance flowing in and the weakening of traditional donors' bargaining position.

Despite the fact that traditional donors still occupy prominent position in international aid architecture, their influence has been quietly challenged by the emerging powers whose development assistance is receiving great amount of support from their partner countries. Apart from giving development assistance based on lesser conditionalities and mutual benefit, what is also attractive about emerging powers' development cooperation is that it is found to be need-based and tailor-made, which is in consultation with the partner countries. This gives the partners a greater leverage as compared to their standing as recipient of Western aid.

The emerging powers, through aid, are trying to alter their Third World status and trying to reposition themselves into a more influential and legitimate position. Hence, they are using a combination of hard and soft powers to lead the developing countries. Though there are varied constraints and challenges in front of the emerging powers, they are showing their readiness to play the leadership role not only in their respective regions but also in the developing Global South. Therefore, this book analyses the roles, motives and strategies of the emerging powers and how this has resulted in far-reaching changes in the international aid architecture, and its implications on international politics.

This book also tries to find answers to the following questions: What is the significance of emerging powers in international aid architecture? What is the nature and volume of aid from Brazil, China and India? What are the factors driving the development assistance policies of the emerging powers, especially Brazil, China and India, towards their recipients? How are the strategies and motivations of emerging powers different from that of established donors? Are the development assistance policies of emerging powers guided by their experience and learnings that they had as aid recipients? What are the implications of the emerging powers' growing influence in the field of international politics?

This book is divided into seven chapters including introduction (this chapter). The second chapter, "The Evolving Bilateral Aid Architecture", deals with both emerging donors and established donors in detail. The goal is to examine and compare their development assistance policy; their motives and agendas behind aid-giving; institutions involved; focus areas; and geographical coverage. The chapter provides an in-depth analysis of the evolving bilateral aid architecture and its functioning and how emerging powers are contributing to its transformation.

The third chapter, "COBRADI: The Rise and Fall of a Southern Provider", analyses the institutional framework, operational components and disbursement pattern of Brazil's development assistance. It also elaborates on the historical background of Brazil's development assistance programme. Even though the focus is on understanding the motives and objectives involved in its development assistance, this chapter also analyses the influence of domestic factors and the leadership in formulating Brazil's development cooperation policy.

The fourth chapter, "China's Development Assistance: Leveraging Deep Pockets", focusses on Chinese development assistance policy, the motives behind their development assistance programme, their strategies, aspirations and interests in aid-giving. This chapter delves deep into China's growing development assistance after the launch of the BRI and what Chinese leadership is aiming to achieve in the coming years through its growing development assistance. It also analyses how China's role as an aid donor has affected its position/status in international politics.

The fifth chapter, "India's Development Cooperation: Aiming High, Falling Short", sketches the historical trajectory of India's aid-giving and further analyses its motives, aspirations, strategies, institutions involved and geographical spread. This chapter also examines the influence of India's development assistance programme on the bilateral aid architecture.

The sixth chapter "Comparisons: Brazil, China and India as Development Assistance Providers", juxtaposes the three case studies and analyses them in comparative perspective. It looks into the similarities and the dissimilarities that the cases offer. This chapter also analyses the areas where the trio cooperates and/or competes.

The concluding chapter summarises the theoretical arguments and the major findings of the book.

References

Alesina, Alberto and Dollar, David. (2000), "Who Gives Foreign Aid to Whom and Why?", *Journal of Economic Growth*, 5(1): 33–63.

Baldwin, D. (1966), *Foreign Aid and American Foreign Policy: A Documentary Analysis*, New York: Praeger.

Bergamaschi, I. and Tickner, Arlene B. (2017), "Introduction: South-South Cooperation Beyond the Myths—A Critical Analysis" in Bergamaschi, I., Phoebe Moore and Arlene B. Tickner (eds.), *South-South Cooperation Beyond the Myths: Rising Donors, New Aid Practices?*, London: Palgrave Macmillan.

Chenoy, Kamal Mitra. (2010), *Plurilateralism and the Global South*, India Brazil South Africa Academic Forum: A Policy Dialogue [Online: web]. Accessed at http://www.ipc-undp.org/pressroom/files/ipc138.pdf.

De Long, J. Bradford and Eichengreen, Barry. (1991), "The Marshall Plan: History's Most Successful Structural Adjustment Program" [Online: web]. Accessed at http://econ161.berkeley.edu/pdf_files/Marshall_Large.pdf.

Dreher, A. et al. (2015), *Apples and Dragon Fruits: The Determinants of Aid and Other Forms of State Financing from China to Africa*, Working Paper 15, AidData [Online: web]. Accessed at http://aiddata.org/sites/default/files/wps15_apples_and_dragon_fruits.pdf.

EXIM Bank. (2015), "Annual Report 2014–15" [Online: web]. Accessed at http://www.eximbankindia.in/sites/default/files/English%20Annual%20Report_0.pdf.

Gabas, Jean-Jacques and Losch, Bruno. (2008), *Fabrications and Illusions of Emergence*, in Jaffrelot, Christophe (eds.), *The Emerging States: The Wellspring of a New World Order*, London: Hurst and Company.

Griffin, K.B. and Enos, J.L. (1970), "Foreign Assistance: Objectives and Consequences", *Economic Development and Cultural Change*, 18(3): 313–327.

Gu, J. et al. (2016), "Introduction: International Development, South-South Cooperation and the Rising Powers" in Gu, J., Alex Shankland and Anuradha Chenoy (eds.), *The BRICS in International Development*, London: Palgrave Macmillan.

Harris, Jerry. (2005), "Emerging Third World Powers: China, India and Brazil", *Race & Class*, 46(3): 7–27.

Hart, Andrew F. and Jones, Bruce D. (2010), "How Do Rising Powers Rise?", *Survival*, 52(6): 63–88.

Hilhorst, Dorothea and Jansen, Bram J. (2010), "Humanitarian Space as Arena: A Perspective on the Everyday Politics of Aid", *Development and Change*, 41(6): 1117–1139.

Hoge, J.F., Jr. 2004. "A Global Power Shift in the Making", *Foreign Affairs*. Accessed at https://www.foreignaffairs.com/articles/united-states/2004-07-01/global-power-shift-making.

Hurrell, Andrew. (2006), "Hegemony, Liberalism and Global Order: What Space for Would-be Great Powers?" *International Affairs*, 82(1): 1–19.

Hurrell, Andrew. (2008), *Playgrounds of Regional Powers: Regional Powers and the Global System*, RPN Conference Paper [Online: web]. Accessed at http://www.giga-hamburg.de/dl/download.php?d=/english/content/rpn/conferences/hurrell.pdf.

Hurrell, Andrew. (2010), "Emerging Powers, Global Order and Global Justice", IILJ colloquium [Online: web]. Accessed at http://www.iilj.org/courses/documents/2010Colloquium.Hurrell.pdf.

IPEA. (2014), "Brazilian Cooperation for International Development 2010", Institute for Applied Economic Research, Brasilia.

Jaffrelot, Christophe (eds.). (2008), *The Emerging States: The Wellspring of a New World Order*, London: Hurst and Company.

Jordaan, Eduard. (2003), "The Concept of a Middle Power in International Relations: Distinguishing between Emerging and Traditional Middle Powers", *Politikon*, 30(2): 165–181.

Kragelund, Peter. (2010), *The Potential Role of Non-traditional Donors' Aid in Africa*, Issue Paper No. 11, ICTSD [Online: web]. Accessed at http://ictsd.org/downloads/2010/03/the-potential-role-of-non-traditional-donors e28099-aid-in-africa.pdf.

Lancaster, Carol. (2007), *Foreign Aid: Diplomacy, Development and Domestic Politics*, Chicago: University of Chicago Press.

Layne, C. (2012), "The Global Power Shift from West to East", *The National Interest*. Accessed at https://nationalinterest.org/article/the-global-power-shift-west-east-6796.

Liska, G. (1960), *The New Statecraft: Foreign Aid in American Foreign Policy*, Chicago: University of Chicago Press.

Manning, Richard. (2006), *Will "Emerging Donors" Change the Face of International Cooperation?*, ODI Lecture [Online: web]. Accessed at http://www.oecd.org/dataoecd/35/38/36417541.pdf.

Mawdsley, Emma. (2012), *From Recipients to Donors: Emerging Powers and the Changing Development Landscape*, London: Zed Books.

Milani, Carlos. (2014), *Brazil's South-South Co-Operation Strategies: From Foreign Policy to Public Policy*, Occasional Paper No. 179, SAIIA [Online: web]. Accessed at http://www.saiia.org.za/occasional-papers/487-brazil-s-south-south-co-operation-strategies-from-foreign-policy-to-public-policy/file.

Mistry, Dinshaw. (2004), "A Theoretical and Empirical Assessment of India as an Emerging World Power", *India Review*, 3(1): 64–87.

Modi, Renu (ed.). (2011), *South-South Cooperation: Africa on the Centre Stage*, London: Palgrave Macmillan.

Morgenthau, Hans. (1962), "A Political Theory of Foreign Aid", *The American Political Science Review*, 56(2): 301–309.

Mthembu, P.M.S. (2018), *China and India's Development Cooperation in Africa: The Rise of Southern Powers*, London: Palgrave Macmillan.

Nel, Philip. (2010), "Redistribution and Recognition: What Emerging Regional Powers Want?", *Review of International Studies*, 36(4): 951–974.

ODI. (2010), *Brazil: An Emerging Aid Player*, Briefing Paper 64 [Online: web]. Accessed at http://www.odi.org.uk/resources/download/5120.pdf.

O'Keefe, Joseph. (2007), "Aid—From Consensus to Competition?", The Brookings Blum Roundtable [Online: web]. Accessed at http://www.brookings.edu/global/aspen/2007o%27keefe.pdf.

Planalto. (2016a), "Brazilian States and Municipalities May Present International Technical Cooperation Projects to the Benefit of Developing Countries" [Online: web]. Accessed at http://www4.planalto.gov.br/saf-projetos/brazilian-states-and-municipalities-may-present-international-technical-cooperation-projects-to-the-benefit-of-developing-countries.

Planalto. (2016b), "Program for Decentralized South-South Technical Cooperation" [Online: web]. Accessed at: http://www4.planalto.gov.br/saf-projetos/south-south-cooperation/program-guidelines/guidelines.

Quadir, Fahimul. (2013), "Rising Donors and the New Narrative of 'South–South' Cooperation: What Prospects for Changing the Landscape of Development Assistance Programmes?", *Third World Quarterly*, 34(2): 321–338.

Sachin Chaturvedi, Thomas Fues and Elizabeth Sidiropoulos (eds.). (2012), *Development Cooperation and Emerging Powers: New Partners or Old Patterns?*, London: Zed Books.

Sahni, Varun. (2012), *Panel Discussion on Rising Powers: From Regional Leaders to Global Players*, NOREF/PRIO Seminar, 25 April 2012, PRIO, Hausmanns Gate 7, Oslo. Accessed at https://www.youtube.com/watch?v=lJ9QWoILPKA.

Sato, Jin et al. (2010), *How Do "Emerging" Donors Differ from "Traditional" Donors? An Institutional Analysis of Foreign Aid in Cambodia*, Working Paper, JICA [Online: web]. Accessed at http://jica-ri.jica.go.jp/JICA-RI_WP_No.2_2010.pdf.

Schirm, Stefan A. (2006), *Leadership in Regional and Global Politics: Why Do Emerging Powers (Sometimes) Fail to Reach Their Goals?*, Working Paper, GIGA [Online: web]. Accessed at http://www.sowi.rub.de/mam/content/lsip/leadership_paper.pdf.

Schweller, Randall. (2011), "Emerging Powers in an Age of Disorder", *Global Governance*. 17: 285–297.

Strange, Susan. (1995), "The Defective State", *Daedalus*, 124(2): 55–74.

Tarp, Finn. (2006), "Aid and Development", *Swedish Economic Policy Review*, 13(2): 9–61.

Woods, Ngaire. (2008), "Whose Aid? Whose Influence? China, Emerging Donors and the Silent Revolution in Development Assistance", *International Affairs*, 84(6): 1205–1221.

CHAPTER 2

The Evolving Bilateral Aid Architecture

Foreign aid has occupied a prominent place in the debates on development since the Marshall Plan of 1948. The mainstream literature and narratives on foreign aid have focussed largely on an international aid architecture that was defined in North-South terms. Brautigam (2010) defines the international aid architecture as "the system of institutions, rules, norms, and practices that govern the transfer of concessional resources for development" (Brautigam 2010, 5). Initially, the only actors that had legitimacy and a standing in international aid architecture were the Organisation for Economic Cooperation and Development (OECD). The definition of aid or official development assistance (ODA) given by the OECD-DAC and the rules and regulations made by them were the norm. Aid flows were considered unidirectional, i.e. from the developed countries of the Global North to the developing or underdeveloped countries of the Global South.

The Global North still remains a formidable force in international development landscape as the power and influence exercised by them on the aid architecture is immense, considering the high volume of aid, scope, geographical reach, modalities and strong institutional structures in place.

The increasing visibility and presence of the emerging powers of the Global South have brought noticeable changes in the structure of development landscape over the years. The Global South, which was always

C. Purushothaman, *Emerging Powers, Development Cooperation and South-South Relations*, International Political Economy Series,
https://doi.org/10.1007/978-3-030-51537-9_2

considered to be on the receiving end of foreign aid, started to reposition themselves as providers of development assistance. Their role and significance have changed dramatically over the years. The emerging powers like China, India and Brazil have been changing the map of development assistance that was largely a dominion of the Global North. These developing countries of the Global South have been making inroads into the international development landscape since long. However, it is recently that they have managed to gain attention with the increasing volume, scope and geographical reach of their development assistance. These countries have been changing the development landscape with their increasing role in international aid architecture, in addition to making their own rules and regulations, and carving out a niche of their own in both the international development landscape and in the development agenda of their partner countries. The emerging powers floated their own idea of development cooperation based on the principle of South-South Cooperation (SSC).

In this chapter, along with an in-depth analysis of the evolving bilateral aid architecture and its functioning, the role of emerging powers as development assistance providers has been explored in detail. This chapter also examines the changing dynamics of international aid architecture, comprised of "institutions and actors, volume and composition, instruments and modalities, and rules and standards", with the increasing momentum in SSC (Brautigam 2010, 5). It also assesses whether the rise of the emerging powers in the development aid architecture challenges the long-standing binary constructions like, "North" and "South", "East" and "West", "developed" and "developing" and "First", "Second" and "Third" Worlds (Sidaway 2012).

The Evolution of Foreign Aid in International Politics

Over the past seven decades, the international aid architecture has transformed to include several actors, institutional structures, changes in definition, modalities and motives from what was of Marshall Plan of 1948. Hence, there is a need to sketch the evolution of international aid architecture that would give a fair idea of how the traditional donors have regulated the aid system for so long and how the developing countries of the Global South have made inroads into this system and the institutions that have been set up by the traditional players as per their own needs and interests.

Pronk (2001) explains the decade-wise changes in the aid structure based on the major developments in international politics and how aid was modified accordingly. According to Pronk, while the early years of aid to developing countries were focussed on the technical assistance, it slowly gave way to supporting community development in the 1950s. In the 1960s, aid was seen filling up the trade and investment gaps and in the following decade, aid was provided for the basic human needs. The 1980s foreign aid programmes were dedicated to structural adjustment and debt relief. The 1990s saw the end of Cold War which led to foreign aid being targeted for humanitarian assistance along with efforts towards conflict prevention, democracy promotion and good governance (Pronk 2001, 612).

Fraser's classification of the periods of aid-giving could be a useful model in understanding how the traditional donors have played out their role after the Second World War (Fraser 2006). Fraser classifies the foreign aid-giving into five neat time periods; "the post-colonial moment (1945-75); the mid-70s turn (1975-1980); the early structural adjustment era (1980s); adjustment after the Cold War (1990s); and presently, the partnership era (2000s)" (Fraser 2006, 6).

By the end of the Second World War, the power structures changed considerably with the new economic powerhouses like the US and the Union of Soviet Socialist Republics (USSR) taking the leadership role that was earlier assumed by major powers like the United Kingdom (UK), France and Germany. To run the Marshall Plan, the Organisation for European Economic Cooperation (OEEC) was created in 1948, which officially started off the process of institutionalisation of the traditional donors' aid. With the success of the OEEC in changing the face of Europe, the US and Canada were keen to expand their aid programme to other parts of the world. This led to the establishment of OECD in 1961, when the US and Canada joined their European partners for replicating their efforts in Europe to Asia, Africa, Eastern Europe and Latin America. In 1964, Japan joined the OECD club of the industrialised West to be a part of the developed donor countries' club.

With the beginning of the Cold War, foreign aid was being used as an instrument for garnering support and forming Cold War alliances by both the US and the USSR. In the Third World, this period was also marked by independence movements from the Western colonisers and also by the struggle to sustain newly gained freedom by some countries. The donor policies towards these newly independent developing countries were driven by the Cold War politics. With the colonial world order nearly coming to an end by 1966, the former colonies realised the importance of foreign aid as harbinger of growth and development, as well as a way to continue influencing their erstwhile colonies. The role of aid in this period largely focussed on the strategies and interests of the superpowers. The superpowers could intervene in the domestic and foreign policy decisions of their recipients at their will despite them agreeing to the norms of self-rule and state sovereignty that are enshrined in the United Nations (UN) Charter. Many developing countries maintained friendly relations with these superpowers who reciprocated in order to safeguard their geopolitical alliances and also to ensure their free access to raw materials in the developing country recipient (Fraser 2006, 7). For instance, Bolivia received maximum aid from the US during 1953–1961. This was the US strategy to discourage Bolivia from joining the Soviet bloc and later, to leverage domestic policy changes in the recipient country (Fraser 2006, 8). The USSR also was very keen to cast itself as a natural ally for the newly independent countries and was providing aid for defence and boosting infrastructure development in the recipient countries. This period was also marked by several new ideas and solidarity initiatives from the Global South, including the Bandung Conference, Colombo Plan, Non-Aligned Movement (NAM) and Group of 77 countries (G-77). These were major initiatives in the direction of SSC and solidarity among the Global South, which was important as there was a general understanding among the countries of the Global South that they are being unnecessarily dragged into the Cold War politics in return for the aid they receive.

In the mid-1970s, the aid flows from the North to South started showing a major slowdown mainly because of the economic crisis faced by the capitalist countries. This had severe impact on the developing world, which was thoroughly dependent on the foreign aid from the West (Fraser 2006, 15). The industrial production in the West dropped which automatically resulted in a sharp decline in the demand for raw materials from the developing countries. This made the situations worse for the aid-dependent countries of the Global South. However, this dependence was not one-sided and the West was quick to realise this with "the Vietnam War, the Organization of the Petroleum Exporting Countries (OPEC) oil cartel and large-scale nationalisation in Chile, Iraq,

Peru, Libya and Venezuela" (Fraser 2006, 12). This "reverse dependence" of the North on the South was mainly due to "geo-strategic advantage", and the need to get access to natural resources and commodities, and for gaining influence on their domestic economy (Fraser 2006, 12). The G77 and NAM, during this period, pushed for a New International Economic Order (NIEO), and through the United Nations Conference on Trade and Development (UNCTAD), worked for the revision of the existing Bretton Woods institutions for an equitable international economic system in favour of the developing countries of the Global South. Hence, in the mid-1970s the solidarity among developing countries brought more strength to their negotiations with the OECD, although the long-term gains remained rather limited. However, a major development in the field of SSC was the conference of the Global South on technical cooperation among developing countries (TCDC) held in Buenos Aires in 1978, which resulted in the adoption of the Buenos Aires Plan of Action (BAPA) for promoting and implementing TCDC. Fifteen focal areas for TCDC were identified and insisted on giving "special attention to the least developed countries, the landlocked developing countries, and the small island developing states" (UNOSSC 2016a).

The energy crisis in the 1970s hit several developing countries hard, which made them overly dependent on external economic assistance. It was in this period that the International Monetary Fund (IMF) and the World Bank introduced the structural adjustment programme (SAPs) which made aid disbursal either through loans or lending conditional on enforcing policy changes in order to reduce inflation and fiscal imbalances in the struggling countries. SAPs focussed on conditionalities like good governance and free market policy that forced the developing countries to liberalise their economies. While SAPs were effective in certain developing countries with an institutional framework, it had adverse effect on the poorest countries with no institutional mechanisms in place, like sub-Saharan Africa, leading to economic crisis, inflation and adverse effects on the social sector. It soon became evident that the SAPs were not focussed on poverty reduction in the recipient country and faced a lot of criticism that forced a change in the SAPs, allowing social spending. In 1999, the World Bank and the IMF replaced SAPs with the Poverty Reduction Strategy Papers (PRSPs). However, the PRSPs were also at a loss to address the flaws within the global economy which rather reinforced and legitimised global inequities (Mosley et al. 2004, F236). This was not making the foreign aid architecture any better for the recipient developing country apart from fortifying the vertical relationship between the donor and the recipient.

With the end of the Cold War, the foreign aid priorities of the traditional donors changed. The US focussed on supporting the smooth transitioning of the Eastern European countries into democratic and free market economies. The OECD donors began to push for democratisation with greater energy and imposed aid sanctions on recipients who do not comply. They increased their focus on surveillance so that their aid brings desired outcomes (Fraser 2006, 13).

The twenty-first-century international aid architecture saw a marked shift, with the increasing presence of the emerging powers as development assistance providers. The international aid architecture witnessed change after development cooperation from the emerging powers like China, India, Brazil and South Africa started increasing. Despite being aid recipients from the traditional donors, these countries have been involved in providing development assistance as early as the 1950s. What is new has not been their role in giving development assistance but the increased volume, scope and nature of their development cooperation. Their dual role as both a recipient and a donor has given them a better understanding of the foreign aid architecture. These emerging economies are bringing in their own perspectives into aid-giving, which is changing the exclusive monopoly enjoyed by the traditional donors and giving more choice to their recipients. The concept of North-South flow of resources as the defining feature of international aid architecture no more held ground as the Global South is increasing their presence as providers of development assistance.

Why Give Foreign Aid?

Different strands of thought bring in diverse views on what drives donors to give foreign aid and their considerations while selecting recipients. For international political economists, foreign aid is driven by the donors' political and economic goals. Factors like culture, institutions, power distribution and the dynamics of competitive interests have a decisive role in determining the donor motivations behind aid-giving (Gilpin 1987; Schraeder et al. 1998). As per the realists, foreign aid was a tool used by the donors during the Cold War period to buy allegiance. Realists consider political hierarchy based on the distribution of strategic capabilities as an important factor in determining and reinforcing the inequalities between the donor and the recipient (Morgenthau 1962; Liska 1960). Liberal internationalists believe that aid acts as a means to fill the gaps existing between the higher and lower stages of economic development (Baldwin 1966; Chenery and Strout 1966). For them, the expansion of international trade and finance is also an important factor in mitigating this gap over a period of time. The critical theorists argue that aid has played an instrumental role in expanding world capitalism, constraining the recipient's development path to mere dependence on the world market and creating a relationship of symbolic domination (Hattori 2001, 639).

Morgenthau (1962) elaborates on six types of foreign aid that have a single commonality, i.e. "the transfer of money, goods and services from one nation to another". These can be classified as humanitarian foreign aid,[1] subsistence foreign aid,[2] military foreign aid,[3] bribery, prestige foreign aid[4] and foreign aid for economic development[5] (Morgenthau 1962, 301). He contends that all types of foreign aid are used by the donors to fulfil their national interest and the only exception in this could be humanitarian aid which could be non-political. However, he does not dismiss the idea that humanitarian assistance could also be used to wield influence if given to the recipients in a political context. Like Morgenthau, Hoy also puts forth 6 different types of aid, i.e. project

[1] Humanitarian aid is provided by governments to those nations which have suffered natural disasters like floods or famines.

[2] Subsistence aid is given by governments to prevent the breakdown of law and order situation in a recipient country.

[3] Aid for military purposes is used by governments to build and strengthen their alliances. Apart from alliance building, military aid has been given for strategic reasons to even neutral countries depending on their strategic positioning in international politics.

[4] Prestige aid is a major form of assistance given mainly to the underdeveloped countries to build infrastructure projects like a highway, airport or a stadium which leads to increase in prestige of both the donor and the recipient. It is rather a show of modernity and power and not a conscious effort by donor to get economic or political dividends. However, donors have gained several political advantages including greater goodwill through their efforts in supporting such projects.

[5] This form of aid has been given based on the proposition that the developed countries have an obligation to support the economically deprived countries by taking them on the path of development.

aid,[6] programme aid,[7] technical assistance,[8] food aid,[9] emergency or humanitarian assistance[10] and military aid[11] (Hoy 1998).

Pierre Bourdieu calls foreign aid as "symbolic domination, or a practice that signals and euphemizes social hierarchies" (Bourdieu 1990, 98). Such practices constitute what he describes as "the gentle invisible violence, unrecognized as such, chosen as much as undergone" (Bourdieu 1990, 98). The donors give those material goods to the recipients which they urgently need or those they desire to have. By giving aid as a gift, the donors aim to transform their status from being dominant to generous. Difficult to reciprocate, the recipients generally become grateful to the donor, which gives foreign aid its social power (Hattori 2001, 640).

While majority of scholars have argued that foreign aid is driven by selfish motives of the donors, ethical or idealist claims for giving aid also exist (Lumsdaine 1993; Riddell 1996). Aristotle's view of "giving as a civic virtue" could be considered one of the important ethical claims. Lumsdaine (1993) also emphasises the moral vision of the donors in giving aid. He argues that "foreign aid cannot be explained on the basis of the economic and political interests of the donor countries alone, and any satisfactory explanation must give a central place to the influence of humanitarian and egalitarian convictions upon aid donors" (Lumsdaine 1993, 35). He emphasises that factors such as colonial history, the democratic status of the recipients and income levels have a decisive role in the direction of the aid flows.

Hattori (2001) puts forth three distinct ethical justifications for foreign aid, i.e. foreign aid as a fundamental human right, as a moral response to difficulties and, finally, as embodying the ideal of humanitarianism. According to him, it is the material inequality between countries that

[6] Project aid constitutes a grant or loan designated for a specific project or outcome.

[7] Programme aid is usually a policy-based loan given to create suitable economic conditions in recipient country.

[8] It involves providing equipment or experts for a specific sector or outcome.

[9] Food aid is given to those countries that suffer natural or man-made disasters, such as floods, famines and armed conflicts.

[10] It includes grants, materials and relief to meet the demands of the victims of any disaster.

[11] It is given to strengthen the military of the recipient governments. It is the least benign form of assistance.

have prompted the rich donors to give foreign aid to their poor recipients who lack the resources essential for their development (Hattori 2001, 639). Like Hattori (2001), Pronk (2001) also maintains that foreign aid is given based on three factors—charity, economic and political. Aid given for eradicating hunger, misery and despair in the recipient country could be branded as charity. The main economic objective of aid is to help the underdeveloped recipient country attain certain levels of sustainable economic growth and the political objectives comprise factors like creating political stability, supporting peace and democracy promotion in the recipient country (Pronk 2001, 613). However, he adds two other factors including preserving political independence of former colonies and maintaining the sphere of influence of the donor country which does not entirely fit into his ethical justification of aid.

Though the ethical justifications for foreign aid continue to be the most favourite among the donors, the actual reason for giving aid captures our curiosity as aid-giving is not simply a function of intent as displayed by the donors. Rather, there are multiple objectives and motivations of aid, some of which can be said to be in conflict with each other. Hence, the complexity of donor motivations makes it difficult to assume that the major objectives behind foreign aid giving are the economic growth and development of the recipient. While humanitarian concerns might drive donors to give aid in certain scenarios, aid largely ensures that donor interests are fulfilled (Boone 1995).

The priority for a donor country while deciding on giving aid to a particular country is strategic considerations. This has been evident from the early Cold War days during which aid was used as an important instrument by the US and the USSR for their strategic benefits without any consideration for the economic development of the recipient country (Radelet 2006). Apart from the Cold War considerations of curbing communism or capitalism, other strategic interests play out as well. For instance, the US has been an important donor to Afghanistan, Israel and Iraq. While there are several underdeveloped countries which are in dire need of external financing, US preferred to give aid to those countries strategically important to the US and therefore they receive a major portion of the US aid.

Foreign policy and political interests also determine the aid from a donor to their particular recipients (Radelet 2006). Aid is also given to gain favour and to influence the domestic and foreign policy of the recipient (Griffin and Enos 1970). In order to get diplomatic support and recognition from countries around the world, Taiwan and China are competing with each other to give aid to several developing countries to choose between Beijing and Taipei. The conflict for recognition between the two has led to an increase in aid to those countries which support them and buying out support through aid. China, with its deep pockets, has been more successful in its efforts compared to Taiwan and has been able to sever links of many countries with Taiwan (e.g. Solomon Islands). In the diplomatic battlefield between China and Taiwan, the recipient countries of one had to accept antagonisms from the other. It makes it difficult for these recipient countries to accept assistance without getting involved in the tussle.

Alesina and Dollar (2000, 33) indicate that a number of factors could drive the donors to give foreign aid, including strategic interests, colonial ties, quest for natural resources, trade and democratic promotion. Sometimes, the donor decisions are also governed by the economic and political interests of the influential groups within the donor country, boosting their benefits (Hopkins 2000). In some cases, therefore, recipient needs rarely figure in the aid picture. A few situations when the humanitarian angle could be spotted are during severe natural calamities (Tarp 2006; Griffin and Enos 1970). Both Griffin and Enos (1970) and Alesina and Dollar (2000) argue that philanthropy is not one of the reasons for giving aid, as foreign aid is generally an instrument in the hands of the donor countries to wield influence. In reality, foreign aid from the rich and powerful to the poor countries reflects the power politics at play in which "the strong can engage in symbolic battles without any physical injury" (Griffin and Enos 1970). Therefore, national interest tops the list of factors driving the donors to give aid. Self-interest of donor countries has always influenced the decision of foreign aid flows (Hook 1998). Before the end of the Cold War, the aid flows were based on political interests. The focus slowly shifted to donors' commercial interests in the recipient countries, including trade and investments (Berthelemy and Tichit 2002, 19). Donor's motives are clearly supposed to have an impact on the recipients, who have little choice or voice in selecting donors, their modalities or the conditionalities that accompany aid.

Evaluating Aid and Development Linkages

Aid and development are closely interlinked because narrative of aid is largely donor-driven, where aid is used for development and economic growth of the recipient. In this scenario, aid effectiveness becomes an important dimension that concerns both the donors and the recipients in deciding any positive role played by aid in development.

The increasing focus on aid effectiveness also sheds light on the conditionalities imposed by donors on the recipients to bring desired results. The rationale for using aid conditionalities is that they prove to be important mechanisms for the growth and development of the recipient country and aid is more beneficial when accompanied by conditionalities. Donors go to the extent of arguing that aid is not given for any monetary benefits of the donor but for "aid to act as a lever for the policy reforms" (Radelet 2006, 13).

With the end of the Cold War, the major donors gained confidence to attach political and economic conditionalities on the recipients without being concerned that they would lose their allies. This period also marked the rise of pro-democracy movements in various parts of the world, including Eastern Europe, Africa and Latin America (Chhotray and Hulme 2007). This gave a push to donors' pursuit of democracy promotion and good governance in recipient countries, which were driven by political considerations.

In fact, there are no set rules for conditionalities imposed by the donors. Collier and Dollar (1999) says "poverty reduction is a function of growth and growth alone". In order to reduce poverty in the recipient country, economic growth is a must. However, the donors assume that aid is more effective when the recipients have democratic institutions that are transparent and accountable, and sound economic policies to support growth and development (Hansen and Tarp 2000; Lensink and White 2000a; Erixon 2005; Radelet 2006). Tarp (2006) argues that aid works only in those countries that have transparent institutions and good policies. While good policies of the recipients helped them get continuous supply of aid, the strategic interests of the donors also played an important role in ensuring this aid flow (Pronk et al. 2004, 12). For the recipients, conditionalities imposed on them are harsh and has had severe domestic consequences. Conditionalities do not always bring policy reforms in the recipient country (Bird 1999; Hoy 1998). Collier et al. (1997, 1406) propose that "aid allocation should reflect ex post growth performance and human development rather than ex ante policy conditionality".

Western donors have increasingly emphasised on good governance as an inevitable condition for foreign aid. While the relevance of good governance on aid architecture has been increasingly emphasised, there exists no single definition for good governance. The most common accepted definition of good governance is the one propounded by the World Bank, according to which governance is "the manner in which power is exercised in the management of a country's economic and social resources for development" (World Bank 1992, 1). The World Bank also refers to good governance as "sound development management and sees it as central to creating and sustaining an environment which fosters strong and equitable development and is an essential complement to sound economic policies" (World Bank 1992, 1). Aubut (2004, 9) argues that governance "not only refers to the rules of the game, but also to the 'players' of the game, such as politicians and bureaucrats". The players are important as they are capable of using the institutions to manage resources that could propel growth and development. Some view good governance in a narrow sense that is limited to improving institutions and their role in development (Aubut 2004).

Both the World Bank and the OECD (1995) have similar definition of what governance is. However, OECD also relates governance with participatory development and democratisation. In order to achieve and maintain high levels of development, the OECD laid down four elements of good governance that are crucial for the recipients to follow: the rule of law, controlling corruption, public sector management and reduction of military spending (OECD 1995). Further, human rights and democracy have also been incorporated as main aspects of governance (Neumayer 2003). As the concept of good governance gained prominence, the donor countries also started adopting their own definitions of good governance. While they consider the World Bank and the OECD definitions as important, the some donors also focussed on specific criteria for governance. For example, the US prioritises "lawful governance" while Sweden emphasises on "public management and administration" (Aubut 2004, 10).

However, the Western notion of governance may not be universally applicable. The claim that aid effectiveness is governed by good policies is not always true (Pronk et al. 2004; Doornbos 2001). Aid could be effective only when the political, economic and the cultural contexts of the recipient are taken into consideration (Doornbos 2001). Donor perspectives on good and bad policy might not work for all recipients and therefore should not be seen as absolutes. Instead, these policies work subjectively based on the level of development and the resource availability of the recipients. If not, the donor conditionalities would have produced similar outcomes everywhere.

The idea of conceptualising governance in aid policy gained momentum with the acknowledgement that the recipient political situation decides the effectiveness of aid. Even though aid has been ineffective in bringing growth and development in several countries, it is supposed to bring positive results when both the donors and recipients meet the quality conditions, of which good governance is one (Barder and Birdsall 2006).

Barder and Birdsall (2006) outlined a mechanism for progress-based aid that ensures accountability and resources are utilised properly in the recipient country. In this mechanism, those countries get more funds that choose better institutions and policy reforms. The aim is to ensure transparency and effectiveness, at the same time reducing the costs. Most importantly, this is supposed to enable recipient countries to strengthen their local institutional capacity that is inevitable for economic growth and development (Barder and Birdsall 2006, 21). However, aid for progress has its own downsides. Countries with poor governance and high levels of poverty need more aid for making any difference in their governance structures. Many countries are entirely dependent on foreign aid to achieve the SDGs. Hence, there is a need to increase aid to these countries despite their poor policies so that they achieve economic growth (Barder and Birdsall 2006, 3). The trend of rewarding good policy reforms existed as early as the 1990s. Many donors decide on their recipients also by the institutional structures and good governance. However, this approach is said to emphasise short-term results "at the expense of long-term institutional development" (Berthelemy and Tichit 2002).

In the mid-1990s, there was a shift among the donors towards "process conditionality". Process conditionality emphasises "minimum levels of corruption, respect for human rights, adherence to the rule of law, and greater accountability of government to its citizens" (Barder and Birdsall 2006, 6). Recipient governments were supposed to ensure local ownership of policy reforms for uninterrupted flow of aid from donors. Indeed, donors began to categorise countries on the basis of one or more political and institutional characteristics. These characteristics also determined the delivery mechanisms adopted by donors to these countries, i.e. bilateral, multilateral or aid through the NGOs. However, this emphasis on process conditionality and selectivity brought new problems with it. Several countries with lack of proper institutions and poor governance were kept out of aid system despite having efficient leaders who can make a difference to the domestic situation of the country with greater funds at disposal.

Furthermore, process conditionality has been instrumental in strengthening civil society groups in the recipient country. According to Barder and Birdsall (2006, 6), "process conditionality may be harder to measure and enforce than policy conditionality".

Conditionality, both political and economic, has been important aspect of aid for long. However, these do not yield desired results most of the time and are fraught with severe problems from the conception stage to the level of implementation.

Boone (1996) compared aid's effect in different regimes, including elitist, egalitarian and laissez-faire political regimes, and concluded that the type of regime in these recipient countries has no effect on the effectiveness of aid. However, aid is found to have an effect on government consumption, which increases without any exception in regimes. Hence, aid is found to be not so effective even in democratic regimes with good policy and governance (Aubut 2004, 18). Peter Bauer (1991) argues that aid is seldom effective and has been used by the donors without any consideration for the development of the recipient. He maintains that aid could only be considered as donor government subsidy to the recipient government that caters to the rich people in the recipient countries and has no impact in lifting the poor people out of poverty. Overall development of the recipient country does not figure in the priority list of both the donor and recipient governments. It is only the political elites in the recipient country who benefit from the flow of aid. The situation in Ethiopia and Burma in the 1980s demonstrated that aid was mostly diverted for the benefit of the rich. By supporting corrupt and inefficient governments, aid has resulted in causing a poverty trap (Boone 1996). These governments, instead of fostering economic growth and development, have diverted it for the benefit of their political elites (Aubut 2004, 12).

Further, many a time the donors decide the institutional specifications for the recipients which are not suitable to their stage of economic growth and do not take into consideration the local needs and demands. These institutions remain in place only until the aid flow continues from that donor. Aid has had diverse effects on the recipient countries. Recipients also find it hard to manage aid flows from several donors as most of these donors impose different conditionalities that make it a huge challenge for them to cope with.

The steady rise of foreign aid since the mid-nineteenth century peaked by 1990. However, with the end of the Cold War, the foreign aid flows fell considerably (Hopkins 2000; Berthelemy and Tichit 2002; Aubut 2004, 1). Another reason for reduced foreign aid flows has been "aid fatigue" syndrome experienced by certain donors (Hoy 1998; Bird 1999; Aubut 2004). Aid fatigue was a result of the realisation among donors that aid has not been able to bring much positive outcomes in the recipient countries. This resulted in debates and discussions on aid effectiveness, and the main concern was that despite giving money and resources to their recipients, most of them still remained poor (Aubut 2004, 1). The lack of effectiveness of aid led to an anti-aid atmosphere in several donor countries (Hoy 1998; Bird 1999). Donor fatigue became an issue and was raised as an important concern in the budgetary discussions of donor countries. Furthermore, this could be also because of the dominant neoliberal ideology which mandated a reduction in government spending and a greater thrust towards private players.

Hopkins offers six strong reasons for the decline of the aid since the last decade of the nineteenth century which include

> the reduced significance of aid with the end of the cold war, growing budget pressures on the donors, disappointment with the effectiveness of aid, weakened popular support for aid in donor countries, donor country's weakened special interest coalitions that supported aid and that the intellectual foundations of aid were challenged by the neo-liberal philosophies. (Hopkins 2000, 7)

Donors consider the factors existing within the recipient country responsible for the alleged failure of foreign assistance, including corruption and incompetence, lack of proper infrastructure facilities and good governance (van de Walle 1999, 350). However, it is good to note that if these factors did not exist in these countries, they would not have needed any external aid.

Even when aid from the OECD countries has shown a decline, what is most interesting is that the aid given by the emerging powers is increasing steadily. Hence, aid fatigue seems to have affected only the traditional donors.

The following sections specifically look into the international bilateral aid architecture and how the emerging powers as development assistance providers are making inroads into the aid system and institutions established and managed by the traditional donors.

Bilateral Aid Architecture

Foreign aid could successfully transform itself with changing times to cater to a variety of aims and objectives that it was supposed to deliver. This made the categorisation of aid too complex and difficult (Burnell 2004). There are three main vehicles through which the donors provide foreign assistance, i.e. bilateral aid, multilateral aid and aid through the non-governmental organisations (NGOs) (Hoy 1998, 4).

Earlier, most aid was given as bilateral aid, i.e. direct flow of resources from one country to another. The major economic powers, like the United Kingdom (UK), France and the US, provided bulk of their foreign aid through bilateral channels. Major colonial powers directed their aid to their former colonies[12] or to countries that are strategically important to them.[13] For example, the US reciprocated Pakistan's support on the war on terror with huge amount of aid. Even now, most donors prefer to give bilateral aid in comparison with multilateral aid, as bilateral aid gives donors direct access to their recipients.

Multilateral development assistance also became one of the platforms for donor countries to provide assistance, especially the UN and its agencies like the United Nations Development Programme (UNDP) and the Economic and Social Council (ECOSOC), playing out a major role in development story of the poorest countries of the world. Furthermore, several donor countries are also making their contributions to NGOs and doling out money through these NGOs gives these donors greater control over their funding and influence the selection process of recipients.

The type of aid flows, be it bilateral or multilateral, has always influenced the types of projects that are being funded by the donor countries. Through bilateral aid, the donors tend to place stricter political, diplomatic or economic conditionalities on the recipients. On the other hand, multilateral aid is considered to be less harsh on recipients in terms of conditionalities as the donor interests are less reflected (Hoy 1998, 4).

[12] For instance, UK gives most part of its aid to its former colonies. Its maximum aid was being diverted to India, a former colony, until 2010. UK's aid to India was reduced when New Delhi declared that it is not dependent on foreign aid. Since then, UK increased its aid to Pakistan and Bangladesh, both former colonies of UK (DFID 2015, 32). In 2018, Pakistan is the top recipient of UK aid at £331 million (DFID 2018).

[13] The US has a history of providing aid to countries it sees as strategic partners. For instance, its increasing aid to South Asia especially, Afghanistan and Pakistan.

However, the history of World Bank and IMF austerity programmes and SAPs amply demonstrated that sometimes multilateral aid can also be as coercive as bilateral aid (Minch 2010).

The following sections in this chapter would examine closely the bilateral development assistance flows, both North-South and South-South.

North-South Cooperation: The Established Donors

The North-South flow of aid is managed by the OECD-DAC, known as the established donors or the traditional donors in the international aid architecture. The standard definition of foreign aid also comes from the OECD-DAC, which defines foreign aid as "financial flows, technical assistance, and commodities that are designed to promote economic development and welfare as their main objective and are provided as either grants or subsidized loans" (Radelet 2006). The official development assistance (ODA) from OECD-DAC was defined as

> those flows to countries and territories on the DAC List and to multilateral development institutions which are "i. provided by official agencies, including state and local governments, or by their executive agencies; and ii. each transaction of which: a) is administered with the promotion of the economic development and welfare of developing countries as its main objective; and b) is concessional in character and conveys a grant element of at least 25 per cent (calculated at a rate of discount of 10 per cent). (OECD 2008, 1)

This definition of aid dates back to 1969 and was further concretised in 1972. Although its interpretation was broadened over the years, it is a definition drafted by donors, without taking into account the concerns or the needs of the recipients and the changing contours of international politics.

The end of Cold War changed the political and economic situations that existed after the Second World War. The transition economies of Eastern Europe had new aid requirements, and the East Asian countries had progressed economically in a big way by this time which reduced their demand for foreign aid. This made the OECD to adopt a new list for potential recipients.

> The consolidated list of recipient countries was divided into two parts until 2005:
>
> Part I: Only aid to "traditional" developing countries was counted as ODA, for which there is a long-standing United Nations target of 0.7% of donors' national income.
>
> Part II: Aid to "more advanced" developing and eastern European countries were recorded separately as "official aid". (OECD 2016a)

From 1970, the UN has set a target for Part I countries, that they should receive 0.7% of donors' Gross National Income (GNI)[14] as aid.[15] Aid to the Part II countries in the list was documented separately as "Official Aid (OA)" which is not included in ODA. Only a few DAC countries cross the 0.7% of their GNI mark. In 2018, only five countries, i.e. Sweden, Luxembourg, Norway, Denmark and UK, met the target and only Sweden crossed the mark of 1.0% of GNI. The giant economy like that of the US provides only 0.17 per cent of its GNI (OECD 2019a). Even though the US falls much below in the list of countries giving aid commensurate with their 0.7% commitment, when it comes to the net ODA disbursements, the country tops the list. This has been mainly because of the size of the US economy which makes even a 0.17% of its aid coming to a sizeable amount of USD34.26 billion (OECD 2019a). Unquestionably, the ODA from the traditional donors will remain a critical source of development finance in the coming years despite the reduction in the amounts of ODA allocated by these countries since the 2008 financial crisis (ECOSOC 2014, 2/20). In 2018, the ODA declined again by 2.7% from the 2017 figures and the most affected

[14] Initially, a target of 1% of aid from developed countries was recommended by the World Council of Churches in 1958. This was followed up by a proposal by Jan Tinbergen who was appointed as the Chairman of the United Nations Committee on Development Planning in 1964. Tinbergen proposed "a target of official flows of 0.75% of gross national product to be reached by 1972 based on the estimated capital inflows developing economies needed to achieve desirable growth rates" (OECD 2010, 1).

The Pearson Commission Report *Partners in Development* in 1969 proposed "a target of 0.7% of donor Gross National Product (GNP) which should be achieved by 1975 and in no case later than 1980"(OECD 2010, 2). In 1993, after the revised System of National Accounts, "gross national product was replaced by gross national income (GNI), an equivalent concept" (OECD 2010, 3).

[15] Only few States give aid according to the UN target of 0.7% GNI of which the most important are the Scandinavian countries that have continuously been trying to keep up the 0.7% mark.

were the neediest countries which would again find it difficult to meet the 2030 agenda if the OECD aid keeps declining (OECD 2019b).

The OECD-DAC, since 2018, has changed the definition of the ODA to

> those flows to countries and territories on the DAC List of ODA Recipients[16] and to multilateral development institutions which are:
>
> i. provided by official agencies, including state and local governments, or by their executive agencies; and
> ii. each transaction of which:
>   a. is administered with the promotion of the economic development and welfare of developing countries as its main objective; and
>   b. is concessional in character. In DAC statistics, this implies a grant element of at least
>   - 45 per cent in the case of bilateral loans to the official sector of LDCs and other LICs (calculated at a rate of discount of 9 per cent).
>   - 15 per cent in the case of bilateral loans to the official sector of LMICs (calculated at a rate of discount of 7 per cent).
>   - 10 per cent in the case of bilateral loans to the official sector of UMICs (calculated at a rate of discount of 6 per cent).
>   - 10 per cent in the case of loans to multilateral institutions (calculated at a rate of discount of 5 per cent for global institutions and multilateral development banks, and 6 per cent for other organisations, including sub-regional organisations). (OECD 2019d)

The new definition has changed the concessionality part to a large extend, especially with the ongoing discussions on reflecting public sector instruments in the ODA (Atwood et al. 2018). This has raised questions on the quality standards and credibility of the new ODA reporting rules, as the newly introduced grant equivalent method is supposed to inflate the actual ODA figures (Scott 2019). The OECD-DAC's definition of ODA still continues to be a major parameter for quantifying and evaluating foreign aid. However, the new definition and statistical measures are yet to be finalised as the discussions are still ongoing among the OECD-DAC members.

[16] For a complete list of ODA recipients for reporting on aid in 2018 and 2019, see (OECD 2019c). The list is revised every three years and the next one is due in 2020.

Though the DAC still occupies the top position in terms of the net flow of aid, recent DAC statistics suggests the increasing presence of developing countries, not belonging to the OECD, as donors in the international aid architecture. With the economic gravity changing, emerging powers like China, India and Brazil are increasingly playing a prominent role in the international aid architecture, though with their own rules and agendas. However, it remains to be seen as to what proportion of the emerging powers' development assistance would qualify as ODA under the OECD-DAC definitions as these countries do not give a clear definition of aid and the sparse data on their assistance makes any classification difficult. But these developing countries are making their presence felt in the international aid architecture. Even though in a limited capacity, these countries have made the Global South a relevant entity in changing the discourse on foreign aid.

South-South Development Cooperation (SSDC)

South-South Cooperation (SSC) is defined as "a broad framework for collaboration among countries of the South in the political, economic, social, cultural, environmental and technical domains" (UNOSSC 2016b). SSC has expanded through the increased volume of trade, foreign direct investment (FDI) and regional integration of the Southern countries apart from technology transfers and capacity-building programmes, sharing of area experts and several other forms of South-South exchanges to achieve economic growth and development of the Global South through their concerted efforts.

Even though SSC is a much wider concept, the purview of this book is the role of the Global South in development cooperation. SSC can operationalise on a bilateral, multilateral, regional, sub-regional or inter-regional basis with the developing countries of the Global South coming together in order to achieve their development goals. The principles of SSC first emerged in bilateral or regional contexts which were slowly incorporated into the global context. In this research, bilateral South-South Development Cooperation (SSDC) is focussed upon to understand emerging powers' development cooperation with countries in the Global South.

SSDC has gained greater momentum with the emerging powers like China, India and Brazil's increasing development assistance volume and scope. In addition, the new ideas and perspectives brought by the

Global South into development cooperation have garnered attention and curiosity, from both the traditional donors and the recipient countries, in their development cooperation activities. Furthermore, the Global South has always emphasised that their definition of SSDC is much wider and different from that of "foreign aid" as defined by OECD-DAC.

The Global South albeit with different histories, political systems, economic capabilities and institutional set-up has been involved in addressing a variety of development challenges they face through SSDC. The driving principles of the SSDC, as observed from the policies and practices of these developing countries as development assistance providers, include "respect for national sovereignty, ownership and independence; non-interference in domestic affairs; alignment with national priorities; and unity, solidarity and equality among partners" (UN 2010; ECOSOC 2014, 11/20). This has been also emphasised in the outcome document[17] of the High-level United Nations Conference on South-South Cooperation (UNDP 2010). The 2nd High-level United Nations Conference on South-South Cooperation termed as BAPA+40, held in Buenos Aires in March 2019, was a major event on SSC and triangular cooperation, which emphasised on the Global South's commitment to the implementation of the 2030 Agenda for sustainable development, the Addis Ababa Action Agenda and endorsing BAPA (UN 2019).

The principles of SSC evolved with geopolitical changes and economic developments in international politics. Developing countries have been pushing for greater SSC in several ways with the changing contexts. Southern countries, with the backing of ECOSOC's Development Cooperation Forum (DCF), have successfully laid down the key features of SSC, including

> the diversity of approaches; horizontality, as a voluntary process and mutually agreed relationship; equal distribution of benefits; non-conditionality; comprehensive vision, cultivating the capacity for longer-term sustained development; results-orientation, aimed at enhancing mutual benefits and promoting win-win outcomes and complementarities; flexibility, in ways of sharing their own development experiences and knowledge; and visibility, with a focus on concrete results and through demand-driven projects that target country needs. (ECOSOC 2014, 11/20)

[17] See, the High-level United Nations Conference on South-South Cooperation, held in Nairobi in 2009 at http://southsouthconference.org/.

Furthermore, certain countries of the Global South have also used an "integrated approach", that encompasses both "non-concessional loans and commercial transactions in trade and investment", as an important aspect of their development cooperation (ECOSOC 2014, 11/20).

Within the Global South, only a few countries have been successful in repositioning themselves from a recipient to a development assistance provider. While over the past decade, some Southern countries have been able to overtake certain Northern economies on economic growth rate, most countries in the Global South are still aid recipients and dependent on OECD aid. Consistent high economic growth of emerging powers like China, India and Brazil has placed them in a different league from other developing nations in the Global South. However, these countries do not fall in the category of the "developed" nor do they align themselves with the North. Even though their growth rates are much higher than that of many developed countries, their per capita income remains much lower. China and India could be considered as major countries involved in the development cooperation to the Global South. Hence, most of the discussions on Southern donors are China-centric, which ignores several other Southern donors including South Africa, Indonesia, Thailand and Colombia, all of which are equally significant in offering development assistance, despite most of them enjoying modest per capita incomes (Mawdsley 2012).

While these emerging powers prefer to distance themselves from the OECD-DAC donors for both political and diplomatic reasons, OECD has shown interest in reaching out to these countries. OECD proposed for "enhanced engagement" procedures with China, India, Brazil, Indonesia and South Africa and termed them as "key partners" of the OECD (OECD 2016b). However, these emerging powers prefer to be called as "development partners" rather than "donors" and identify their "development cooperation" as very different from the "foreign aid" of the traditional donors.

Furthermore, the Global South is not a homogenous entity. Inequality as well as diversity within as well as between nations suggests that even within the Global South there exists a "North of South" and "South of South", just like every country has its own North and South (Chisholm 2009, 4). Even though the emerging powers as development assistance providers are similar in many ways, they are equally diverse. Within this context, a renewed call for South-South development cooperation has emerged based on equality and mutual benefit for transforming the growth trajectory of its partners.

Emerging Powers vs. the OECD

This section analyses both the policies and positions of both the traditional donors and emerging powers as donors. It also explores the possible differences between North-South cooperation and SSC in their approach and outcomes.

One of the biggest challenges in analysing the developing cooperation programmes of the emerging powers like China, India or Brazil is that they do not have a clear official definition of development cooperation. Similarly, what constitutes development cooperation might differ from country to country and the lack of a single definition demands taking up individual country case studies for analysing development cooperation of the Global South. Emerging powers are not a monolithic group and there is limited availability of data regarding their development assistance volume and scope. This makes the task of calculating their development cooperation volume further difficult.

The volume of development assistance from emerging powers is found to be steadily increasing. However, they do not meet higher standards for governance and transparency (O'Keefe 2007, 7). For example, Chinese government has been hesitant to disclose information on its development cooperation. Even though they have come up with two[18] White Papers on Chinese Foreign Aid, there are several gaps in the data and the data is not published regularly. This is the case with most of the emerging powers, including Brazil and India, that are not part of the OECD.

These emerging powers, which are development assistance providers, are yet to develop institutions that exclusively focus on their development assistance. In contrast, the OECD has strict rules for its member countries and their institutions have evolved over the last several years. Sato et al. (2010) observe that "the lack of institutional constraints" gives the emerging powers "a certain level of freedom to pursue their short-term national interests" through development cooperation (Sato et al. 2010, 24). Emerging powers' development cooperation is also accompanied by trade and investments. In order to increase the trade flows, they pay

[18] The First White Paper on Chinese Foreign Aid was published in 2011 and the second one in 2014.

particular attention to trade-related development cooperation, support big infrastructural projects and provide training and technical assistance for capacity-building (Kragelund 2010, 23). This policy of commercial engagement through aid could also be mutually beneficial to both the partners. Since these donors are not constrained by standard rules or regulations, they have a free-hand in taking decisions and making rules, which makes the development assistance of emerging powers tailor-made to a certain extend. The increased involvement and support of the emerging powers in disaster relief and post-conflict resolution efforts reflect their readiness to support their peers during crisis as well as their enduring need-based support to the Global South (Dreher et al. 2010, 1).

Besides, emerging powers' development cooperation is found to be affirmative in several ways. Given their own experience as a recipient of foreign aid from the traditional donors, the emerging powers have competitive advantage in providing development cooperation which could be both need-based and merit-based (Dreher et al. 2010, 1). Their no-conditionalities approach also makes it more lucrative for their partners in the Global South (O'Keefe 2007, 6). Rather than adhering to conditionalities attached to OECD aid, the recipient countries find it comfortable in taking development cooperation from emerging powers.

Furthermore, the emerging powers' development cooperation is said to be "tailor-made" as they are found to be comparatively more considerate about their partner's domestic situations and policies. They also act based on the demands of the partners and this demand-driven approach favour the partner countries. Their assistance is more predictable, which helps the beneficiary country tremendously in running projects without many hurdles. Since the inception of the SAPs in the 1980s, traditional donors' aid has been characterised by a "one-size-fits-all" approach (Kragelund 2010, 22). This policy was applied to almost all the aid recipient countries on an equal footing. In order to make the economies of the developing countries market-oriented, apart from being encouraged to move towards privatisation, they forced them to concentrate more on trade and production to boost their economy. Many developing countries, especially in Africa, were burdened by these programmes that were hard to be implemented in those countries because of the lack of required infrastructure and experience in dealing with such situations, which worsened the domestic situations of the recipient countries.

When compared to the OECD countries, the emerging powers' speedy response to the demands of the recipients has been seen in a positive light by the beneficiary countries. DAC rules and regulations to enhance the quality and effectiveness of aid make aid-giving a time-taking process. Emerging powers are rather quick with their decisions in providing development cooperation. For example, China is famous for responding much quicker to the demands of its partners. They are also known to complete their development projects within the timeline for completion. However, democratic countries like India and Brazil take somewhat longer than the Chinese to respond to the call for help from their partner countries. However, India is known for being quick during emergencies and its humanitarian assistance are found to be effective and beneficial to its partners.

Sato et al. (2010, 34) argue that "emerging donors are beginning to serve as real alternatives to traditional donors". However, the development cooperation volumes and programmes of the emerging powers are still very small when compared to that of the traditional donors' aid and some of the developing countries are severely dependent on foreign aid for their subsistence which cannot be met with the modest assistance coming from the emerging powers alone. The emerging powers are not yet equipped to replace aid from traditional donors. However, what is interesting is that the emerging powers are "offering recipients a choice, thereby initiating a healthy competition" (Sato et al. 2010, 34).

Another reason for the emerging donors' development cooperation getting more attractive is their generosity when compared to the established donors whose aid has become less generous and therefore, less attractive (Woods 2008). The OECD countries' aid is dwindling, making it important for the recipients to look out for aid from other countries.

The rise of the emerging powers has also led to rising tension between the North and the South (Schirm 2006, 2). Woods (2008) hints at "a new silent revolution" that is bound to take place with the increasing presence of emerging powers in international aid architecture. However, the emerging powers' efforts have not been focussed on overturning or replacing the rules set by the traditional donors. Rather, they have been offering more choice to the recipient countries thereby "introducing competitive pressures into the existing system and are weakening the bargaining position of Western donors" (Woods 2008). This is more so with the changing power dynamics in the international system, where the emerging powers are trying to rise to a more influential position. For the partner countries, they seem to be responsible and their behaviour more legitimate, as they increase their development cooperation in areas where the partner countries demand assistance.

Conclusion

The efforts of the Global South in expanding SSC have resulted in sizeable changes in the international aid architecture that was designed and set up by the developed countries of the Global North. The Global South has brought, not one, but several new approaches to development cooperation based on the core principles of SSC. Even though the development assistance from the emerging powers is not new, their increased presence and visibility in the international aid architecture has brought a greater interest in their development assistance programmes. The change in approach from unequal and conditionality-based aid to a more equal and balanced engagement with beneficiary countries was rather novel. Furthermore, their "dual" position as that of a donor and recipient at the same time brings an edge to their assistance programme as they have an understanding of the needs and constraints of developing countries as aid recipients (ODI 2010, 2; Brautigam 2009, 311). This has helped them garner more support than criticisms from the recipients, unlike the case of traditional donors.

The emerging powers are trying to create a new discourse on development assistance based on SSC. The emerging powers of the Global South are putting effort to transform their development assistance programme by making their own definitions, institutions, development cooperation policies, modalities and agendas. By distancing themselves from the OECD-DAC agenda, these emerging economies are trying to create a unique identity as a "partner" in development assistance. The emerging powers, through their development assistance, are trying to alter their status and trying to reposition themselves into a more influential and legitimate players within the international system. Hence, they are using a combination of "hard" and "soft" power to "lead" the developing countries. Though there are varied constraints and challenges in front of the emerging powers, they are showing their readiness to play the "leadership" role not only in their respective regions but also in the Global South. Hence, the emerging powers are instrumental in bringing about systemic change in international aid architecture and international political economy.

Even when these countries are asserting their Third World identities and positioning themselves as equal partners, the reality of power relations still haunts the development landscape. Often the principle of equality is enunciated at the policy level but struggle to materialise at the practical level. This further brings us to the issues of inequalities within the Global South and the existence of a "South within the South". The weak and poor countries of the Global South cannot match the political and economic clout of the powerful countries within the Global South.

The growing economic and political relevance of the South in global affairs will be the hallmark of the twenty-first century. With the decline in foreign aid from the OECD-DAC, and the growing development cooperation from the emerging powers, they are making their presence felt in the development landscape (Sotero 2009). Today, there are more countries receiving aid than ever before. One cannot disagree with the claim that "the sun does not set on foreign aid" (Burnell 1997). With the increasing presence of emerging powers, the flow of resources has definitely increased. However, SSC is perceived to be "at best a complement, and not a replacement", for North-South cooperation (Nel 2010, 958). To replace traditional donors' development assistance, the emerging powers have to go a long way in terms of increasing the volume and scope, setting up institutions, formulating clear-cut definitions and policies, and tackling issues of effectiveness, impact assessment and evaluation. However, it can be said that SSDC has eroded the exclusive competence of the West on matters of development (Six 2009, 1117).

Nevertheless, emerging powers' development cooperation efforts have brought a fresh air into the development landscape. These countries have been bringing more choice for the recipient countries and creating competition in the international aid architecture. However, the emerging powers in the Global South are not a homogenous group and have different approaches to SSDC. This makes generalisations of emerging powers' development cooperation an arduous task. Yet, development cooperation is an inevitable component of the emerging powers' economic diplomacy. These countries have been enhancing their economic diplomacy efforts in order to rise in the international system.

In the subsequent three chapters, the role of the three key emerging powers of the Global South, i.e. Brazil, China and India, is analysed in detail to understand their development cooperation policies, agendas and motivations. Brazil, China and India will act as a lens for building a general understanding of the emerging powers' development cooperation, their nature, behaviour, motives and markedly their changing identities. It would be interesting to see what new approaches and ideas does the emerging powers bring to the table of international aid architecture, which would be instrumental in understanding the changing landscape of international politics.

References

Alesina, Alberto and Dollar, David. (2000), "Who Gives Foreign Aid to Whom and Why?", *Journal of Economic Growth*, 5(1): 33–63.

Atwood, J.B, Manning, R. and Riegler, H. (2018), "Don't Undermine the Basic Architecture of OECD/DAC Statistics: A Letter of Warning", Brookings. Accessed at https://www.brookings.edu/blog/future-development/2018/12/21/dont-undermine-the-basic-architecture-of-oecd-dac-statistics-a-letter-of-warning/.

Aubut, Julie. (2004), *The Good Governance Agenda: Who Wins and Who Loses. Some Empirical Evidence for 2001*, LSE working Paper Series No. 04-48 [Online: web]. Accessed at http://www2.lse.ac.uk/internationalDevelopment/pdf/WP48.pdf.

Baldwin, D. (1966), *Foreign Aid and American Foreign Policy: A Documentary Analysis*, New York: Praeger.

Barder, Owen and Birdsall, Nancy. (2006), *Payments for Progress: A Hands-Off Approach to Foreign Aid*, Working Paper 102, Centre for Global Development [Online: web]. Accessed at http://www.cgdev.org/content/publications/detail/11550/.

Bauer, P. (1991), *The Development Frontier: Essays in Applied Economics*, Cambridge: Harvard University Press. Cited in Aubut, Julie. (2004), *The Good Governance Agenda: Who Wins and Who Loses, Some Empirical Evidence for 2001*, LSE working Paper Series No. 04-48 [Online: web]. Accessed at http://www2.lse.ac.uk/internationalDevelopment/pdf/WP48.pdf.

Berthelemy, Jean-Claude and Tichit, Ariane. (2002), *Bilateral Donor's Aid Allocation Decisions: A Three Dimensional Panel Analysis*, Discussion Paper No. 2002/123, World Institute of Development Economics Research, United Nations University, Finland [Online: web]. Accessed at http://www.wider.unu.edu/stc/repec/pdfs/rp2002/dp2002-123.pdf.

Bird, Graham. (1999), "The Political Economy of Foreign Aid: Fatigue or Regeneration?", *Zagreb International Review of Economics and Business*, 2(2): 1–24.

Boone, P. (1995), *Politics and the Effectiveness of Foreign Aid*, Discussion Paper No. 272, Centre for Economic Performance, London School of Economics and Political Science, London [Online: web]. Accessed at http://cep.lse.ac.uk/pubs/download/dp0272.pdf.

Boone, P. (1996), "Politics and the Effectiveness of Foreign Aid", *European Economic Review*, 40(2): 289–329.

Bourdieu, Pierre. (1990), *The Logic of Practice*, Cambridge, UK: Polity.

Brautigam, Deborah. (2009), *The Dragon's Gift: The Real Story of China in Africa*, New York: Oxford University Press.

Brautigam, Deborah. (2010), *China, Africa and the International Aid Architecture* [Online: web]. Accessed at http://www.american.edu/sis/faculty/upload/Rev-working-paper-china-africa-aid-architecture-August-2010.pdf.

Burnell, Peter. (1997), "The Changing Politics of Foreign Aid—Where to Next?", *Politics*, 17(2): 117–125.

Burnell, Peter. (2004), *The Domestic Political Impact of Foreign Aid: Recalibrating the Research Agenda*, Working Paper [Online: web]. Accessed at http://www.essex.ac.uk/ecpr/events/generalconference/marburg/papers/26/4/Burnell.pdf.

Chenery, Hollis B. and Strout, Alan M. (1966), "Foreign Assistance and Economic Development", *American Economic Review*, 56 (4): 679–733.

Chhotray, Vasudha and Hulme, David. (2007), *Contrasting Visions for Aid and Governance in the 21st Century: The White House Millennium Challenge Account and DFID's Drivers of Change*, Working Paper [Online: web]. Accessed at http://economics.ouls.ox.ac.uk/14023/1/gprg-wps-062.pdf.

Chisholm, Linda. (2009), "Introduction: Rhetoric, Realities, and Reasons", in Chisholm, Linda and Steiner-Khamsi, Gita (eds.), *South-South Cooperation in Education and Development*, Teachers College Press: New York.

Collier, P. and Dollar, D. (1999), *Aid Allocation and Poverty Reduction*, Policy Research Working Paper No. 2041, World Bank, Washington, DC.

Collier, P. et al. (1997), "Redesigning Conditionality", *World Development*, 25 (9): 1399–1407.

DFID. (2015), "Statistics on International Development 2015". Accessed at https://www.gov.uk/government/uploads/system/uploads/attachment_data/file/482322/SID2015c.pdf.

DFID. (2018), "Final UK Aid Spend 2018". Accessed at https://assets.publishing.service.gov.uk/government/uploads/system/uploads/attachment_data/file/832541/Statistics-on-International-Development-final-aid-spend-2018.pdf.

Doornbos, M. (2001), "Good Governance: The Rise and Decline of a Policy Metaphor?", *The Journal of Development Studies*, 37(6): 93–108.

Dreher, Axel et al. (2010), *Are 'New' Donors Different? Comparing the Allocation of Bilateral Aid Between Non-DAC and DAC Donor Countries*, CEGE

Discussion Paper No. 96 [Online: web]. Accessed at http://papers.ssrn.com/sol3/papers.cfm?abstract_id=1574789.

ECOSOC. (2014), "Trends and Progress in International Development Cooperation", Report of the Secretary-General, High level Segment: Development Cooperation Forum, United Nations Economic and Social Council [Online: web]. Accessed at https://www.un.org/ecosoc/sites/www.un.org.ecosoc/files/publication/n1440507.pdf.

Erixon, Fredrik. (2005), "Aid and Development: Will It Work This Time?", The Jamestown Foundation [Online: web]. Accessed at http://www.policynetwork.net/development/publication/aid-and-development.

Fraser, Alastair. (2006), *Aid-Recipient Sovereignty in Global Governance*, Working Paper [Online: web]. Accessed at http://cambridge.academia.edu/AlastairFraser/Papers/254/Aid_recipient_Sovereignty_in_Historical_Context#Share.

Griffin, K.B. and Enos, J.L. (1970), "Foreign Assistance: Objectives and Consequences", *Economic Development and Cultural Change*, 18(3): 313–327.

Gilpin, R. (1987), *The Political Economy of International Relations*, Princeton: Princeton University Press.

Hansen, Henrik and Tarp, Finn. (2000), "Aid Effectiveness Disputed", *Journal of International Development*, 12(3): 375–398.

Hattori, Tomohisa. (2001), "Reconceptualizing Foreign Aid", *Review of International Political Economy*, 8(4): 633–660.

Hook, Steven W. (1998), "Building Democracy Through Foreign Aid: The Limitations of United States Political Conditionalities, 1992–96", *Democratization*, 5(3): 156–180.

Hopkins, Raymond F. (2000), "Political Economy of Foreign Aid" [Online: web]. Accessed at http://www.swarthmore.edu/SocSci/rhopkin1/research/PolEconFA.pdf.

Hoy, Paula. (1998), *Players and Issues in International Aid*, Sterling, VA: Kumarian Press.

Kragelund, Peter. (2010), *The Potential Role of Non-traditional Donors' Aid in Africa*, Issue Paper No. 11, ICTSD [Online: web]. Accessed at http://ictsd.org/downloads/2010/03/the-potential-role-of-non-traditional-donors e28099-aid-in-africa.pdf.

Lensink, Robert and White, Howard. (2000a), "Assessing Aid: A Manifesto for Aid in the 21st Century?", *Oxford Development Studies*, 28(1): 5–18.

Liska, G. (1960). *The New Statecraft: Foreign Aid in American Foreign Policy*, Chicago: University of Chicago Press.

Lumsdaine, David. (1993), *Moral Vision in International Politics: The Foreign Aid Regime, 1949–1989*, Princeton, NJ: Princeton University Press.

Mawdsley, E. (2012), *From Recipients to Donors: Emerging Powers and the Changing Development Landscape*, London: Zed Books.

Minch, Kevin J. (2010), "Bilateral Vs Multilateral Aid", International Debate Education Association [Online: web]. Accessed at http://www.idebate.org/debatabase/topic_details.php?topicID=392.

Morgenthau, Hans. (1962), "A Political Theory of Foreign Aid", *The American Political Science Review*, 56(2): 301–309.

Mosley, Paul et al. (2004), "Aid, Poverty Reduction and the 'New Conditionality'", *The Economic Journal*, 114 (496): F217–F243.

Nel, Philip. (2010), "Redistribution and Recognition: What Emerging Regional Powers Want?", *Review of International Studies*, 36(4): 951–974.

Neumayer, E. (2003), *The Pattern of Aid Giving: The Impact of Good Governance on Development Assistance*, Routledge: New York.

O'Keefe, Joseph. (2007), "Aid—From Consensus to Competition?", The Brookings Blum Roundtable [Online: web], Accessed at http://www.brookings.edu/global/aspen/2007o%27keefe.pdf.

ODI. (2010), *Brazil: An Emerging Aid Player*, Briefing Paper 64 [Online: web]. Accessed at http://www.odi.org.uk/resources/download/5120.pdf.

OECD. (1995), *Participatory Development and Good Governance*, Development Co-operation Guideline Series, Organisation for Economic Cooperation and Development, Paris [Online: web]. Accessed at http://www.oecd.org/dataoecd/27/13/31857685.pdf.

OECD. (2008), "Is it ODA?", Factsheet [Online: web]. Accessed at http://www.oecd.org/dac/stats/documentupload/IsitODA.pdf.

OECD. (2010), "History of the 0.7% ODA Target" [Online: web]. Accessed at http://www.oecd.org/investment/stats/45539274.pdf.

OECD. (2016a), "History of DAC Lists of Aid Recipient Countries" [Online: web]. Accessed at http://www.oecd.org/dac/stats/historyofdaclistsofaidrecipientcountries.htm.

OECD. (2016b), "Members and Partners" [Online: web]. Accessed at http://www.oecd.org/about/membersandpartners/.

OECD. (2019a). "ODA 2018 Preliminary Figures." Accessed at http://www.oecd.org/dac/financing-sustainable-development/development-finance-standards/official-development-assistance.htm.

OECD. (2019b), "Development Aid Drops in 2018, Especially to Neediest Countries." Accessed at http://www.oecd.org/dac/financing-sustainable-development/development-finance-data/ODA-2018-detailed-summary.pdf.

OECD. (2019c), "DAC List of ODA Recipients." Accessed at http://www.oecd.org/dac/financing-sustainable-development/development-finance-standards/DAC-List-of-ODA-Recipients-for-reporting-2018-and-2019-flows.pdf.

OECD. (2019d), "What Is ODA?". Accessed at https://www.oecd.org/dac/financing-sustainable-development/development-finance-standards/What-is-ODA.pdf.

Pronk, Jan. (2001), "Aid as a Catalyst", *Development and Change*, 32(4): 611–629.

Pronk, Jan et al. (2004), *Catalysing Development? A Debate on Aid*, Malden, MA: Blackwell.

Radelet, Steve. (2006), *A Primer on Foreign Aid*, Working Paper 92 [Online: web] Accessed at www.cgdev.org/files/8846_file_WP92.pdf.

Riddell, R.C. (1996), "The Moral Case for Post-Cold War Development Aid", *International Journal*, 51(2): 191–210.

Sato, Jin et al. (2010), *How do "Emerging" Donors Differ from "Traditional" Donors? An Institutional Analysis of Foreign Aid in Cambodia*, Working Paper, JICA [Online: web]. Accessed at http://jica-ri.jica.go.jp/JICA-RI_WP_No.2_2010.pdf.

Schirm, Stefan A. (2006), *Leadership in Regional and Global Politics: Why Do Emerging Powers (Sometimes) Fail to Reach Their Goals?*, Working Paper, GIGA [Online: web]. Accessed at http://www.sowi.rub.de/mam/content/lsip/leadership_paper.pdf.

Schraeder, P.J., Hook, S.W. and Taylor, B. (1998) "Clarifying the Foreign Aid Puzzle: A Comparison of American, Japanese, French and Swedish Flows", *World Politics*, 50(2): 294–323.

Scott, S. (2019), "A Note on Current Problems with ODA as a Statistical Measure", Brookings. Accessed at https://www.brookings.edu/blog/future-development/2019/09/26/a-note-on-current-problems-with-oda-as-a-statistical-measure/.

Sidaway, J. (2012), "Geographies of Development: New Maps, New Visions?", *Professional Geographer*, 64(2): 1–14.

Six, C. (2009), "The Rise of Post-colonial States as Donors: A Challenge to the Development Paradigm?", *Third World Quarterly*, 30(6): 1103–1121.

Sotero, Paulo. (2009), "Emerging Powers: India, Brazil And South Africa (IBSA) and the Future of South-South Cooperation", Woodrow Wilson International Centre for Scholars [Online: web]. Accessed at http://www.wilsoncenter.org/topics/pubs/IBSA%20Publication.pdf.

Tarp, Finn. (2006), "Aid and development", *Swedish Economic Policy Review*, 13(2): 9–61.

UN. (2010), "Nairobi Outcome Document of the High-level United Nations Conference on South-South Cooperation", United Nations General Assembly A/RES/64/222, 64th Session, Agenda item 68(b). Accessed at http://ssc.undp.org/content/dam/ssc/documents/Key%20Policy%20Documents/Nairobi%20Outcome%20Document.pdf.

UN. (2019), "Report of the Second High-Level United Nations Conference on South-South Cooperation", United Nations. Accessed at https://www.unsouthsouth.org/wp-content/uploads/2019/07/N1920949.pdf.

UNDP. (2010), "Nairobi Outcome Document." Accessed at http://ssc.undp.org/content/dam/ssc/documents/Key%20Policy%20Documents/Nairobi%20Outcome%20Document.pdf.

UNOSSC. (2016a), "Background" [Online: web]. Accessed at http://ssc.undp.org/content/ssc/about/Background.html.

UNOSSC. (2016b), "What Is South-South Cooperation?", United Nations Office for South-South Cooperation [Online: web]. Accessed at http://ssc.undp.org/content/ssc/about/what_is_ssc.html.

van de Walle, Nicolas (1999), "Aid's Crisis of Legitimacy: Current Proposals and Future Prospects", *African Affairs*, 98(392): 337–352.

Woods, Ngaire (2008), "Whose Aid? Whose Influence? China, Emerging Donors and the Silent Revolution in Development Assistance", *International Affairs*, 84(6): 1205–1221.

World Bank. (1992), *Governance and Development*, Washington, DC: World Bank.

CHAPTER 3

COBRADI: The Rise and Fall of a Southern Provider

Increasingly being termed as an emerging power with enormous potential for economic growth and development, Brazil has come a long way from being a Portuguese colony and an underdeveloped country to an upper-middle-income country with a growing GDP per capita (World Bank 2016). Despite alarming rates of poverty and income inequality, Brazil has ensured its position as one of the most influential emerging powers in the global order. The Brazilian economy is the ninth largest economy in the world and the largest in Latin America with a GDP share of 41.4% in 2017 (Deloitte 2018). After a lull in 2015 and 2016, Brazil is expected to get back on the path of economic growth by 2020 if it is able to raise its industrial productivity, competitiveness and investments (IMF 2019). As Brazil has embedded its position among the largest economies in the world, it has ensured that it uses its soft power in order to increase its political and economic clout both in its region and around the world.

In the international aid architecture, Brazil was increasingly viewed as an ODA recipient from the OECD-DAC and continues to receive aid from them, in certain sectors like environment and climate change. However, like several other emerging economies, Brazil also transformed itself from a recipient to "a development cooperation partner". Development cooperation to the Global South was slowly but steadily incorporated into the foreign policy considerations of the Brazilian government.

C. Purushothaman, *Emerging Powers, Development Cooperation and South-South Relations*, International Political Economy Series,
https://doi.org/10.1007/978-3-030-51537-9_3

As early as 1950s, Brazil had modest beginnings in the field of development cooperation and, since then, it has been expanding steadily to include most sectors and geographical zones into its development cooperation agenda. This agenda got a boost in the twenty-first century with the coming into power of Luiz Inácio Lula da Silva government in 2003. The next decade could be defined as the golden period for Brazil as a development assistance provider as its involvement in shaping the development discourse of its peers in the Global South grew manifold. Considering the significant role played by Brazil in international development during this period, even the federal government in its report acknowledged the use of development cooperation as "an instrument of foreign policy" (IPEA 2011, 11). The growing importance of development cooperation clearly demonstrated Brazil's increasing emphasis on its soft power as the key driver of its foreign policy.

With development cooperation becoming a foreign policy priority, Brazil has been careful in both its usage and definition. The Brazilian officials assert that Brazilian development cooperation is personalised and does not adhere to any traditional definitions or norms set by the developed countries. Ambassador Celso Amorim, who was the Minister of External Relations under President Lula, concluded that "the country is today characterised by an innovative diplomacy, but which does not stray from the fundamental values of the Brazilian nation-peace, pluralism, tolerance and solidarity" (IPEA 2011, 9). What promoted Brasília to initiate its development cooperation programme is said to be Brazil's own development experiences that had been successful in rescuing millions of Brazilians out of extreme poverty. Brazil boasts of successfully dealing with the inequalities of income and the promotion of opportunities leading to "introducing similar measures in other developing countries facing similar challenges" through its development cooperation projects (IPEA 2011, 9). Moreover, Brazil's readiness to replicate the best practices in order to address the pressing issues faced by other countries has also been the reason for initiating and expanding its development cooperation. Furthermore, Brazil's development cooperation policy with the Global South is also fostered by its own experiences as a recipient of foreign aid.

As an emerging power in the world order with its own foreign aid programme, it is pertinent to analyse the origin and development of its foreign aid policies, patterns and modalities, the motivations and agendas behind its position as a development assistance provider and the factors driving the selection process of its recipients/partners. This chapter tries to address the following questions: What does Brazilian development cooperation look like and where does it mostly go? What drives Brasília to be a development assistance provider? Does Brazil bring to the table a new agenda for development cooperation? And if yes, then how is it different from the OECD aid? What principles and paradigms, in comparison with the existing structures, is Brazilian development cooperation based on? Does Brazil's own experience of being a foreign aid recipient shape Brazilian development cooperation? Is Brazil a revisionist power or status-quoist in international aid architecture? As a global player in development assistance, does Brazil bring its own norms and agendas at play? Hence, this chapter aims to focus on Brazil as an emerging power which is also a development assistance provider, in order to delve deep into how countries like Brazil bring changes into how foreign aid is traditionally understood and operationalised.

Evolution of Cobradi

For Brazil, the concept of development is nothing new. Development as a concept gained weight in both the national and foreign policy landscape since the birth of the Brazilian constitution, which upholds development not only in its preamble and Article 3 as the "Fundamental goals of the Federative Republic of Brazil", but also repeats the term over 50 times throughout. This makes the idea of development "a fundamental value with great political and policy resonance within Brazil's political discourse" (Dauvergne and Farias 2012, 906). Even though not all previous governments have promoted developmental activities with same degree of intensity, the idea of development has always been prominent in Brazil's national and foreign policy considerations.

In the domestic realm, the focus on development began in the 1930s, when Brazil adopted the national-developmentalist paradigm. This was formally articulated in the late 1940s, particularly through the work of the Economic Commission for Latin America (CEPAL).[1] The primary

[1] CEPAL is the Spanish acronym for the Economic Commission for Latin America, established in 1948, with its headquarters in Santiago, Chile. CEPAL is one of the five regional commissions of the UN. In 1984, the commission's work was broadened to include the Caribbean countries, and hence, it was called the Economic Commission for Latin America and the Caribbean.

aim was the economic development of Latin America and strengthening economic ties among nations of the region and with the outside world (CEPAL 2016). This also meant adopting an industrialisation model based on import substitution along with active state intervention in the country's economy (Dauvergne and Farias 2012, 907). Many of these ideas gradually spilled into foreign policy.

The origins of Brazil's international development cooperation policy date back to the 1950s (IPEA 2011, 16). The end of the military regime brought about significant changes in the Brazilian political-institutional order, like "the strengthening of social movements, the consolidation of democracy, constitutional reform, the reshaping and consolidation of social policies, international recognition and a greater economic and financial stability", that guaranteed growing volume and visibility of Cobradi (IPEA 2011, 16). The main priority throughout the 1960s and 1970s was the overall development of the country and its economy to gain economic power in the international arena. Brazil's then Minister of Foreign Affairs, Joao Augusto Araujo Castro (1963–1964), had explained Brazil's ambitions of economic power as follows: "for Brazil the quickest, most direct path for the strengthening of its national power is the path of its own economic development and industrial expansion" (Dauvergne and Farias 2012, 907). For this, the government strongly emphasised foreign trade and improving economic ties with the region and the outside world. The outcome of this policy was Brazil's active engagement with multilateral groupings with other developing countries, such as the G77 and joining the call for a New International Economic Order (NIEO).

In 1978, the Buenos Aires Plan of Action (BAPA) for Promoting and Implementing Technical Cooperation among Developing Countries (TCDC) was signed and became a turning point for developing countries of the Global South as providers of technical cooperation.[2] Since then, Brazil underscored the importance of delivering technical assistance between developing countries as an essential component of its foreign policy. Many developing countries pushed for an inter-governmental consensus on international technical cooperation between developing countries to be achieved through the UNDP platform. Their efforts materialised when the UN World Conference on Technical Cooperation among Developing Countries (TCDC) was held in Buenos Aires in

[2] BAPA provided the conceptual underpinnings as well as a practical guide for realising the objectives of TCDC (UNDP 1994).

September 1978. The Buenos Aires Action Plan adopted at this conference introduced technical cooperation among developing countries into the international system. Thereafter, Brazil, with its scientific and technological advances, became a confident technical cooperation partner for developing countries of the Global South with its increasing focus on horizontal cooperation among developing nations. Hence, Brazil maintained its own position on international cooperation and did not follow the traditional concept of foreign aid, given by the OECD, since the very beginning.

With the establishment and expansion of TCDC programs, Brazil began to reach out to countries in its neighbourhood and also to the African continent. Therefore, most of its initial projects and technical cooperation agreements were negotiated with countries in Latin America and Africa. From the mid-1970s, Brazil's policy towards the Portuguese-speaking African countries (PALOPs) also took a positive turn with the independence of PALOPs. Earlier, Brazil could not build ties with these countries as the Treaty of Friendship between Brazil and Portugal restricted Brasilia from doing so (Vaz and Inoue 2007, 5). With their independence, the PALOPs, having linguistic, cultural and historical ties with Brazil, became a foreign policy priority for the Brazilian government. Technical cooperation between Brazil and the PALOPs opened new avenues for political, social, cultural and economic cooperation. This, however, did not change Brazil's focus on its region, Latin America, which continued to be the foremost priority and sphere of influence.

International development cooperation gained weight in Brazil's foreign policy considerations, which further led to the creation of the ABC in 1987. This agency was created within the Ministry of External Relations (MRE).[3] This was an attempt to provide central coordination for international development cooperation or more specifically, technical cooperation, at that point of time. Brazil, as a recipient of foreign aid, was supposed to implement its own delivery of technical assistance, keeping in mind the lessons it learned as a recipient, working on the limitations of the North-South flow of aid and improving on it.

Brazil's efforts to promote development in its foreign policy slowed during the domestic economic crisis of the 1980s and the revival of

[3] MRE is also famously referred to as Itamaraty.

the Cold War. By the 1990s, the meaning and importance of development for domestic and international policy strategies were shifting. The path towards national development was detaching from the national-developmentalist economic model of state intervention and import substitution. Brazil's financial instability was also undermining such efforts and pushing aside those wanting to position Brazil as a 'leader' of developing nations (Dauvergne and Farias 2012, 907).

Major shifts in Brazilian foreign policy came about with the election of Lula da Silva as president in 2003. However, the domestic and foreign policy of Lula (2003–2010) was not so much of a departure from Fernando Henrique Cardoso's (1995–2002), particularly if we look at Cardoso's last years in office. The major difference between the two was in their approach to development and the mechanisms that would enable Brazil gain a better position in the world order. While Cardoso focussed on strengthening alliances with developed countries, Lula's approach underlined or rather questioned the international status quo that he found was impeding development (Dauvergne and Farias 2012, 907). What makes the Lula administration different from its predecessors was the degree to which he aimed to project Brazil as an emerging power, which had SSC as the cornerstone of its foreign policy.

Even though Brazilian technical cooperation started to grow in the 1980s, it did not get a boost in the 1990s and remained almost stable until Lula came to power. It was only during the second term of Lula (2006–2009) that TCDC got much-needed push from the administration (Inoue and Vaz 2012). Under President Lula, SSC was underscored as the driving factor behind Cobradi. The SSC was recognised by the government as a broader concept that not only constitutes technical cooperation but also non-technical aspects of cooperation including humanitarian assistance and economic cooperation (Inoue and Vaz 2012, 510). Brazil's South-South Cooperation reinforced the idea of horizontal partnerships that envisages equality among partners that goes against the donor-recipient hierarchy advocated by the OECD.

Under the Lula government, there was a clear increase in volume of Brazilian development cooperation. Lula influenced the shift in Brazilian foreign policy from "autonomy through participation" to "autonomy through diversification", which promoted SSC and increased participation of the country in multilateral forums (Suyama et al. 2016). While Brazil has been giving more emphasis to SSC, regionalism, multilateralism and universalism in its foreign trade, the "liberal economic orthodoxy" it had adopted in mid-1990s continues to remain the basis for economic policy, both domestic and foreign (Vaz and Inoue 2007, 4). Despite this, Cobradi has remained an important component of its foreign policy that has been inevitable for it to advance its international cooperation efforts. Brazil has underscored the importance of the concept of international development cooperation over the Western concepts like foreign aid or ODA. It considers itself as a partner for other developing countries in the Global South. Lula's Brazil was able to create more partnerships with other developing countries, with great emphasis on solidarity that made it one of the important providers of development cooperation in the developing world. Presidential diplomacy played a major role in exhibiting Brazil's achievements and its willingness to share its experiences with other developing countries (Suyama et al. 2016).

After a proactive policy of development cooperation under the Lula administration, President Dilma's first term in office saw a major shift in priorities from external affairs to domestic issues. One common concern raised by the officials of the MRE and ABC during President Dilma's tenure was the increasing focus on the domestic affairs that led to the decline in the funds for development cooperation, with not many new projects initiated and very few foreign visits to the partner countries made during her tenure. Her second tenure was the most turbulent period in the twenty-first-century Brazil's political landscape.

Inoue and Vaz (2012) classify the evolutionary phase of Cobradi into four periods based on the shifts in its development cooperation policies and priorities: the first (1969–1978),[4] the second (1978–1987),[5] the third (1987–2003)[6] and the fourth phase (2003–present)[7] (Inoue and Vaz 2012, 509). While this classification is a useful division of time frames, the period from 2003 has seen major shifts in the foreign policy

[4] During this period, Brazil's efforts were in the direction of creating a national system for coordinating its technical cooperation. It also signed its first agreements with partner countries during this phase (Inoue and Vaz 2012, 509).

[5] This phase is marked by a considerable increase in the number of aid projects funded by Brazil in other countries of the global south (Inoue and Vaz 2012, 509).

[6] This was a major turning point in Cobradi as the Brazilian Cooperation Agency (ABC) was set up in 1987 as an important step in the institutionalisation process of Cobradi. This phase continued till 2003 when President Lula came to power.

[7] This phase started when President Lula took office. It was the golden period in the history of Brazilian development cooperation so far (Inoue and Vaz 2012, 509).

considerations of the successive government under Lula. Although the period from 2003 has seen an enormous increase in the development cooperation from Brazil, this was a change attributed rather exclusively to the Lula government which took a special interest in promoting Brazil's development cooperation agenda. Therefore, after Lula, this trend almost discontinued. Five years of the Dilma government, 2011–2016, was a gradual shift from Lula's proactive development cooperation policy and have seen a downfall in Brazilian development cooperation. Between 2012 and 2015, there was a reduction in ABC's budget by 25% that led to a drop in the number of projects funded by ABC, from 253 in 2010 to 161 in 2014 (Marcondes and Mawdsley 2017, 685). Therefore, the fourth phase would rather be from 2003 to 2010, and the fifth phase (2011–present) could be added to this classification in order to denote the major shifts in the development cooperation policies under Dilma Rousseff, since her coming to power in January 2011.

After the domestic turmoil followed by impeachment of President Dilma in early 2016 for the charges of allegedly manipulating the public funds, the new government that formed under interim President Michel Temer (earlier, the vice-president) also focussed on domestic policies. With several corruption charges levelled against him and his involvement in scams, questions were raised on his legitimacy and integrity to remain as the president, and domestic politics took centre-stage with foreign policy getting relegated to the background. Brazil, during this period, was also going through the worst economic recession that further restricted its allocation of funds for development cooperation. However, the most important development was the shift in Brazil's position of being a Southern Donor to moving closer to OECD for a membership, which could redefine Brazil's long-standing principles on development cooperation and its approach to its recipient countries. In 2017, Brazil formally approached the OECD for a membership that is still pending with the organisation which demands certain standards to be met, especially environmental standards. The foreign aid policy of the new government formed under Jair Bolsonaro in January 2019 is yet to unfold. However, Bolsonaro being a right-wing president and an appeaser to the Western world, especially the US, would most likely move forward with the OECD membership. However, his complete disdain for environment, evident from his response to the fires in the Amazon forest, can stall Brazil's progress for membership in the OECD, which gives priority to issues on environment and climate change (Boadle 2019). Furthermore, the structural and political challenges confronting the state are likely to retard its growth story; taking away its status of an emerging power and its decision to join the developed country club could be considered as a decision to belong to the group of the developed and powerful. This can change how Brazil has been traditionally viewed by its peers in the Global South, and the major tenets of Cobradi would need to be redefined in the coming years that would adhere to the recommendations and rules governing the OECD.

Brazilian Development Cooperation: An Instrument of Brazil's Economic Statecraft

With the Brazilian government committing to contribute to "the promotion of global development, with emphasis on Latin America, Africa and Asia", international development cooperation was prioritised as a major component of Brazilian foreign policy (IPEA 2011, 10). The stated position of the government was that the cooperation for development was not limited to the interaction between donors and recipients; they considered it "as an exchange between equals, with mutual benefits and responsibilities" (IPEA 2011, 8).

Brazil's efforts in sharing of knowledge and successful experiences, and its capacity to replicate best practices in supporting other developing countries to overcome development challenges point to the fact that Brazil, through its horizontal cooperation, hopes to play an important role in correcting the "social and economic asymmetries" in other developing countries (IPEA 2011, 9). Cobradi's focus has mostly been on sectors in which Brazil has expertise, such as the technical and infrastructural support in the agricultural sector[8] or conditional cash

[8] Major examples of Brazil's support to other developing countries in agriculture sector have been the Mozambique Tropical Savannah Agricultural Development Project (ProSavana) and the Cotton-4 Project. ProSavana has been an attempt to replicate Brazil's success in its Cerrado (Savannah) region, where it could achieve high agricultural productivity using appropriate technologies, in Mozambique's Savannah region. This project has been a triangular cooperation project between Brazil, Mozambique and Japan. Cotton-4 project has been executed in four African partner countries of Benin, Burkina Faso, Chad and Mali. This project focusses on improving the production of cotton as well as improving its quality thereby giving the economies of these countries a boost.

transfer programmes like the Bolsa Familia[9] programme (Usher 2011, 2). Furthermore, the aim was to make use of domestically created solutions, especially in priority sectors like agriculture and education, in order to support countries' similar stages of development as that of Brazil's.

The major tenets of Cobradi are respect for sovereignty, non-interference and the defence of self-determination that has traditionally defined Brazilian diplomacy. Brazil's official position does not allow it to impose conditionalities, nor does it aim at immediate political goals (IPEA 2011, 8). This was a major shift from the traditional concept of foreign aid or development assistance endorsed by the OECD countries, as Brazilian development cooperation was based on the idea of SSC and horizontal partnership that enabled Brazil to engage in the development story of the fellow developing countries, thereby also forging stronger bilateral ties and regional arrangements with them.

The two reports jointly published by the IPEA and ABC with other arms of the Federal government in 2011 and 2014 give a comprehensive assessment of Cobradi for the years 2005–2010 (IPEA 2014, 13). These are the only official reports available on Cobradi and more reports are expected to be released by the IPEA in future. However, Brazil has not been keen to disseminate its Cobradi data on a regular basis which makes it difficult to undertake an overall assessment, which also raises questions about its transparency.

The following sections look at how Brazil defines its international development cooperation, the institutions involved and the policy-framework guiding Cobradi.

What Is Cobradi?

The lack of a definition for development cooperation is one of the biggest challenges faced by most emerging powers that provide development assistance. This has also been observed in the case of Brazil. It did not have a definition until 2011, when the Cobradi report was released

[9] Bolsa Familia has been Brazil's flagship social programme, based on conditional cash transfer, started during the Cardoso regime that got tremendous boost from the subsequent Lula administration. Initiated to stimulate growth and social development, it has been considered as one of the success stories with a large number of people coming out of extreme poverty in Brazil.

jointly by MRE, ABC and IPEA. The responsibility to define and quantify Brazilian international cooperation for development rested with the MRE which in turn proposed to the Presidency of the Republic (PR) the need for a survey of Cobradi, which later initiated the development of the Cobradi report in 2011 and later in 2014, for years 2005–2009 and 2010, respectively. This report is the first to acknowledge what development cooperation means for Brazil.

The major challenge facing Brazil in defining the volume of Cobradi was the lack of coordination among different institutions of the federal government that also posed difficulty in quantifying the volume and defining Brazilian development cooperation with precision and clarity. However, the IPEA report mentions that the federal government agencies and entities catalogued the amount allocated by Brazil to other developing countries, so as to put to rest the lack of transparency conundrum raised by the traditional donors (IPEA 2011, 11).

The MRE, ABC and the IPEA worked towards defining Brazilian development cooperation; understanding various modalities and their characteristics; identifying, recovering and systematising the data and information on federal government investments for projects and programmes (IPEA 2011, 11). Eventually, they arrived at a common definition for Brazilian development cooperation on the basis of which the data was collected and organised in order to finalise the report. As per the definition given by the ABC and IPEA, Cobradi is:

> The total funds invested by the Brazilian federal government, entirely as non-repayable grants, in governments of other countries, in nationals of other countries in Brazilian territory or in international organizations with the purpose of contributing to international development, understood as the strengthening of the capacities of international organizations and groups or populations of other countries to improve their socio-economic conditions. (IPEA 2011, 11)

For the Brazilian federal government, financing[10] and debt pardons do not constitute development cooperation and were therefore omitted from

[10] This mainly constitutes investments with varying rates of returns. If financing was to be considered as a part of Cobradi, the actual figures would have been much higher than what was given in the IPEA report as Brazil's development cooperation.

the expenditures calculated as a part of Cobradi (IPEA 2014, 14). There are mainly two types of expenditures made by the federal government for Cobradi: firstly, expenditures on federal government officials and collaborators, “including airfares, per diems, salaries, work hours, scholarships and donations”, and second, those expenditures “resulting from commitments and obligations of the Brazilian federal government with international organizations” (IPEA 2014, 14).

The position of the Brazilian government to define its development cooperation as only grants clearly demonstrates that it doesn’t identify itself with the OECD’s definition of foreign aid or development assistance. For the OECD, ODA could have a grant element of 10% and above as per its latest definition (OECD 2019). However, Brazil categorically states that its Cobradi would include only those funding with 100% grants. This takes out the investments and commercial lending and loans out of the purview of Cobradi. However, this definition does not prevent either ABC or the Federal government from signing trilateral cooperation agreements with the OECD-DAC countries[11] or with other international organisations.

Cobradi: Institutional Structures

Like most emerging powers, Brazil does not have a single agency to manage development cooperation which could have brought coherence into its development cooperation efforts. Despite numerous efforts by the Federal government to set up a centralised structure for Cobradi, nothing bore fruit. Several government institutions are still a part of Brazilian development cooperation without much coordination with each other. Apart from the federal government, there are several provincial and non-state actors involved in Brazil’s international development cooperation. This makes it hard for the ABC and the IPEA to calculate the volume of Cobradi and hence make the volume quoted in the Cobradi report problematic and inaccurate by a huge margin.

[11] Brazil has several trilateral cooperation projects running, in Latin America and Africa, with the Japan International Cooperation Agency (JICA), the US Agency for International Development (USAID), German Federal Ministry of Economic Development and Cooperation (BMZ) and French Development Agency (AFD).

Since the mid-1980s, Brazil has been involved in institution-building efforts in order to organise and institutionalise its development cooperation. The creation of ABC, in 1987, points to the efforts of the Federal government in the direction of establishing a centralised system in order to coordinate Brazilian development cooperation. Before the creation of ABC, Brazil's technical cooperation was managed by two institutions within the Federal government; first, the Division of International Technical Cooperation (DCOPT) linked to the MRE that had the responsibility to undertake and establish Brazil's technical partnerships with other countries, and second, Sub-secretariat for International Technical and Economic Cooperation (SUBIN) related to the Secretariat for Planning (SEPLAN) that looked after the national coordination of Cobradi. Centralising the institutional structure was considered important for a greater coordination of its internal development needs and the external development assistance (more of which was in the nature of technical cooperation in the 1980s), which led to the idea of merging these two institutions (Inoue and Vaz 2012, 512). And in 1987, these institutions were finally merged and ABC was set up with the following functions at its disposal:

> The ABC, established by the Decree n° 94,973 of September 25th, 1987, under the Ministry of External Relations (MRE), is responsible for the coordination, negotiation, approval, monitoring and evaluation, at national level, of cooperation for development in all areas of knowledge; both that received by Brazil from other countries and international organizations, as well as that given by Brazil to other developing countries. (IPEA 2014, 26)

Despite the creation of the ABC, the centralised coordination of Brazilian development cooperation remained a distant dream. The state actors involved in Cobradi also include the "non-traditional" state actors like domestic ministries, federal agencies[12] and subnational

[12] Like the Brazilian Agricultural Research Corporation (Embrapa), which is linked to the Ministry of Agriculture or the Oswaldo Cruz Foundation (Fiocruz), related to the Ministry of Health.

entities[13]; non-state actors who defend public and national interests; and private sector businesses (Milani 2014, 5).[14] These actors do not work under the authority of the Presidency of the Republic of Brazil. They could advance their own agendas, different from that of the state agenda, which could affect the authority of the state as the real centre of power in executing development cooperation policy of the state (Milani 2014, 5). For example, the state of Rio de Janeiro has been granting scholarships, especially to students from African countries, to study in different universities in their state, which is in addition to the scholarships given by the Federal government to study in Brazil. Similarly, the state of Sao Paulo has been actively involved in rehabilitation of the refugees, especially from Syria, coming to Brazil and has been allocating funds for this purpose from their budget. This has not been taken into account while measuring the volume of Cobradi. The plurality of actors and agendas makes it a herculean task to manage, quantify and access accurate data on Brazilian development cooperation. This rather becomes impossible with no state control on the international agendas of the non-state and private sector actors.

Different individual ministries continue to be in charge of administering different modalities of cooperation. For instance, the scientific and technological cooperation is coordinated by the Ministry of Science and Technology (MCT) along with its arm National Council for Scientific and Technological Development (CNPq).

Decentralisation of the Brazilian development cooperation was further encouraged and legitimised by the federal government in 2012 through the Decentralised Programme for South-South Technical Cooperation.[15]

[13] This includes federated states and municipalities.

[14] Prof. Carlos Milani, during an interview with him on 3 April 2015 at Rio de Janeiro, explained this issue in detail. Similar views were expressed by the interviewees in the MRE, ABC and IPEA. However, the IPEA officials said that they are trying to get this data for incorporating it into the next report that they are planning to come up with. But this is a very time-taking process and data is not shared publicly and there are not any options to access it unless it is provided by the authorities on request of the Federal government.

[15] The main objective of this programme was to encourage Brazilian states and municipalities to develop international technical cooperation projects with their counterparts in other developing countries (Planalto 2016).

This allowed further diversification of actors and agendas in the sphere of Brazilian foreign policy in general and its development policy in particular. The debate on building centralised institutional structures for Cobradi was further diluted with this move and Itamaraty further lost its monopoly over its development cooperation programme. With growing international actions embarked by the federated states and municipalities, it is now "difficult to find a ministry or governmental agency that does not have its own budget devoted to international affairs" (Milani 2014, 11).

Cobradi: Defining Principles

Brazil's Federal Constitution (FC) envisages cooperation for "the progress of humanity" in the "Article 4 of the FC of 1988" as an important principle of Brazilian foreign policy (IPEA 2014, 13). Hence, Cobradi has also been driven by these principles underlined in its constitution, leading to the usage of ideals like equality and social justice as guiding principles of its foreign policy and economic diplomacy. The positive results of its social policies like Bolsa Família, which lifted thousands out of extreme poverty, were well received around the world. Broadening of these social policies domestically had a great impact on Brazil's economic development and social well-being which raised demands from the outside world to replicate similar policies in other developing countries. Brazil, then, incorporated these successful domestic policies into its Cobradi thereby sharing its experiences, best practices and technological transfer with its partner countries in the similar stages of development. Several principles began to characterise Cobradi that also had resonance with the priorities of the countries in the Global South.

Non-Intervention and SSC

Brazil started associating itself with the Global South since mid-nineteenth century, and therefore, its development cooperation programmes also resonated the idea of SSC. As mentioned in the previous sections, the definition and the concept of Brazilian cooperation for international development varied considerably from that given by the OECD-DAC donors and Brazil's position was a clear demonstration of how it did not want to be identified as belonging to the traditional donor club. Minister Marco Farani (2011), former Director of ABC, laid out the basic difference between Brazilian international cooperation for development and the OECD aid:

> In Brazil, when we talk about aid, we are talking about cooperation: South-South Cooperation (SSC). This involves collaboration and knowledge-sharing through a horizontal structure, not the vertical structure that is at the core of developed countries' approaches and embodied in the terms 'aid' and 'assistance'. (Farani 2011, 3)

He also suggested that the Cobradi has gained popularity among developing countries as a result of Brazil's non-intervention policy and its involvement in peaceful conflict solution, their multicultural and multiethnic society, Brazil's positive economic growth and finally their efforts for international development which is based on SSC (Farani 2011, 4). Farani also emphasised Brazil's position as an active supporter of development and solidarity in the international arena (Farani 2009).

President Lula focussed his efforts on positioning Brazil "not only as a developing country but as a leader among them" (Dauvergne and Farias 2012, 909). Brazil's policy of strengthening its ties with other developing countries through its policy of SSC is "in tandem with the idea of 'development-as-goal' and 'development-as-identity'" (Dauvergne and Farias 2012, 909).

Solidarity, Regional Cooperation and Building Alliances with the Global South

Celso Amorim, former Minister of Foreign Affairs (2003–2011) under President Lula, considered Brazil's efforts to build strong ties with other developing countries as a crucial component in advancing Brazil's international position. He explains his take on SSC and building alliances with the Global South in his article "*Brazilian Foreign Policy under President Lula (2003-2010): An Overview*" where he emphasises that:

> South–South cooperation is a diplomatic strategy that originates from an authentic desire to exercise solidarity toward poorer countries. At the same time, it helps expand Brazil's participation in world affairs. Cooperation among equals in matters of trade, investment, science and technology and

> other fields reinforces our stature and strengthens our position in trade, finance and climate negotiations. Building coalitions with developing countries is also a way of engaging in the reform of global governance in order to make international institutions fairer and more democratic. (Amorim 2010, 231)

Building Southern coalitions became important for Brazil in the wake of twenty-first century and a pioneer in this regard was IBSA, a major player in advancing SSC in poorer countries. IBSA Fund, which was established in 2004 and became operational in 2006, is financing or has financed development projects[16] in Haiti, Guinea-Bissau, Cape Verde, Cambodia, Palestine, Sierra Leone and Vietnam. Even though the budgets are extremely small when compared to other multilateral development organisations, such South-South flows remain notable (IBSA Fund 2016).

With greater budgets and more hype, BRICS has evolved into an important coalition of the Global South where the most important Southern countries have come together. The rise of BRICS as a coalition has been phenomenal in recent years.

President Dilma's former Foreign Affairs Minister, Antonio Patriota (2011–2013), also adopted a similar stand on SSC and reiterated the prominent role that SSC would continue to have in Brazil's foreign policy. It was during her tenure that BRICS countries strengthened their engagement with each other that saw an increase in the intra-bloc trade and setting up of the New Development Bank and the Contingent Reserve Arrangement, all of which got active support from the government (Suyama et al. 2016).

Furthermore, Latin America and the Caribbean are the priority for Brazil. Being the largest economy in the region, it hopes to boost its political and economic clout through its development cooperation activities and forming coalitions with neighbouring countries in the region. Brazil is a proactive member of the regional organisations, including Southern Common Market (MERCOSUR), Union of South American Nations (UNASUR), Organisation of American States (OAS) and Community of Latin American and Caribbean States (CELAC), for free trade and free

[16] However, the exact details on the projects are unavailable as the website has these relevant sections password-protected, leading to much speculation on the lack of transparency. The annual reports issued by IBSA Fund are another link to look into the projects running or already completed (IBSA Fund 2016).

movement of people. Brazil has been supportive of regional integration and has tried to maintain cordial relations with its neighbourhood, and its development cooperation is geared towards that agenda.

Triangular Cooperation, Multilateralism and Legitimacy
Successful implementation of sound domestic policies, innovative programs and new development approaches that saw a great improvement in the socio-economic indicators of Brazil has been a significant aspect of Cobradi, which it hopes to replicate in other developing countries. Gradually, some of these programmes that showed positive result in Brazil were converted into forms of international cooperation; initially bilateral and later, triangular cooperation with both developed and developing countries. Although the bilateral South-South Cooperation has always been a priority for Brazil, triangular partnerships began to be considered as a valuable mechanism that could enhance the impact of the development projects in the partner countries (Corrêa 2009, 3). Triangular cooperation, therefore, emerged as primary modality of Brazil's international development cooperation (Corrêa 2009; Inoue and Vaz 2012). While there has been no internationally agreed definition of triangular cooperation, the term has gained credence since the Buenos Aires Plan of Action and has evolved over time (OECD 2013, 9). The ABC has defined triangular cooperation as:

> an international cooperation modality for the development of a complementary nature of South-South bilateral cooperation, with shared governance, value-added and identifiable comparative advantages, which can take different arrangements of implementation involving developing countries, developed countries and /or international bodies. (ABC 2016a)

For Brazil, triangular cooperation is a platform which favours "the optimized use of the comparative advantages of the partners involved" (Corrêa 2009, 4). Brazil's comparative advantage could be counted in terms of its cultural diversity, multi-ethnic composition and its experience in using development as a tool for reducing social and economic asymmetries (Corrêa 2009, 4; Inoue and Vaz 2012, 522; IPEA 2014, 27). Besides, Brazilian technology and knowledge have been considered to be easily adaptable to the developing country realities. On the other hand, the comparative advantage of the other partner, usually a traditional donor, remains to be mobilisation of greater resources and technical assistance, expanding the scale of the projects and focussing on bigger impact (Corrêa 2009, 4).

Japan has been the most important triangular partner for Brazil, followed by Germany and the United Kingdom (UK) (ABC 2016a). Apart from these three countries, France, Canada, Argentina and Spain are also involved in triangular cooperation with Brazil (IPEA 2014, 27). Triangular cooperation projects of Brazil range from health, public administration, reforestation and professional education. The beneficiaries of these projects are Latin American Countries (especially Haiti and Bolivia) and Portuguese-speaking countries in Africa (Inoue and Vaz 2012, 522).

Brazil has also been successful in establishing triangular cooperation[17] with several multilateral organisations, including the UNDP, the International Labour Organization (ILO), the UN Population Fund (UNFPA), the Amazon Cooperation Treaty Organization (ACTO), the Ibero-American States Organization (IASO), the World Food Program (WFP), the Food and Agriculture Organization of the UN (FAO), the World Bank, the European Union (EU), the Inter-American Institute for Cooperation in Agriculture (IICA) and others (IPEA 2014, 27; Inoue and Vaz 2012, 523).

One of the major achievements of Brazil in the field of international cooperation is that it could break "the North-South-South pattern" of triangular cooperation and bring in the "South-South-South" triangular cooperation that has taken SSC a step ahead. For example, Brazil collaborated with Argentina and Chile to assist Haiti after the acute political crisis in 2004; a Memorandum of Understanding (MoU) was signed between Brazil and Egypt in 2009 for promoting technical cooperation in African countries. The focus areas of South-South-South triangular cooperation have been capacity-building, knowledge sharing and information exchange, and technical support (Inoue and Vaz 2012, 525).

For Brazil, OECD-DAC has never been an ideal platform to discuss and debate their development cooperation. In an interview with a senior official from ABC on 9 March 2015 at Brasilia, the interviewee maintained that Brazil views OECD as a forum for Western countries where the concerns and interests of the emerging powers are not taken into

[17](ABC 2016b).

consideration. Brazil's idea of development assistance has been different from the OECD definitions and guidelines, which remains the dominant strand in international aid architecture. OECD's enduring influence on the aid architecture has pushed the emerging powers to look for other platforms where their voices are heard.

The lack of a neutral body which accepts different points of view on development has been a major hurdle in bringing the South to the development debate. However, Brazil has been more than ready to be a part of the multilateral set-up to discuss development under the UN umbrella. Brazil considers UN as a better platform to discuss SSDC and maintains that the UN could do more to promote SSC, which works closely towards understanding the priorities and needs of the developing countries of the Global South. Brazil has actively supported the UN in shaping the ECOSOC's Development Cooperation Forum (DCF), which they consider as a legitimate forum for discussions on Cobradi (Inoue and Vaz 2012, 516). Brazil has been rather careful to avoid imitating the traditional North-South patterns of foreign aid. It has been keen on following the principles of SSC in triangular cooperation and even supports it in different multilateral forums.

Patterns and Modalities of Cobradi

While the exact data on the aid flows is not available, there have been two reports released by the IPEA in coordination with the ABC and the External Affairs Ministry, and this official data has been used throughout this section as the base data to analyse the trends of Cobradi. The expenditure headings under which Brazil gives its development cooperation include:

> the provision of personnel, infrastructure and financial resources, by training individuals and strengthening organizations and institutions abroad; organizing or participating in missions or peacekeeping operations; managing of joint scientific-technological programs and projects with other countries and research institutes; offering humanitarian cooperation; supporting the integration of refugees in national territory; paying contributions and participation shares in international organizations, and official donations, organized by modalities according to prevailing international terminology. (IPEA 2014)

Cobradi also includes money spent on Brazilian government officials who have the responsibility to carry out "treaties, conventions, agreements, protocols, institutional acts or international commitments". Hence, in order to obtain the data on Cobradi disbursements, the federal government had to involve "approximately 91 federal institutions" that were involved directly or indirectly in Cobradi. The process to get hold of the data must have been a daunting task for both IPEA and ABC, which coordinated with all these organisations for data. As per the government, more than 250 government officials and collaborators were deployed to get the Cobradi data records from these institutions, which points to how Brazil was keen to assess and evaluate Cobradi (IPEA 2014).

While these reports came as innovative and positive move from Brazil, which was a clear deviation from its earlier policy of not disclosing the data to the international community that had led to speculations from the developed countries regarding the motivations driving Cobradi and its lack of transparency. Even though these reports have helped Brazil create a positive opinion in front of the international community, what has been alarming is that these reports have been identified with several discrepancies, which the IPEA and ABC hope to correct in future. The major cause for these discrepancies has been the large number of organisations involved in development cooperation apart from the ABC. It was hard to bring together data from these organisations which range over a hundred in number.

As per the IPEA reports, the total amount given as Cobradi is approximately USD 923 million in 2010, with maximum assistance given to Latin America and the Caribbean followed by Africa and Asia (IPEA 2014). However, the OECD figures suggest that Cobradi was only USD 369 million in 2009 which increased to about USD 500 million in 2010 (OECD 2016a).[18] The huge difference between the IPEA and OECD figures results from the different mechanisms used by both these organisations. OECD has used the data given by IPEA as the base, even though the components of OECD aid are different from Cobradi's definition given by Brazil. However, from this total amount of Cobradi mentioned

[18] The OECD has given Cobradi figures based on the IPEA report and has not be able to come up with independent data on Cobradi. Hence, Cobradi figures from 2010 to present are not available as it has not yet been published by IPEA, the only agency that disseminates the official data on Cobradi.

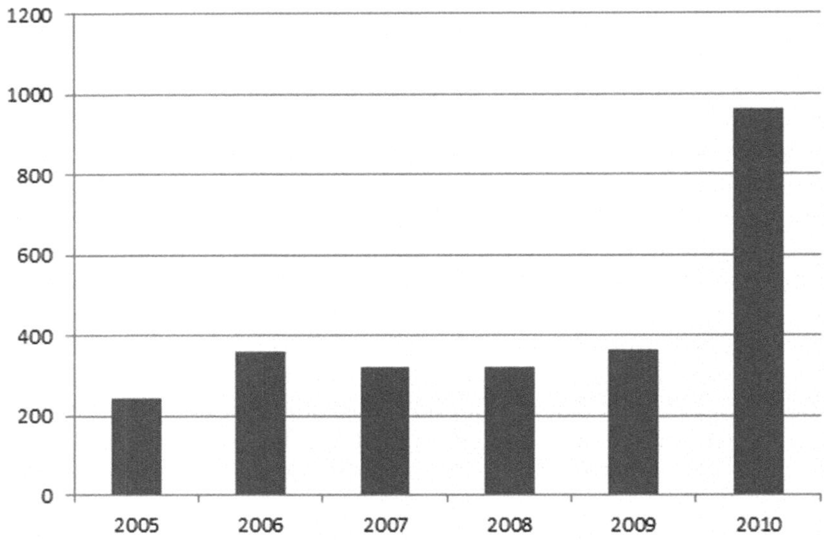

Fig. 3.1 Brazilian development cooperation, 2005–2010 (in USD million) (*Source* IPEA 2011, 2014)

in IPEA reports, they have deducted that component of multilateral assistance given by Brazil, which is not used for economic development of any developing country and omits the expenditures incurred for Brazil's bilateral peace-keeping activities from its data on Cobradi (OECD 2016a) (Fig. 3.1).

Geographical Patterns

Geographical distribution of Brazilian development cooperation suggests that Brazil's focus has been predominantly on its region, the Latin America and the Caribbean, as its neighbouring countries have received the maximum development assistance (see Fig. 3.2). However, Africa is also a priority for Brazil and it has been increasing its foothold in Africa. Earlier, it was just the PALOPs that used to be the foci but Brazil has been spreading its wings to other parts of the continent with Brazil's expanding political and economic clout as an emerging power with a global role as well as its increasing trade and commercial interests in the region. During

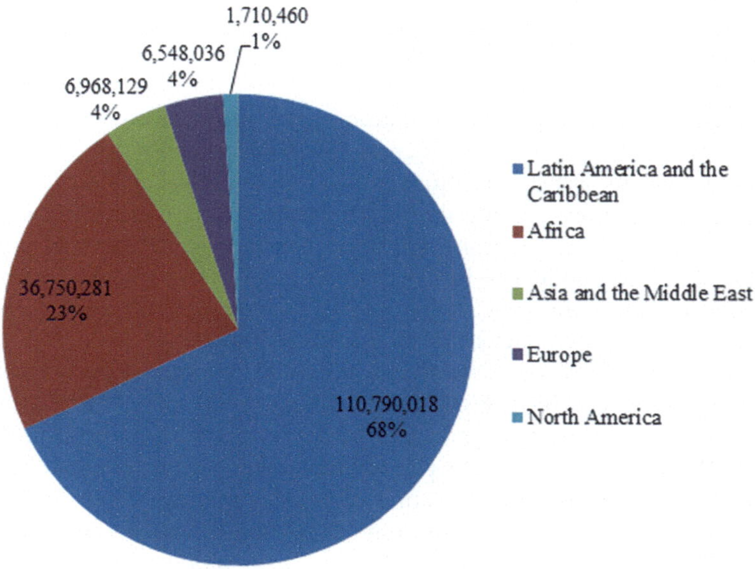

Fig. 3.2 Geographical distribution of Brazilian development cooperation, 2010 (in USD) (*Source* IPEA 2014, 19)

Lula's period, Productive Development Policy (2008–2010) was incorporated with the aim to boost trade, investment and cooperation with Africa (Suyama et al. 2016). Furthermore, Brazil aims to diversify its partners and hence has been slowly expanding its influence in other parts of Africa based on its "new commercial promotion strategy" initiated by President Dilma (Abdenur and Neto 2014). In December 2013, Brazilian Development Bank (BNDES) opened its first overseas office in Africa, in Johannesburg, after Brazil decided on debt relief as a major component of Brazil's economic relations with Africa. It was President Dilma who unveiled an Africa Agenda that pushed for strengthening Brazil's ties with the African continent (Suyama et al. 2016, 42).

Latin America and the Caribbean

President Lula clarified the importance Brazil attaches to its region during his first term in office:

> South America is a priority in Brazilian external policy. Our region is our home. (de Freitas Barbosa et al. 2009, 65)

For Brazil, its foreign policy and economic diplomacy have been focussed on its region for long. Brazil has increasingly been considered as a regional power despite its global ambitions and efforts in realising its dream of being a global power. Undoubtedly, Brazil is the largest political and economic entity in the region and exerts considerable amount of political and economic influence in its neighbourhood. The fact that around 68% of Cobradi is diverted to the region underscores Brazil's priorities and interests that are attached to its neighbourhood.

Even though President Cardoso (1995–2002) adopted more idealistic policy in multilateral relations, his approach was more pragmatic as far as Brazil's neighbourhood was concerned (de Freitas Barbosa et al. 2009, 64). In 2000, his foreign policy priority was rather made clear with Brazil hosting the first High-Level Meeting of South American countries. This continued under Lula administration (2003–2010) when the Cobradi funds to South America increased tremendously along with the overall increase in total Cobradi in the first decade of the twenty-first century. President Lula used Cobradi as "a tool for regional integration" (Inoue and Vaz 2012, 518). Brazil has incorporated both regional and bilateral projects as a part of its Cobradi in South America. The following countries receive maximum Cobradi in Latin America and the Caribbean (see Table 3.1).

Table 3.1 Country-wise distribution of Brazilian development cooperation in Latin America and the Caribbean, 2010

Country	*Values (USD)*	*Proportion*
Haiti	52,534,130	47.4
Chile	18,087,052	16.3
Argentina	9,481,047	8.6
Peru	4,958,115	4.5
Paraguay	3,962,262	3.6
Colombia	3,726,054	3.4
Uruguay	2,847,684	2.6
Cuba	2,663,593	2.4
Bolivia	2,504,251	2.3
Jamaica	1,992,043	1.8

Source IPEA (2014, 20)

Haiti has been the most important beneficiary of Cobradi with 47.4% of all assistance to Latin America and the Caribbean in 2010 (IPEA 2014). Brazil is actively involved in efforts towards political stabilisation and maintaining peace and security in Haiti since the political crisis of 2004. To promote peace and security in Haiti, the UNSC had formed the United Nations Stabilisation Mission in Haiti (MINUSTAH) under the leadership of the Latin American countries including Brazil, Argentina and Chile. Following the 2010 earthquake, the efforts of MINUSTAH further intensified for the rehabilitation and reconstruction of the devastated country (MINUSTAH 2016). Since 2004, Brazil has been actively involved in supporting Haiti through both multilateral and bilateral efforts (Vianna Braga 2010). Under the Lula government, Brazil has expanded its Cobradi, and Haiti became the major recipient of Cobradi in the region. Between 2005 and 2010, Brazil is expected to have given approximately USD 7 billion to Haiti as development cooperation (Feldmann et al. 2011). The earthquake became far more challenging scenario for all the donors, including Brazil, with whatever they had done starting in 2004 washed away within no time. Apart from providing immediate relief measures on the aftermath of the earthquake, President Lula committed to "a 100% increase in its military presence in MINUSTAH" (Hirst 2011). In 2010 alone, Brazil had given USD 52.53 million as Cobradi to Haiti (IPEA 2014, 29). It was also the first country to contribute to the Haiti Reconstruction Fund (HRF), USD 55 million was contributed in this regard (World Bank 2010). Apart from defence support and police training, technical assistance, agriculture, infrastructure, public health and environment were important areas of cooperation with Haiti (IPEA 2011, 50). The 2010 earthquake was followed by a cholera epidemic which forced the Ministry of Health (MS) to increase its assistance to Haiti. All the agencies involved in Cobradi coordinated their efforts for assisting Haiti to recover from the crisis.

Aside Haiti, the top beneficiaries of Cobradi is Brazil's immediate neighbours in South America, including Chile, Argentina, Peru and Paraguay. In the case of Chile, maximum assistance is given in the field of education, and science and technology. For Brazil, Argentina is not only a beneficiary of Cobradi but also a partner in trilateral cooperation. It gives assistance to Argentina in sectors like education, science and technology, and humanitarian assistance (IPEA 2011). Peru became one of the largest recipients of Brazil's humanitarian assistance in 2005–2009 after the earthquake and the floods (IPEA 2011, 26). It also receives considerable amount of Cobradi as technical assistance, education, and science and technology. Jamaica and Cuba were the beneficiaries of humanitarian assistance from Brazil after the hurricane that jolted both the countries.

Brazil has been actively involved in strengthening its regional ties and creating goodwill in its neighbourhood. Development cooperation has been an important instrument of Brazil's economic statecraft in the region.

Africa

Brazil has had close economic, political and cultural relations with several countries in Africa from the colonial period. Brazil initiated its efforts towards reviving these ties with African countries in the 1960s and 1970s (de Freitas Barbosa et al. 2009, 59). However, President Lula's foreign policy engagements could be counted as a step forward as far as Africa is considered. According to him, Brazil's earlier attitude towards Africa was "turning our back to Africa" and this had to be changed in order for Brazil to maintain and strengthen its ties with the region. In the article written by President Lula in *Valor Economico* in October 2007, he emphasised that "Brazil has all the conditions to contribute to this 'African Renaissance'" (de Freitas Barbosa et al. 2009, 73). President Lula also said:

> We feel ourselves connected to Africa through cultural and historical threads. Having the second largest black population in the world, we are committed to share the challenges and the destiny of the region. (de Freitas Barbosa et al. 2009, 65)

President Lula, during his term (2003–2010), visited 27 countries in Africa, which is higher than any other president of Brazil had managed to do. Lula's proactive foreign policy and economic diplomacy towards Africa were seen as a way "to consolidate Brazil as a global player" (Inoue and Vaz 2012, 518). However, priority was given to the PALOPs and several efforts were made in consolidating Brazilian relations with all of the Lusophone countries in Africa. For example, President Lula was quick to set up an embassy at Sao Tome and Principe in 2003, the same year he came to power. Sao Tome and Principe was the only PALOP country where Brazil did not have an embassy. The embassy was set up the same year on an urgent basis. PALOPs continue to be the largest beneficiaries

Table 3.2 Country-wise distribution of Brazilian development cooperation in Africa, 2010

Country	*Values (USD)*	*Proportion*
Cape Verde	8,953,437	24.4
Guinea-Bissau	7,804,779	21.2
Mozambique	4,901,040	13.3
Sao Tome and Principe	3,812,296	10.4
Angola	2,643,276	7.2
Senegal	1,237,643	3.4
Democratic Republic of Congo	700,433	1.9
Liberia	689,111	1.9
Mali	563,953	1.5
Benin	509,903	1.4

Source IPEA (2014, 21)

of Cobradi in Africa and have the most number of projects in the region. Even though Brazil has started giving assistance to other countries in Africa, linguistic affinities still continue to be a driving factor in deciding Brazil's development cooperation partners in Africa. For country-wise distribution of Cobradi in Africa, see Table 3.2.

Even though African continent receives just 23% of the total Cobradi,[19] the PALOPs topping the list of the countries receiving maximum Cobradi to Africa re-emphasise Brazil's efforts to strengthen its historic, cultural and linguistic ties with the continent. The top five beneficiaries are the PALOPs including Cape Verde, Guinea-Bissau, Mozambique, Sao Tome and Principe and Angola.

Cape Verde gets one-fourth of all Cobradi given to Africa in 2010 (IPEA 2014). The sectors include technical assistance, urban infrastructure, health, environment, and science and technology. In order to solve the housing infrastructure problem in Cape Verde, Brazil replicated its successful urban infrastructure programme called "Minha Casa Minha Vida (My House, My Life)" in Cape Verde.[20] This project garnered a lot of positive response from Cape Verde that was going through a huge housing crisis.

[19] See Fig. 3.2.

[20] In Cape Verde, this programme was called "Casa para Todos (Homes for All)" (IPEA 2014).

With 21.2% of the total Cobradi allocated for Africa going to Guinea-Bissau, the country could be considered as one of the most important partners for Brazil in Africa. The most important areas of assistance include education, technological support and humanitarian assistance. Brazil's oldest bilateral development cooperation project has been for Guinea-Bissau, for a project that helped registering and documenting birth in Guinea-Bissau (IPEA 2014, 35).

Mozambique, Sao Tome and Principe, and Angola receive much less than what Cape Verde and Guinea-Bissau get. In Mozambique, agriculture has been the priority sector for cooperation. The ProSavana project has been the landmark project of Brazil, based on its own innovative agricultural practices, skills and technology for increasing the agricultural productivity of Mozambique. This project is also an instance of Brazil's triangular cooperation with Japan. Other areas of cooperation with Mozambique have been education, science and technology and health.

Brazil's focus on Africa has been driven by the efforts to strengthen linguistic and historical ties. PALOPs receiving more than 75% of all Cobradi to Africa is a testimony to that. The linguistic similarities have helped in deepening the level of understanding between these countries and have increased the prospects of sharing technology and expertise through the SSC platform.

Apart from strengthening historical and cultural bonds, Brazil definitely has geopolitical and economic interests in the region. Support from African countries is of vital importance to fulfil its dream of a permanent seat in the UNSC (de Freitas Barbosa et al. 2009, 72). Boosting trade with the continent is also a major concern for Brazil. Furthermore, the quest for natural resources and the search for new markets have also made Africa an important region. Brazil has increasingly been keen to maintain its relations with Africa and with the mounting pressure from the private sector to maintain these ties; the engagement with Africa is only expected to increase.

Modalities

The Brazilian development cooperation has increased steadily over the first decade of the twenty-first century and ranges across a growing number of areas, including health, education, technical cooperation, humanitarian assistance, peace-keeping operations, refugee assistance, and science and technological cooperation. The modalities of Cobradi in the year 2010, as given by the IPEA report, give a clear picture of the priorities of Brazil (see Fig. 3.3). Peace-keeping operations (36%) and funding for international organisations (34%) combined make 70% of total Cobradi. Humanitarian cooperation forms the third largest component with 17% of all expenditure from Cobradi (IPEA 2014).

The data of each modality of Cobradi remains highly dispersed mainly because of the numerous governmental agencies involved in the process causing a lack of coordination and monitoring. However, the IPEA reports are the only available data from over 100 agencies involved in Cobradi.

The modalities of Cobradi are decided as per the priorities and interests of Brazil that also depend on domestic and international factors; Brazil's capacity to deliver; its experience and expertise in relevant sectors as well as its bilateral relations with the beneficiary country.

Domestic sectoral interests also play a prominent role in deciding the foreign policy priorities of Brazil as in certain cases the interests of political parties and bureaucratic organisations are taken into consideration when development assistance patterns and modalities are decided.

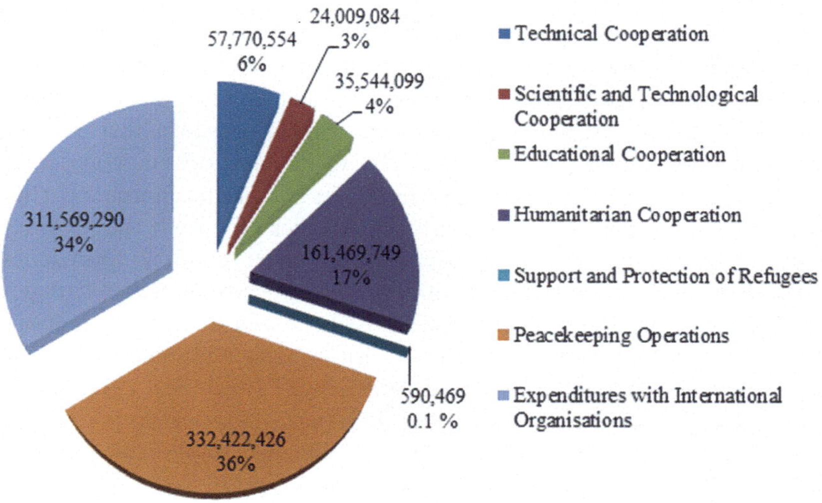

Fig. 3.3 Modalities of Brazilian development cooperation 2010, expenditures (in USD) (*Source* IPEA 2014, 17)

Several organisations such as EMBRAPA, Fiocruz and National Service for Industrial Training (SENAI)[21] that play an inevitable role in Cobradi are especially proactive in advocating for increased external cooperation ties.

Technical cooperation has been an important component of Cobradi since its early days. More than 170 institutions of the federal government, "including ministries, public entities, foundations and companies", are responsible for carrying out Brazil's technical cooperation. All the technical cooperation of Brazil is overseen by the MRE, through the ABC; different ministries; and the embassies abroad. It is provided in areas as diverse as "agriculture, education, vocational education, health, environment, public administration, transportation, energy, sanitation, construction of popular housing, culture and justice" (IPEA 2014, 26). The responsibility to send and supervise the technical missions to the partner countries rests with the ABC. These missions are usually composed of Brazilian experts from its own institutions that prepare technical programmes for its partners. The ABC overlooks all preparations for the smooth execution of these technical cooperation programmes, including their assessment as well as financing the projects. The main features of Brazilian technical cooperation include its emphasis on horizontality and demand-driven approach. The demands of the partners who need technical assistance from Brazil reach "through embassies and Brazilian delegations abroad, the embassies and offices of international organizations in Brasília, or visits to Brazil made by foreign official missions" (IPEA 2014, 26). Despite the official position that Brazil's technical cooperation component is always demand-driven, competing claims exist. In several cases, Brazil advised its partner to choose a particular programme that would be mutually beneficial for both the provider and the beneficiary. In certain cases, the partner country approaches without any particular demands and these countries are bound to get funding for projects chosen by Brazil. It is also noted that technical cooperation has helped open new markets for Brazilian businesses thereby paving way for indirect commercial gains. Brazil's technical cooperation is linked to its global aspirations, both for a permanent seat in the UNSC and for ensuring senior positions for the Brazilian diplomats (Suyama et al. 2016).

[21] SENAI is a non-profit organization that provides formal training and education for workers in the industrial sector.

In 2010, more than half of Brazil's total technical cooperation was for Latin America and the Caribbean (53.3%), followed by Africa (39.5%) and Asia (7.0%) (IPEA 2014, 29). Haiti and Peru topped the list of partner countries that received maximum technical assistance from Brazil. The figures suggest that the technical cooperation budget of Brazil has seen a four-fold increase from 2005 (USD 16 million) to 2010 (USD 58 million) (IPEA 2014, 28). Last one decade would have seen several changes in the composition of Cobradi. However, the lack of authentic data prohibits any analysis on the changing modalities and its geographical spread.

Through its South-South technical cooperation, Brazil aims at knowledge transfer from its social and economic development experiences and success stories, notably with regard to health, agriculture and professional education sector. Through technical cooperation agreements, Brazil has been fortifying its bilateral relations in the Global South (Dauvergne and Farias 2012, 909). President Lula considered technical cooperation with developing countries as a way to strengthen Brazil's bilateral ties with the rest of the world, thereby elevating the country's profile in international politics.

Brazil's educational cooperation forms just 4% (USD 63 million) of its total Cobradi in 2010 (IPEA 2014). However, it is an important form of cooperation with the African countries, mainly the PALOPs, and in Latin America and the Caribbean. Several students from low-income countries get scholarships for studying in Brazil. The students from PALOPs coming to Brazil find it easy to adjust to a new country setting because of language and cultural similarities. Most universities in Brazil have students from Africa smoothly integrating into the Brazilian set-up. In April 2015, during my field visit to University of Brasilia (UnB), University of Sao Paulo (USP) and Federal University of Rio de Janeiro (UFRJ), there were several students from PALOPs and Latin American countries in all the three campuses. Many of the foreign professors who teach in these universities have also been students in these universities earlier who preferred to stay back in Brazil. The main institutions involved in disbursing education cooperation are the Ministry of Education (MEC), MRE and the Ministry of Science and technology (MCT). However, the federal units also have the capacity to offer scholarships separately as per their discretion. For example, the state of Rio de Janeiro extends scholarships to students from Africa and Latin America to study in the State University of Rio de Janeiro (UERJ), which comes under its administration. This was clarified by Professor Carlos Milani of the UERJ during an interview with him on 26 March 2015 at the UERJ campus, Rio de Janeiro. All the development assistance given by the federal units has not been included in the volume of Cobradi as depicted in the IPEA report. In case this gets included in future reports, the Cobradi volume would be much higher than what it is projected now.

The scientific and technological cooperation (STC), though less (2% of total Cobradi), has also been a component for Brazil's cooperation with the Global South. In the IPEA 2011 report, it was clubbed into the technical cooperation component. In the IPEA 2014 report, scientific and technological cooperation was separated from what was called technical and scientific cooperation earlier. It is the Ministry of Science, Technology and Innovation (MCTI) that is responsible for STC. However, the MEC and MRE are also involved in Brazil's cooperation efforts abroad. Latin America and the Caribbean countries are the largest beneficiaries of STC, with 43.6% (IPEA 2014, 65).

Brazil has supported several countries in emergency situations and political distress through its humanitarian cooperation that forms 17% of the overall Cobradi (IPEA 2014). The main tenets of Brazil's humanitarian cooperation are "humanity, impartiality, neutrality and independence" (IPEA 2014, 71). It is also inspired by programmes initiated by President Lula in 2003 to fight against hunger and extreme poverty, like Zero Hunger Programme (Fome Zero). Under the coordination of MRE, an Inter-ministerial Working Group on International Humanitarian Cooperation (GTI-CHI), comprised of fifteen ministries of the Federal government, was set up in 2006 to manage the humanitarian cooperation efforts of Brazil. In 2012, Brazil's contributions to the United Nations Office for the Coordination of Humanitarian Affairs (OCHA) increased to USD54.4 million when compared to its contribution in 2010, which amounted to USD 26.6 million (Marcondes and Mawdsley 2017, 688).

Another challenge for Brazil in the twenty-first century the increasing flux of refugees and support given to them was incorporated into Cobradi. While the Ministry of Justice has been the most important Federal agency involved in formulating Brazil's refugee policy, the National Committee for Refugees (Conare)[22] has been the agency involved in its execution. Because of Brazil's relaxed refugee laws, there has been a huge influx of

[22] Conare is an agency affiliated to the Ministry of Justice.

refugees, especially from Haiti and Syria. The Venezuelan crisis has also increased influx of refugees to Brazil that has brought new challenges for the country. While the relaxed immigration rules for nationals of countries suffering humanitarian crisis have helped several people to stay and work in Brazil, the major concern is that the country is not yet equipped to deal with such mass migration and has been finding it difficult to support the refugees with their rehabilitation and settlement.

Brazil's increasing presence in peace-keeping operations under the UN umbrella demonstrates its commitment to peace and security around the world. The authorisation from the Congress is mandatory for deploying troops for peace-keeping operations. The MRE and Ministry of Defense (MD) have to initiate the process after which they have to get the nod from the president before submitting it to the Congress for approval. Brazil has been involved in several peace-keeping missions in countries including Haiti, Cyprus, Sudan, East Timor, Ivory Coast, Lebanon and Liberia.

Thirty-four percentage of total Cobradi is given as contributions to international organisation. These contributions are managed by the Secretariat of International Affairs in the Ministry of Planning, Budget and Management (MP). These contributions are made to both multilateral organisations like the UN and multilateral development funds like African Development Fund (ADF).

The different modalities of Cobradi suggest that Brazil is most actively involved in multilateral development cooperation. More than 70% of Cobradi is provided through the UN or its agencies. The survey of geographical patterns and modalities of Cobradi suggest that (1) Brazil's focus has been on Latin America and the Caribbean, and Africa and (2) that it prefers multilateral cooperation to bilateral cooperation. The following section will focus on what prompts Brazil to give development cooperation to its peers in the Global South.

What Drives Cobradi? Motivations and Aspirations of an Emerging Power

In the twenty-first century, the strategies and practices of international development cooperation have witnessed changes with the emerging powers increasingly playing an instrumental role in this transformation. As Brazil provides more development cooperation to the Global South and gets more actively engaged in international cooperation, it becomes important to understand whether Brazil is using its development cooperation for political and economic gains or is it more altruistic in nature. As noticed in the case of traditional donors or other emerging powers, the motivations and agendas of Brazil is varied and complex, which forms the crux of this section.

The official position of Brazil about its development cooperation is that its cooperation is horizontal, demand-driven and has no similarity to the North-South pattern of foreign aid flows. Brazilian officials claim that Cobradi is motivated not by economic or political interests, but based on international solidarity and its sincerity towards its Southern partners. While the official position points mostly to the altruistic motivations, the research on Cobradi shows that national interest plays an important role in Brazil's development cooperation initiatives and it is not completely divorced from the broader foreign policy objectives. Many of the senior diplomats from ABC and MRE, interviewed in Brasilia during the first two weeks of March 2015 by the author, were of the opinion that Brazil is more concerned of its solidarity, equality and support to the Global South. However, some of them did not cast-off the idea that Brazil might have mixed motivations for providing development assistance. However, most of them were hesitant to admit that there could be clear motivations behind Brazil's development cooperation endeavours. A senior diplomat from ABC, interviewed on 9 March 2015, explained that Cobradi is based on SSC and horizontality which makes it more altruistic. He clarified that if Brazil is gaining something out of its development cooperation efforts, it is coincidental.

The detailed analysis of Cobradi makes it clear that it inevitably entails a degree of national interest and is not just philanthropy. However, one cannot discount Brazil's role in bringing positive change for the partner countries. Like Inoue and Vaz (2012) have maintained, "the dual motivations of altruism and national interest are not necessarily mutually exclusive. International relations could be seen as a positive sum game, in which there is some room for mutual gains" (Inoue and Vaz 2012, 509). Based on the available data on Cobradi and the changing trends in Brazil's development cooperation policy, the following priorities of Brazil can be discussed.

Regional Solidarity and the Neighbourhood First Policy

The geographical distribution of Brazil's development cooperation signifies the priority it attaches to its region. The fact that Latin America and Caribbean gets around 68% of Cobradi is in itself an evidence of how the growth and development of its region continue to be a key tenet of Brazilian foreign policy. While there are several factors driving Brazil's development cooperation, including trade and investments, search for new markets and historical linkages; regional solidarity and stability in the region is of utmost importance. Because it is the largest country in the region in terms of area, population, economic growth as well as political and economic clout, Brazil's role in regional integration and stability is huge. Brazil's role in Pacific Alliance and Mercosur is also reminder of the fact that together, these two account for more than 90% of LAC's GDP, trade and FDI flows, which make it important for Brazil to forge ties with these regional groupings that can define its position in the region (OECD/CAF/ECLAC 2018). Brazil's willingness to shoulder the responsibility of supporting other countries in the region through development cooperation has been evident from its foreign policy considerations based on enhanced economic diplomacy in the neighbourhood.

Linguistic, Cultural and Historic Affinity

One of the important driving factors in deciding Brazil's development cooperation partnership has been its emphasis on close cultural and historic relationship with other developing countries, especially in Latin America and the Caribbean, and in the PALOPs (Corrêa 2009, 1). Apart from the regional stability factor, Latin America and the Caribbean's historical linkages and cultural similarities with Brazil have been important for Brazil.

Despite Brazil's long-lasting historical ties with Africa, it was never so much of a priority until President Lula revived Brazil's ties with the continent. The decision to build closer ties with Africa was a direct outcome of President Lula's adoption of "solidarity diplomacy as a guiding principle of its foreign policy" (Pino and Leite 2010). Under Lula, Brazil's global aspirations got a boost from his style of presidential diplomacy. Lula considered SSC as a way to strengthen the bilateral ties with the

Global South thereby promoting Brazil's image as a developing country with huge potential.

Around 80% of total development cooperation to Africa goes to the PALOPs and other countries in Africa receive less than 20% of Cobradi.[23] Even when Brazil's focus has been on the PALOPs, which share linguistic, cultural and historical links with Brazil, other countries in the continent also gained importance in the twenty-first century.

Trade, Business and Search for Markets

With the increasing amount of Cobradi flowing into Africa in the first decade of the twenty-first century, there were more trade prospects emerging between Brazil and Africa. Under President Lula, trade "multiplied five-fold between 2002 and 2008" with Africa (de Freitas Barbosa et al. 2009, 73). Brazil's trade with Africa grew from USD 6 billion to USD 24 billion under President Lula (BBC 2010, July 4). From 2002 to 2012, their trade increased from USD 4 billion to USD 27 billion.

Brazil's 36 embassies in Africa show its renewed commitment to Africa. President Lula made record number of visits to Africa. Brazil opened 12 new embassies in Africa between 2003 and 2006 (the first tenure of President Lula) and on a whole 17 embassies during President Lula (2003–2010) (Abdenur and Neto 2014). President Lula travelled far and wide in Africa during his tenure, made at least 12 trips covering 27 countries. Brazil, in turn, received 47 visits of African leaders from 27 nations (IPEA 2011, 3).

There are several countries which were visited more than once by President Lula thereby emphasising Brazil's priorities as well as political and economic interests in the region. Within Africa, South Africa became the most visited country with President Lula visiting it thrice. Being the most powerful country in the region and the main export destination of Brazilian goods in Africa, South Africa was on top of Lula's list for high-level visits. Furthermore, South Africa is also a partner in both the BRICS and the IBSA initiative, which is aimed at promoting SSC and bringing together the emerging powers of the Global South to collaborate on important issues of global concern. Some countries were visited twice by Lula, including Angola, Nigeria, Sao Tome and Principe and

[23]These values have been calculated on the basis of the figures given in the IPEA report 2014.

Ghana. Angola is the most favoured destination of Brazilian investments in Africa which made Lula visit this Lusophone country twice. Brazil has one of its largest current account deficits with Nigeria, as a consequence of oil imports (de Freitas Barbosa et al. 2009, 73). Ghana is important as it is the headquarters of Embrapa's office in Africa, which is located in Accra. Even though Lula visited Mozambique and Gabon only once, these visits were considered as most important from the economic diplomacy perspective as the rationale behind this strategic visit was to back Companhia Vale do Rio Doce (CVRD) investments in these countries.

President Lula's economic diplomacy endeavours were welcomed by a growing number of private sector companies as they reaped the benefits of Brazil's trade and investment in Africa. Lula has always been supportive of the expanding interests of Brazilian businesses (Marcondes and Mawdsley 2017) and his team for bilateral visit always included a group of businessmen interested in investing in Africa (de Freitas Barbosa et al. 2009). Despite this, the businesses are getting more demanding for government support in expanding their interests abroad. They have been disappointed at times with the insufficient support from the government. Therefore, the Brazilian businesses have been pushing the government for boosting its economic diplomacy endeavours in Brazil that could be mutually beneficial for both.

During Dilma'spresidency—even though Africa remained a priority—economic diplomacy was not pursued as intensely, which is evident from the fact that she visited only 6 countries—Angola, Mozambique, South Africa, Nigeria, Equatorial Guinea and Ethiopia—during her tenure (Marcondes and Mawdsley 2017). Even though these six countries are strategically important for Brazil's trade and investments, she put little efforts to push presidential diplomacy to the levels of her predecessor. However, her approach and engagement towards the Global South were largely driven by the economic context that had changed drastically after she came to power. The new economic realities defined by falling economic growth at home and worsening international financial crisis have had an influence on the priorities of the leadership. Despite supporting SSC, she emphasised on building commercial ties with the Global South that could be a market for Brazilians goods (Marcondes and Mawdsley 2017; Suyama et al. 2016). After 2014, the economic crisis hit so hard that it was impossible for the government to even financially support the existing embassies in several countries (Marcondes and Mawdsley 2017). The rumours that Temer government has decided to close down few embassies in the Caribbean and Africa raised alarm among the diplomatic community in Brazil and were taken up by the media, which led to the government clarifying that these are false rumours. Any such closures would have compromised Brazil's earlier efforts in SSC.

Expanding the reach of Brazilian companies became part and parcel of country's external strategy since the Lula government, the policy that continued under Dilma. Brazil's foreign direct investments (FDIs) have increased at an average of 14% a year since 2005 (Cervo 2010, 19). Brazil has promoted domestically-owned firms through its economic diplomacy efforts; for example, Gerdau (steel) has operated in 13 countries, Vale (mining) in 25, Petrobras (energy/oil) in 26, Votorantim (various sectors) in 14, Camargo Correa (various) in 13 and JBS (meat) in 14 countries (Baumann 2010, 46). The Federal government has adopted an explicit policy to stimulate investment abroad. To strengthen the smaller Brazilian private firms in specific sectors and to equip them to handle international competition, the BNDES has financed mergers with and acquisition of larger companies (Baumann 2010, 47). However, this move to combine aid with trade and investments did not go well with the civil-society organisations that criticised the blurring of lines, especially in the mining, agriculture and construction sectors in Africa and Latin America (Marcondes and Mawdsley 2017).

Diplomatic Reciprocity

One of the major agendas in Brazil's economic diplomacy has been garnering diplomatic support from partner countries in international platforms, where numbers matter. Pino and Leite (2010) argue that Brazil uses its development cooperation as an instrument that can be used to "disseminate a particular image of modernity" of Brazil that would help in getting support for Brazil gaining a permanent seat on the UNSC. Apart from establishing a strategic partnership among the emerging powers of the Global South, one of the reasons driving multilateral groupings like the IBSA is their common interest in gaining a permanent seat at the UNSC. However, these countries have not been able to tap on the potential of their economic and political ties and take it towards this goal. They seem not to go much beyond informal consultations and small-scale technical partnership agreements (de Freitas Barbosa et al. 2009, 66). Both Brazil and India, along with two major OECD countries, Germany and Japan, created G4 to support each others' bid for a permanent seat in the

UNSC. Even though there is little progress in the reform of the UNSC permanent membership, groupings like G4 are important in projecting the aspirations of emerging powers to play a greater role in international politics.

Brazil's development cooperation programme has helped Brazil tremendously in internationalisation of its economic, political, diplomatic and commercial interests. President Lula's foreign policy priorities have always been clear with him placing more "emphasis on North-South cleavages" and pushing for bilateral relations with the Global South. The main reason behind this has been the quest for a multipolar international political order as well as to shape a "new trade geography" (de Freitas Barbosa et al. 2009, 66). An important feature of this relatively new approach in Brazilian economic diplomacy has been the attempt to link diplomatic agreements with business missions and supported by Brazilian government agencies and enterprises such as the BNDES, Petrobras and the Brazilian Agricultural Research Cooperation (EMBRAPA).

Lula government's efforts in building bilateral ties were rather impressive with a 30 per cent increase in the number of countries where Brazil maintains diplomatic representations (Inoue and Vaz 2012, 529). Even though Lula was criticised for his foreign policy moves such as opening new embassies in supposedly "unimportant" countries in Africa, he had been sure about Brazil's strategic interests in Africa, despite him not stating it explicitly. President Lula defended his position in the country by saying that his approach was not informed by utilitarian interests and that such measures could create new economic ties with the Global South. However, his foreign policy was diplomatically sound with a great understanding of the changing geopolitics.

Under Dilma, the foreign policy priorities shifted both due to the political and economic changes that Brazil was going through and due to the difference in personality of the president. The role of leadership in deciding Brazil's foreign policy and economic diplomacy is crucial as evident from the foreign policy shift from Lula to Dilma, despite belonging to the same party and ideology (Burges and Bastos 2017; Suyama et al. 2016). However, SSC was considered as an inevitable part of their foreign policy, which could aid them in climbing the ladder of power. Brazil was willing to take up this responsibility that it thought came with the status of an emerging power that is aspiring for great power status (Malamud 2011).

Conclusion

Over the years, Brazil's development cooperation has evolved drastically, from a recipient of the OECD-DAC aid to a major development assistance provider of the Global South to presently aiming to join the club of the developed and the influential. Until recently, Brazilian development cooperation was anchored on SSC. It has been a conscious effort on the part of Brazil to distance itself from the traditional aid, which is believed to be based on donor-recipient hierarchy and conditionalities. Therefore, it latched on to its identity as a "Third World" country which helped it garner legitimacy and support from other developing countries of the Global South. By placing SSC as the cornerstone of its development cooperation, Brazil's efforts have been in the direction of making the emerging powers' voice getting heard in international politics dominated by the Global North. The emerging powers of the Global South are demanding for a new discourse on development that takes into account the demands and needs of developing countries.

While development cooperation from Brazil focussed on the principles of SSC and Third World Solidarity, the informed recipient choices of Brazil clearly demonstrate the strategies of Brazil towards advancing its national interest and leveraging the recipient countries for political, economic and diplomatic gains. The geographical patterns of development cooperation flows from Brazil signify the factors driving its financial outflows. Brazilian development cooperation should be seen in relation to the country's broad policy objectives as well as in the context of international power shifts in which Brazil is an emerging power capable of shaping the global governance architecture. Brazil uses development cooperation as an instrument of economic statecraft that also serves to enhance its international power. Brazil's long-standing tradition of attracting allies through its development cooperation, multilateral initiatives and diplomacy has been commendable. Through its development cooperation efforts, it aims to achieve its foreign policy goals.

The definition and structure of development cooperation propounded by Brazil have clearly been first of its kind from any emerging power.

Despite not being a part of the Paris Declaration,[24] Brazil has initiated its efforts for more transparency in its development cooperation. It is a model still under construction, which despite revealing a few of its features still lacks greater systematisation and debate. Despite Brazil's comprehensive involvement in SSC, the government has not established a central agency for national coordination of its development cooperation. Nor has it set up a nationally coordinated and standardised system to collect, process and publish information about its development assistance. Brazil also lacks an official external development cooperation policy or any regulations on how its contributions should be reported (Inoue and Vaz 2012, 531). However, Cobradi is still a global model in waiting.

Brazil's development cooperation policy has to be attributed to the political leadership and the strength of its economy. Even though different governments contributed to the formation and consolidation of Cobradi, it was under the presidency of Lula that it got a face of its own. Brazil began to be considered as an important development assistance provider of the Global South during this period. However, the changing domestic and international scenarios pushed the subsequent governments to focus more on domestic politics and foreign policy became secondary. This has had a negative influence on SSC as well as Brazil's political and economic clout that Lula had managed to bring in through his presidential diplomacy. While Dilma tried to follow Lula's path, she was constrained by the economic and political crisis that left very little space to pursue foreign policy goals. The recent developments in Brazilian domestic affairs have put serious questions on Brazil's SSC and the very principles on which Cobradi was based on. Brazil has initiated its accession into the OECD that will alter the narrative of SSC on which Cobradi was built. President Bolsonaro is keen to align Brazil with the Global North and the decision to join OECD would alter Brazil's role as a Southern Donor. The changing preferences of the leadership have had a profound influence on Brazil's foreign policy. However, Brazil joining OECD would place it in

[24] Paris Declaration on Aid Effectiveness is a roadmap for improving the effectiveness of aid. It was signed in 2005 by the OECD countries. Brazil voiced its opinion against this declaration stating that it is harsh and unfair on the recipients and does not take into consideration the voice of emerging powers who are development assistance providers. The major tenets outlined in this declaration are "ownership, alignment, harmonization, managing results and mutual accountability" (OECD 2016b).

the league of Mexico and Chile that have joined OECD and make it distant from emerging powers like China and India that have chosen to remain outside the OECD and make their own rules in the international aid architecture.

References

ABC. (2016a), Trilateral Cooperation with Countries [Online: web]. Accessed on 28 June 2016, http://www.abc.gov.br/Gestao/TrilateralPaises#.

ABC. (2016b), Trilateral Cooperation with International Organisations [Online: web]. Accessed on 28 June 2016, http://www.abc.gov.br/Gestao/TrilateralOrganismo#.

Abdenur, A.E. and de Souza Neto, D. (2014), "Brazil's Growing Relevance to Peace and Security in Africa", Norwegian Peacebuilding Resource Centre Report [Online: web]. Accessed on 26 December 2015. https://www.ciaonet.org/attachments/24877/uploads.

Amorim, C. (2010), Brazilian Foreign Policy Under President Lula (2003–2010): an Overview, Revista Brasileira de Política Internacional, Special Edition, 53: 214–240. Accessed on 20 December 2015, http://www.scielo.br/pdf/rbpi/v53nspe/v53nspea13.pdf.

Baumann, R. (2010), "Brazilian External Sector So Far in the 21st Century". *Revista Brasileira de Política Internacional*, 53: 33–53.

BBC. (2010: July 4), Brazil's Lula Pays Tribute to Africa's historic Role [Online: web]. Accessed on 28 June 2016, http://www.bbc.com/news/10500100.

Boadle, A. (2019), Amazon Fires Could Burn Brazil's Bid to Join OECD Rich Nations Club. *Reuters*. https://www.reuters.com/article/us-brazil-environment-wildfires-oecd/amazon-fires-could-burn-brazils-bid-to-join-oecd-rich-nations-club-idUSKCN1VD2A9.

Burges S. and Bastos F.H.C. (2017), "The Importance of Presidential Leadership for Brazil's Foreign Policy", *Policy Studies*, 38(3): 277–290.

CEPAL. (2016), About ECLAC [Online: web]. Accessed on 28 May 2016, http://www.cepal.org/en/about.

Cervo, A. (2010), "Brazil's Rise on the International Scene: Brazil and the World", *Revista Brasileira de Política Internacional*, 53: 7–32.

Corrêa, M.L. (2009), Policy Dialogue on Development Co-operation Mexico City, 28–29 September 2009 [Online: web]. Accessed on 25 December 2015, http://www.oecd.org/dac/dac-global-relations/43876987.pdf.

Dauvergne, P. and Farias, D.B. (2012), "The Rise of Brazil as a Global Development Power", *Third World Quarterly*, 33: 903–917.

de Freitas Barbosa, A., Narciso, T. and Biancalana, M. (2009), "Brazil in Africa: Another Emerging Power in the Continent?", *Politikon*, 36 (1): 59–86.

Deloitte. (2018), Brazilian Position on Regional Groupings: BRICS and Latin America. https://www2.deloitte.com/br/en/pages/doing-business-brazil/articles/brazil-brics-and-latin-america.html.

Farani, M. (2009), 'Agência Brasileira de Cooperação (ABC) e a Cooperação Técnica do Brasil a Países em Desenvolvimento'. In: Rosangela Elias (ed.). *Atuação Governamental e Políticas Internacionais de Previdência Social*, Brasília: MPS, pp. 19–26. As cited in Inoue, Cristina Yumie Aoki and Vaz, Alcides Costa. 2012. "Brazil as ' Southern Donor ': Beyond Hierarchy and National Interests in Development Cooperation ?", *Cambridge Review of International Affairs*, 25(4): 507–534.

Farani, M. (2011), "Brazil's Global Development Agenda", Chatham House, Meeting Summary [Online: web]. Accessed on 25 July 2016, http://www.chathamhouse.org/sites/files/chathamhouse/271011summry.pdf.

Feldmann, A.E. et al. (2011), "Lost in Translation: ABC Cooperation and Reconstruction in Haiti", *Journal of Peacebuilding and Development*, 6(3): 45–60.

Hirst, M. (2011), Brazil's Renewed Responsibilities for Cooperation in Development and International Security. In: Jake Sherman et al. (eds.), *Engagement on Development and Security: New Actors, New Debates*. Center on International Cooperation, New York University, http://debatt.fn.no/wp-content/uploads/2012/02/engagment_book.pdf#page=33.

IBSA Fund. (2016), [Online: web]. Accessed on 20 July 2016, http://tcdc2.undp.org/ibsa/.

IMF. (2019), Six Charts on Boosting Growth in Brazil. IMF Country Focus, July 25, https://www.imf.org/en/News/Articles/2019/07/25/NA072519-Six-Charts-on-Boosting-Growth-in-Brazil.

Inoue, C.Y. and Vaz, A.C. (2012), "Brazil as 'Southern Donor': Beyond Hierarchy and National Interests in Development Cooperation?", *Cambridge Review of International Affairs*, 25(4): 507–534.

IPEA. (2011), *Brazilian Cooperation for International Development 2005–2009*, Brasilia: Institute for Applied Economic Research.

IPEA. (2014), *Brazilian Cooperation for International Development 2010*, Brasilia: Institute for Applied Economic Research.

Malamud, A. (2011), "A Leader Without Followers? The Growing Divergence Between the Regional and Global Performance of Brazilian Foreign Policy," *Latin American Politics and Society*, 53(3): 1–24.

Marcondes, D. and Mawdsley, E. (2017), "South-South in Retreat? The Transitions from Lula to Rousseff to Temer and Brazilian Development Cooperation," *International Affairs*, 93(3): 681–699.

Milani, C. (2014), "Brazil's South – South Co-Operation Strategies: From Foreign Policy to Public Policy", Occasional Paper No. 179, SAIIA [Online: web]. Accessed on 8 July 2015, http://www.saiia.org.za/occasional-papers/

487-brazil-s-south-south-co-operation-strategies-from-foreign-policy-to-public-policy/file.

MINUSTAH. (2016), [Online: web]. Accessed on 28 June 2016, http://www.un.org/en/peacekeeping/missions/minustah/mandate.shtml.

OECD. (2013), "Triangular Cooperation: What's the Literature Telling Us?" Accessed on 30 December 2015, http://www.oecd.org/dac/dac-global-relations/OECDTriangularCo-operationLiteratureReviewJune2013.pdf.

OECD. (2016a), Brazil's Development Co-operation [Online: web]. Accessed on 15 May 2016, http://www.oecd.org/dac/dac-global-relations/brazil-development-co-operation.htm.

OECD. (2016b), Paris Declaration and Accra Agenda for Action [Online: web]. Accessed on 28 June 2016, http://www.oecd.org/dac/effectiveness/parisdeclarationandaccraagendaforaction.htm.

OECD/CAF/ECLAC. (2018), *Latin American Economic Outlook 2018: Rethinking Institutions for Development*, Paris: OECD Publishing. https://www.oecd-ilibrary.org/development/latin-american-economic-outlook-2018_leo-2018-en.

OECD. (2019), What is ODA?. Accessed at https://www.oecd.org/dac/financing-sustainable-development/development-finance-standards/What-is-ODA.pdf.

Pino, A. and Leite, I. (2010), "The South- South Cooperation of Brazil: Instrument of Foreign Policy or Manifestation of International Solidarity," *Mural Internacional*. Accessed at https://www.e-publicacoes.uerj.br/index.php/muralinternacional/article/view/5262.

Planalto. (2016), Brazilian States and Municipalities May Present International Technical Cooperation Projects to the Benefit of Developing Countries [Online: web]. Accessed on 28 June 2016, http://www4.planalto.gov.br/saf-projetos/brazilian-states-and-municipalities-may-present-international-technical-cooperation-projects-to-the-benefit-of-developing-countries.

Suyama, B. et al. (2016), Brazil as a Development Partner Under Lula and Rousseff: Shifts and Continuities. In J. Gu et al. (eds.). *The BRICS in International Development*, London: Palgrave Macmillan.

Usher, K. (2011), "BRAZIL: Aid from Below", *International Affairs Review*, XX(1).

Vaz, A.C. and Inoue, C.Y. (2007), "Emerging Donors in International Development Assistance: The Brazil Case", IDRC-CRDI [Online: web]. Accessed on 10 May 2015, http://scholar.google.com/scholar?hl=en&btnG=Search&q=intitle:Emerging+Donors+in+International+Development+Assistance+:+The+Brazil+Case#0.

Vianna Braga, C.G. (2010), "MINUSTAH and the Security Environment in Haiti: Brazil and South American Cooperation in the Field", *International Peacekeeping*, 17: 711–722.

World Bank. (2010), Brazil Becomes First Country to Contribute to Haiti Reconstruction Fund, Accessed on 19 June 2016, http://www.worldbank.org/en/news/press-release/2010/05/11/brazil-first-country-contribute-haiti-reconstruction-fund.

World Bank. (2016), Brazil [Online: web]. Accessed on 28 June 2016, http://data.worldbank.org/country/brazil.

CHAPTER 4

Chinese Development Assistance: Leveraging Deep Pockets

In recent years, China's emergence as an economic superpower has been the most important development in the international political economy. Since China discarded its centrally planned economy for a market-oriented economy beginning in 1978, it has experienced rapid economic growth which averaged 10% a year, to become the second-largest economy after the US (World Bank 2016a). Despite its high economic growth and improving GDP per capita,[1] China is still an upper-middle-income country that has several challenges at home (World Bank 2016b). With 1.3 billion population, the largest in the world, China has challenges including extreme poverty and income inequality, which has to be tackled effectively for it to rise to the status of a great power in international politics.

Earlier, there were doubts over China's capability to play a global role in international politics that could challenge the global governance architecture dominated by the West. Zbigniew Brzezinski argued that "China was still a developing country and therefore no serious challenge to the United States" (Brzezinski 2004). However, in just more than a decade's time, China evolved itself into a formidable economic powerhouse that is

[1] Even though China's GDP per capita is increasing, it is nowhere near the GDP per capita of the developed countries of the Global North.

C. Purushothaman, *Emerging Powers, Development Cooperation and South-South Relations*, International Political Economy Series,
https://doi.org/10.1007/978-3-030-51537-9_4

capable of creating not only economic but also political outcomes. Therefore, the dynamic rise of China as a global economic and political power is a major topic of current academic and political discussion around the globe.

As China's economic clout increases, it has not been hesitant to use economic instruments as a way to shift the power dynamics in the international system in its favour. Even when the scale and style of China's economic diplomacy has changed over the years, development assistance continues to be one of the important instruments of economic statecraft for China. Until recently, China has been a net recipient of aid, but has gradually made a transition from an aid recipient to a development assistance provider. Chinese development assistance expanded dramatically, both in volume and geographical scope, in the twenty-first century. Historically, Chinese development cooperation was focussed on Southeast Asia. However, this has changed with China's expanding focus on Africa and Latin America, containing varied activities from commercial investment to humanitarian assistance (White Paper 2014). As per the data from the Chinese White Paper on Foreign Aid, China's foreign aid volume was 89.34 billion Yuan (USD 14.41 billion) in 2010–2012 period which amounts to USD 4.8 billion annually, if the volume is equally distributed over the three years. Maximum assistance went to Africa (51.8%) followed by Asia (30.5%), and Latin America and the Caribbean (8.4%).

The primacy of development assistance in Chinese foreign policy indicates how China uses its soft power capabilities to enhance its political clout. Its growing economic and military capabilities, diplomatic power, increasing presence in regional and global financial institutions and its own initiatives in setting up new institutions for global governance are all indicative of China's increasingly ambitious foreign policy goals (Shambaugh 2004/2005, 64). Both domestic and international factors have played in favour of China's rise that has allowed it to navigate the power struggle without any direct confrontation from the great powers. The domestic leadership has played the most significant role in deciding China's role in the world order. President Xi Jinping's meteoric rise in the Communist Party of China (CPC) has given a new impetus to what his predecessors aimed to achieve for China. Xi's flagship Belt and Road Initiative (BRI) launched in 2013 is widely seen as a project to increase China's global influence.

China's increasing economic growth and expanding global influence has made it pursue its interests and priorities more aggressively than ever before. It has been using different economic instruments from aid to trade to investments that has created dependencies, both economic and political, which has given China the power to dictate terms. Furthermore, the centralised governing system in China has helped it pursue its interests more efficiently when compared to several other emerging powers that are democracies. Even when China is on the path to overtake the US as the largest economy in the world, it has emphasised on its role as an emerging power of the Global South. The decision not to join the OECD-DAC also stems from its reluctance in being identified as a member of the developed country club. Instead, it pushes an identity as an emerging power, and its foreign aid narrative revolves around the principles of SSC. Moreover, China's increasing economic and political clout has enabled China to create its own development cooperation programme without being pulled into the institutions created by the Global North that neither accommodates the concerns of the developing countries nor allows the developing countries of the Global South to play any constructive role in these institutions.

This chapter explores China's increasing role as a development assistance provider, with an emphasis on its development assistance policy, institutional set-up, geographical reach, modalities and the motivations and agendas behind its recipient selection and development cooperation. The aim is also to understand how China has used aid as an instrument of economic statecraft and what role it has played in enhancing its global influence.

The following section gives an overview of the evolution and growth of foreign aid as a major tenet of China's foreign policy and economic diplomacy.

Historical Overview of Chinese Development Assistance

Though often branded as "new donors", most of the emerging powers are not really new to development cooperation. China is no misnomer. It began its development assistance to other developing countries since its birth as People's Republic of China (PRC) in 1949 (Woods 2008, 1205).

In 1950, China started by giving assistance to its close neighbours, the Democratic People's Republic of Korea (DPRK) and Vietnam, with whom China had friendly relations. This was also ideological-driven as both the recipient countries belonged to the Communist bloc. Chinese assistance in Vietnam and DPRK included infrastructure projects like building railways, roads, ports and bridges; assistance for agriculture and industrial development, and technical cooperation, thereby making significant contributions to their post-war reconstruction and economic development. The origin of concessional loans, an important modality of China's foreign aid even in the present times, dates back to 1950 when its assistance to Vietnam and DPRK was tied to goods and services from China (Li et al. 2014, 25). China, during this period, focussed on its region and hence maximum assistance was directed to the Asian countries.

Raposo and Potter (2010, 179) have classified Chinese foreign aid into five phases based on the changing trends in nature of assistance and the recipients over a period of time. These include first phase (1950–1955), second phase (1956–1978), third phase (1979–1982), fourth phase (1983–1999) and fifth phase (2000–present). The period from 1950 to 1955 could be considered as the first phase of Chinese external aid-giving. This was the period when China sensed the threat from the West and decided to strengthen its relations with its neighbouring Communist countries (Cooper 1976, 120). Foreign aid became an important instrument to build strong bilateral ties with neighbouring countries with similar ideologies. In exchange, China received international recognition and support from these developing countries.

Following the Bandung Conference of 1955,[2] the scope of Chinese development assistance expanded from the socialist countries to other developing countries of the Global South. China increased its efforts to build strong bilateral ties with countries in Asia and Africa. The aim was to change its image among the Afro-Asian nations (Cooper 1976, 15). China began to project its image as a developing country without any ideological considerations when it came to supporting its partner countries when need be. Also, it was in need of diplomatic recognition for its one-China policy against Taiwan, which prompted it to build relations with those countries that might lend it diplomatic support. China realised the importance of the developing countries' support in international organisations, and its forays into the African continent began in 1956 with its development assistance to Egypt (Brautigam 2010).

[2] The Asian-African Conference of the Non-Aligned Movement (NAM) in Bandung, Indonesia (1955).

Another crucial factor that changed China's development assistance priorities was the Sino-Soviet dispute in the 1960s, which forced China to move away from ideological motives, thereafter focussing on economic diplomacy. The basic tenet for China's development assistance was formulated in this decade with China declaring the Eight Principles for Economic Aid and Technical Assistance[3] to Other Countries in 1964, the main content of which includes equality, mutual benefit, respect for sovereignty of the recipient and assistance without any conditionalities. Henceforth, these three decades, starting 1950, proved important for China in consolidating its development assistance that began to be considered as an important instrument of economic statecraft.

In 1971, China regained its permanent seat in the UNSC from Chinese Taipei with the support from friendly developing countries. Most of the developing countries, 51 out of 76 that voted for China were found to be recipients of its foreign aid (Li et al. 2014). This prompted China to establish close links with more developing countries, through development assistance and economic cooperation. China increased its technical cooperation during this period and funded many important infrastructure projects. Brautigam (1998, 4) finds that China had development cooperation activities in more African countries than the US during this period. Hence, the 1970s was a period when China expanded its development assistance commitments to most countries in the Global South in order to strengthen its diplomatic ties. China also provided assistance to several developing countries in their efforts to achieve independence from colonial rule and assisted them in achieving economic development and growth.[4] This was instrumental in laying a strong foundation for "its long-term friendly cooperation with developing countries" of the Global South (White Paper 2011).

With the economic reforms and adoption of market-based economy in 1978, China renewed its focus on the economic aspect of its domestic and foreign policy, and worked towards strengthening its economic ties with other developing countries through SSC. Even though China maintained its economic ties with partner countries, the volume of external development assistance showed a decline during this period mainly because of

[3] See, Annexure 1.

[4] China provided economic as well as military aid to these countries under the colonial rule to fight for their independence (Li et al. 2014).

its increased focus on its domestic economy that was changing under the reforms (Li et al. 2014).

In the early 1980s, the focus was on sustaining and consolidating its projects in developing countries, even when the quantity of Chinese assistance had dipped (Brautigam 2010, 4). China's development assistance policy also got a much-needed push after the visit of Chinese Premier Deng Xiaoping to Africa in 1982. By emphasising cooperation and mutual benefit, he proclaimed China's commitment to SSC that respects the sovereignty of the partners, non-interference in their domestic affairs and no-conditionalities attached (Brautigam 1998, 49–50). During this period, China also expanded its development assistance to include loans and grants, apart from concessional loans that were in place since the beginning of China's development assistance (Li et al. 2014).

Initially, China focussed on funding small and medium development projects in agriculture, industry, infrastructure, technical support and capacity-building. Since the 1990s, China's economic cooperation diversified to include sectors like large-scale infrastructure projects, manufacturing, trade and investments, finance, mining and quarrying, and telecommunications (Raposo and Potter 2010, 180). China's foreign aid volume showed continuous increase from 1990 and it has only grown ever since (Li et al. 2014).

China evolved as a major development cooperation partner in the twenty-first century with tremendous increase in its development assistance volume and scope. Moreover, China's increasing economic might has complemented Chinese development assistance thereby raising its volume to the level of some of the OECD-DAC donors. Kitano and Harada (2014, 17) find that China was the sixth-largest donor, just behind US, UK, Germany, Japan and France, in both 2012 and 2013, out of the list comprised of all the OECD-DAC donors' ODA and China's foreign aid.

China's "multidimensional approach" to development assistance, embracing cooperation in political, economic, commercial, social and cultural spheres, has made it one of the most important players in international development finance (Alden 2007, 27). Since the launch of the century's largest infrastructure and investment initiative, the BRI, including Silk Road Economic Belt and the 21st Century Maritime Silk Road in 2013 that spreads across three continents—Asia, Europe and Africa—there is an increasing realisation that this is an effort by the Chinese leadership to alter the global balance of power. It blends aid, trade and investments in a way that is difficult to assess the outcomes of each. This ambitious project will put China in a position of global influence that even the US might find difficult to challenge significantly. As the projects under BRI get chalked out and are operational in the coming years, we would get to know who gains out of this project and how much. This new era of Chinese aid is most significant as it will play a major role in deciding how smooth the power shift in international politics could be in the twenty-first century.

Chinese Development Assistance: Spreading the Wings

China's growing presence and visibility in international development landscape has been because of its proactive development assistance policies and programmes that span the globe. The lack of transparency has always been a hurdle in analysing China's development assistance programme. Neither does China adhere to the Paris Declaration on Aid Effectiveness (2005) which advocates transparency, accountability, impact evaluation and monitoring of aid, nor does it want to be in the league of the developed donors. China also opted out of the aid transparency reporting initiatives of the Western powers, such as the International Aid Transparency Initiative (IATI).[5] The reasons for the reluctance to publicly disseminate Chinese development assistance data might range from the diplomatic row with Taiwan over its one-China policy to its domestic concerns about backlash from its citizens over its burgeoning external development assistance (Brautigam 2009, 167, 168; Lum et al. 2009, 4).

However, the release of two White Papers on Foreign Aid, in 2011 and 2014 respectively, points to China's readiness to bring certain level of transparency into its development assistance. Its efforts in the direction of sporadically publishing its development assistance data and slowly moving towards transparency indicate its willingness to shoulder more responsibilities as a development assistance provider and ensuring its position as one of the important players in international development finance. Because China has not released any White Paper on Foreign Aid after 2014, it is difficult to assess the changes in the foreign aid volume and geographical

[5] IATI aims at enhancing donor coordination and minimising duplication and waste.

spread after the coming of BRI, which would prove to be a milestone in China's history of development finance.

Defining Chinese Development Assistance

There is no officially stated definition of what development assistance means for China. The only way to characterise its development assistance is by identifying the main components of Chinese development assistance. China's foreign aid includes grants, interest-free loans and concessional loans.

Grants are generally aimed at financing social welfare schemes in the partner countries. The projects that come under grants could range from small to medium-scale projects. This could include building hospitals, schools and houses, as well as projects for ensuring food and water supply to the needy. Grants are also used to finance "human resources development cooperation, technical cooperation, assistance in kind and emergency humanitarian aid" (White Paper 2011).

Interest-free loans are given to partner countries to help them construct public amenities to improve life of the common people in that country. The partner country is expected to pay back the loan amount within 20 years that includes "five years of use, five years of grace and ten years of repayment" (White Paper 2011).

Concessional loans are the most important component of Chinese development assistance, constituting more than half of its total assistance. These loans have a low annual interest of 2–3%, mainly used for the purpose of financing industrial and infrastructure projects in partner countries. The repayment of these loans is expected to be completed within a time span of 15–20 years along with a grace period of five to seven years (White Paper 2011).

Institutional Set-up

The institutional structures responsible for China's development assistance have been gradually established and improved on (White Paper 2011). The institutionalisation of Chinese development assistance took a major turn with the setting up of the China International Development Cooperation Agency (CIDCA) in March 2018.

Earlier, several ministries and agencies coordinated China's development assistance. The decision-making power on Chinese development assistance rested with the central government. The main institutions that shared the responsibility of Chinese Development Assistance were the Ministry of Commerce (MOFCOM), Ministry of Finance, Ministry of Foreign Affairs and the Export-Import Bank of China (China Exim Bank).[6] The cooperation among these agencies as a part of the governance structure of Chinese aid could be considered as a perfect juxtaposition of both economic and diplomatic objectives (Rudyak 2019). The Department of Foreign Aid within the MOFCOM of China was the governmental department authorised by the State Council to administer its development assistance. It was responsible for the formulation of foreign aid policies, regulations, annual plans, examination and approval of foreign aid projects and management of the project execution. Other departments of the MOFCOM that were involved in implementing China's foreign aid projects, especially technical assistance and capacity-building and training programmes, include the Executive Bureau of International Economic Cooperation, Academy of International Business Officials, and China International Center for Economic and Technical Exchanges. The departments that take care of commercial activities at the local level also cooperate with the MOFCOM to manage China's development assistance that comes within its jurisdiction. The China Exim Bank deals with the concessional loans to developing countries. It is also entrusted with the allocation of these loans and its recovery (White Paper 2011). The work on ground is directly coordinated and managed by the Chinese embassies or consulates located in the partner countries along with the support of Chinese companies based in the partner country.

All the related government departments involved in Chinese development assistance used to communicate and cooperate with each other regularly. In drafting development assistance programmes for each partner country, the MOFCOM communicated with the Ministry of Foreign Affairs, Ministry of Finance and China Exim Bank and sought suggestions. Help also came from other departments of the State Council in managing those foreign aid projects that require better professional expertise. Furthermore, China also established a foreign aid inter-agency liaison mechanism in 2008 to strengthen the coordination of different

[6] China Exim Bank is one of three "policy banks", the other two being the China Development Bank and China Agricultural Development Bank, both set up in 1994 "to better enable the government to directly finance its development goals as it transitioned to a market economy" (Brautigam 2010, 4).

government departments involved in China's foreign aid. In 2011, China upgraded its inter-agency liaison mechanism into an inter-agency coordination mechanism (White Paper 2011).

The Ministry of Finance, which is the central governmental body in charge of the overall expenditure of the state, also allots the budget for China's external development assistance to different government agencies involved in aid-giving. Each ministry that was involved in running foreign aid projects was allocated money for running different projects in their respective jurisdiction on a yearly basis. Each of these departments used to draw up a budget for foreign aid projects every year and submitted it to the Ministry of Finance for examination, and then to the State Council and the National People's Congress for approval and implementation. The foreign aid funds that were given to these government departments were supervised and audited by the National Audit Office with the help of Ministry of Finance (White Paper 2011). Despite the involvement of several institutions in the disbursal of Chinese development assistance, China was able to bring certain degree of coherence into its development assistance programme mainly because of its disciplined institutional framework for assistance flows and the interconnectedness of these institutions involved. However, there was ongoing competition between different actors involved in execution and implementation of China's aid projects for greater role and influence (Zhang and Smith 2017). Moreover, issues like corruption, major problems in budget management and tender procedures, and illegal spending had plagued Chinese aid (Rudyak 2019). This did not come out in the public because of the nature of the governance structures in China that demands high degree of discipline and cooperation among all the agencies involved.

The creation of CIDCA is an indication of the prominence of foreign aid in Chinese foreign policy and the need to bring in greater structure, coherence, coordination and accountability into its burgeoning foreign aid programme. As per the official press release of the government, the role of CIDCA encompasses formulating strategic guidelines on China's foreign aid, makes recommendations, determines projects, formulates policies and decides foreign aid programme, coordination and management of China's assistance, the execution of which still rests with several actors as before (People's Daily Online 2018). In November 2018, CIDCA came up with a document titled "Measures for the Administration of Foreign Aid" (China Aid Blog 2018) that gives a detailed list of policies from which the Chinese development cooperation could benefit.

An agency like CIDCA, which will exclusively look at China's foreign aid, is expected to reduce these limitations in Chinese aid programme and make it more streamlined so as to complement China's foreign policy priorities and its growing role in international politics (Purushothaman 2018a). However, it would take some time for CIDCA to take full charge of China's foreign aid programme as the foreign aid budget is still managed by the MOFCOM (Sun 2019).

China's Development Assistance Policy

The official position on China's foreign assistance was elucidated in the two White Papers released in 2011 and 2014. The White Paper (2011) clarifies that China's development assistance falls into the category of SSC and considers itself as a development assistance provider of the Global South. Despite the fact that Chinese development assistance is increasing in volume and scope, China does not want to be associated with the traditional donors thereby striving to create a niche of its own in the international development finance.

China upholds the principle of "mutual respect, equality, keeping promise, mutual benefits and win-win" in its foreign aid to other developing countries (White Paper 2014, 1). White Paper (2011) also lists five basic tenets of China's foreign aid policy: helping the recipient countries build up their self-development capacity, no-conditionalities, equality, mutual benefit and common development, maintaining a tailor-made approach to assistance and focussing of reform and innovation in accordance with the changing times (White Paper 2011). China's official position on foreign aid underscores its position as a development assistance provider that has altruism at the core of its foreign aid policy. However, this does not divulge the real motivations driving China's external aid, and continues to be far from reality.

China claims to give development assistance without any political or economic conditionalities. However, Chinese development assistance is not entirely devoid of conditionalities as some economic and political conditions do apply. Chinese aid, especially its concessional loans, is tied to goods and services from China, and is only given to those countries with which it has strong diplomatic ties (Brautigam 2010, 23). Even though China does not emphasise on democracy promotion or good governance,[7] its development assistance conditions mainly include the recipient country's adherence to the "one-China" policy. For China, Taiwan is its integral part. Therefore, it does not provide development assistance to any country that recognises Taiwan as an independent country. The aid rivalry between China and Taiwan has been mainly concerned with diplomatic recognition for themselves (Lin 2001). This has created problems for the recipient countries as they are forced to choose one donor at the expense of the other (Raposo and Potter 2010, 197). The recipient country's affinity to one donor would distance the other, making it necessary for them to take a political stand to ensure continuous flow of aid from their preferred donor.

Another important tenet of China's foreign aid has been its policy of non-interference in the domestic affairs of its partners. This is in sharp contrast to the traditional donors who emphasise institutional transformation and good governance as an inevitable condition for giving foreign aid to their recipients. The White Paper (2011) clearly mentions that "China never uses foreign aid as a means to interfere in recipient countries' internal affairs or seek political privileges for itself". Non-interference has been an important concept in Chinese foreign policy since the "Five Principles of Peaceful Coexistence" initiated in 1953 by China, India and Myanmar. These principles include,

> Mutual respect for each other's territorial integrity and sovereignty; mutual non-aggression; mutual non-interference in each other's internal affairs; equality and mutual benefit; and peaceful co-existence (UN 1958, 70)

This has been the cornerstone of Chinese foreign policy since then. These principles were also incorporated into its "Eight Principles of Economic Aid and Technical Assistance to Other Countries"[8] that form the basis of Chinese foreign aid policy. Furthermore, China also asserts that it encourages every recipient country to discover a development path that suits its actual conditions at home. Here, the emphasis was on the freedom that China gives to its recipients to choose their path of development and how Chinese assistance is need-based or demand-driven. However, there

[7] Democracy promotion and good governance are the conditionalities inherent to OECD-DAC aid to development countries.

[8] See, Annexure 1.

is no clarity as to how much of Chinese assistance is provided based on demands from its recipients.

Nonetheless, Beijing's emphasis on non-interference and no-conditionalities approach has helped add legitimacy into their development assistance policy as the recipients would want no interference from their donors in their domestic affairs. Furthermore, China is keen to project itself as a partner of developing countries that is genuinely interested in their welfare. In 1964, Chinese Premier Zhou Enlai stressed that China focussed on "experience sharing" with its partner countries (Li et al. 2014, 29). This was later used by the successive governments as an important dimension of Chinese foreign aid. China's efforts continue to be in the direction of showcasing itself as a reliable partner, sharing its economic growth and development experience with the partner countries for their overall development.

China also asserts that its development assistance strives to make the recipient more self-reliant by fostering technical assistance and capacity-building, building infrastructure and developing and utilising domestic resources (White Paper 2014).

However, there has been backlash in several countries in Africa as most of the projects funded by China have Chinese workers on ground, bringing no potential employment opportunities or technical know-how to the local population. However, a study on the Chinese workers in Africa suggests that China does not hesitate to take African workers in its projects, even though the percentage of Chinese and local workers might vary widely (SAIS-CARI 2016a).

Regarding the distribution of its foreign aid, China claims to give assistance depending on the level of economic development of the partner country. According to the White Paper (2014), the recipients of China's development assistance are mainly low-income developing countries (see, Fig. 4.1). However, the White Paper does not clarify as to which Least Developed Countries (LDCs) get how much assistance and what kind of projects and programmes are running in those countries. The overall figures on the assistance going to LDCs do not allow us to conclude that Chinese development assistance is purely altruistic. There might be several other important factors—political, economic and strategic—driving Chinese assistance to these countries.

In the twenty-first century, China has expanded its development assistance to fulfil its economic interests like trade, investments, energy and

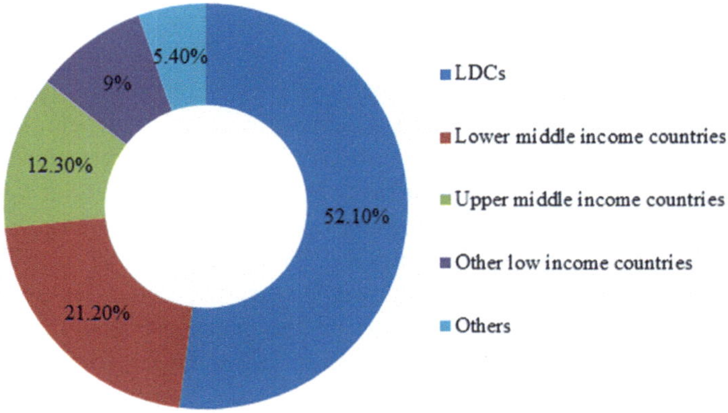

Fig. 4.1 Distribution of Chinese development Assistance according to the income level of the recipient countries, 2010–2012 (*Source* White Paper [2014])

search for markets as well as political interests in terms of diplomatic reciprocity at international organisations and multilateral groupings. China's development assistance policy based on horizontal cooperation, non-interference and no-conditionalities has helped China make a favourable image among its partners in the Global South that are looking forward to get assistance for their development. This has proved to be of great advantage for China to spread its wings to other countries of the Global South, especially in Africa which is still dependent on aid for sustenance and find China a better choice of funding when compared to the traditional donors. However, this has not gone well with the traditional donors who accuse China of supporting authoritarian regimes and nullifying their efforts to push for democracy and good governance in these countries. Furthermore, China's rise as a supplier of arms to Africa and Asia has also been a source of concern for many countries (Tull 2006, 476). For instance, China has been increasingly giving military aid to Pakistan and Sudan. This has been of great concern for even other developing countries in Africa and South Asia. China is Pakistan's close ally and has been providing aid to Pakistan for a very long time. This has created tensions between India and China as India considers this move as a threat to its security. Also, China has increased its assistance to Nepal, a sign of strengthening ties between the two neighbours. Nepal has also been accused of using "China Card" after India's blockade on Nepal. China has come to help Nepal during this difficult period that has not gone down well with India.

China maintains that its development assistance is driven by the concept of mutual help. Apart from fulfilling its own interests, the recipient countries' interests are accommodated into the broader framework of aid (White Paper 2011). China has been keen to use its soft power capabilities to push for stronger diplomatic ties with other developing countries. China's efforts in this direction have mostly been successful as China could get diplomatic support from other developing countries at various international platforms and China has shown great readiness to reciprocate with greater economic cooperation and political support on various occasions. China has also been able to create an alternative source for multilateral funding including the Asian Infrastructure Investment Bank (AIIB) and the New Development Bank (NDB) of the BRICS grouping.

Proposed by Chinese President Xi Jinping in 2013, the AIIB is an international financial institution aimed at promoting interconnectivity and economic development through large-scale infrastructure projects and development of productive sectors. This China-led[9] USD 100 billion strong multilateral organisation got the support of countries from both the Global South and North. AIIB is a bold move by China to create alternate financial institutions as against those existing ones dominated by the Western countries, like the IMF and the World Bank. Even though AIIB was made to finance the infrastructure and developments needs of Asia, it is expected that AIIB would expand in future to include Africa and Latin America.

Established by BRICS countries, with an initial capital of USD 50 billion, NDB is expected to be an important source of financing for the developing countries. Both AIIB and NDB are expected to finance the increasing demand for infrastructure development in developing countries. While both these institutions might expand their mandate to include more countries, the current focus of AIIB is financing projects in Asia and NDB is to finance projects in the Global South. China's role in these organisations is crucial, both for expanding its economic diplomacy endeavours abroad and to cement its role as potential leader in development financing.

[9] China has the maximum voting shares, 26.65%, followed by India, 7.65%.

Clearly, China does not want to be identified as another member of the rich countries' aid club. Beijing has always wanted to be perceived as a developing country of the Global South. This resonates with its policy of SSC and the idea is to bring credibility into its principle of horizontal partnership in development assistance where both the partners are deemed equal, belong to similar stages of development and face similar concerns. China is keen to project its distinctive image as a developing country of Global South, with a clear understanding of the issues and concerns of other developing countries (Lancaster 2007).

The following sections in this chapter will analyse the expanding geographical reach of China around the globe and its changing priorities in terms of its partner countries as well as its motivations and agenda behind its development assistance.

Geographical Outreach and Modalities of Assistance

China has been expanding its footprint around the globe through its economic prowess and diplomatic endeavours. Chinese development assistance has expanded tremendously, both in volume and scope, with special focus on certain countries and regions of the Global South.

While the White Paper on Chinese foreign aid remains the primary source of data to analyse Chinese development assistance; the major hurdle in analysing the trends is that it does not disseminate its development assistance data regularly. Also, the figures given in both the White papers, for the years 2009 and then 2010–2012, do not give a real picture of how much goes where, when and in what form. This section explores the geographical reach of Chinese development assistance and the different modalities used by China. The focus would be to analyse the changing patterns and understand whether China prioritises certain regions over the other and the kind of projects and programmes.

Geographical Patterns

Chinese development assistance flows to most of the developing countries in Asia, Africa, Latin America, the Caribbean, Oceania and Eastern Europe. Even though Chinese development assistance was focussed on its neighbouring region in the earlier times, there has been a shift in its priorities in the twenty-first century. As per the White Paper, the focus has

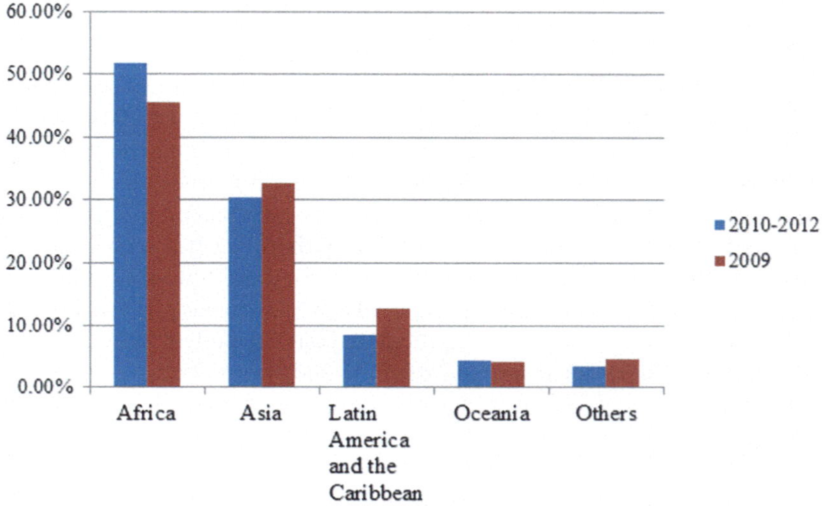

Fig. 4.2 Geographical distribution of Chinese development assistance, 2010–2012 and 2009 (*Source* White Paper [2011, 2014])

shifted to Africa with 51.8% of overall assistance flowing to the continent (White Paper 2014).

From 2010 to 2012, China's total development assistance amounted to 89.34 billion Yuan (USD 14.41 billion). This would amount to USD 4.8 billion per year, if considered on a yearly basis. Out of this, 51.8% went to Africa, 30.5% to Asia, 8.4% to Latin America and the Caribbean. When compared, the data published in two White Papers suggests that Chinese development assistance to Africa has been increasing while its assistance to other continents has seen a decline (see, Fig. 4.2). This confirms that Africa has become a priority for China and its stakes in Africa are expected to increase in the coming years.

Africa

Apart from other components of economic diplomacy like trade and investments, China's focus on Africa is indicated by its growing development assistance to the continent. As per the White Paper on Chinese Foreign Aid (2014), maximum assistance from China went to the African continent in the years 2010–2012. In 2009, Chinese assistance to Africa amounted to 45.7% of its total aid flows (White Paper 2011). The SAIS-CARI study on Chinese development assistance notes significant rise in Chinese foreign aid[10] to Africa. From 2000 to 2010, Chinese assistance to Africa has grown four times (SAIS-CARI 2016b). Since 2010, there is a steady increase in Chinese assistance to Africa indicating the growing importance of Africa in China's foreign and economic policy.

However, China's growing development assistance to Africa is attributed to several factors. China's trade with Africa has seen tremendous growth in the twenty-first century. In the past ten years, China's trade with Africa has increased more than sixfold, making it imperative for Beijing to maintain and strengthen its bilateral and multilateral ties with the region in order to expand its trade and secure its assets. China's expanding trade and aid in Africa are invariably linked. To sustain its growing trade, China supports its trading partners with economic assistance that would enable Beijing to increase its trade volume. Henceforth, majority of assistance is provided for infrastructure development, especially for building roads, highways, railways, ports and airports that would link different trade hubs, which would in turn make things easier for China to improve its trade and diversify markets.

From 2000 to 2014, the top five bilateral trade partners of China in Africa were South Africa, Angola, Nigeria, Egypt and Sudan, all of which are resource-rich countries (SAIS-CARI 2016c). Nigeria, Angola, Egypt and South Sudan[11] are the highest oil-producing countries in Africa. Further, South Africa is rich in minerals, which are important for feeding China's burgeoning industries. Chinese presence in mining sector in Africa has also seen a major rise in the second decade of the 21st century.

China has been accused of using varied strategies for strengthening economic and diplomatic ties with the resource-rich and energy-rich countries in Africa. Gu et al. (2007, 286) claim that China's interests in Africa are overwhelmingly resource-based and consider China's increased ties with African countries like Sudan, Zimbabwe, Nigeria as "energy

[10] These figures are supposedly devoid of China's medical assistance, scholarship assistance or contributions to international organisations. Hence, if those figures were to be included in its development assistance, the amount disbursed might be much higher than projected (SAIS-CARI 2016b).

[11] Sudan was the second-largest oil producer in Africa before splitting into Sudan and South Sudan in 2011.

driven" foreign policy. China's increasing presence in Africa is also considered as its effort to find resources to sustain its rapidly growing population as well as its economy (Gu et al. 2007).

In Africa, Chinese projects range from large infrastructure projects[12] to priority sectors like agriculture,[13] public welfare facilities[14] and health.[15] China's approach to various sectors in recipient countries resembles the Western donors except that China has shown less interest in environmental issues (Strange et al. 2013). China is also accused of using African leaders' historic suspicion of Western intentions for its benefit in the continent (Taylor 2006, 938). China has to a large extent benefitted from its image as a colony and not a coloniser that makes China a "returning friend"[16] for several African countries (Kjollesdal and Welle-Strand 2010, 8).

However, there are diverse views on why China gives assistance to Africa. Some argue that Chinese development assistance is not always driven by selfish interests and have been at times beneficial to the recipients. According to Woods (2008, 1206), the intensified trade links with China might have helped Africa in reaching "higher growth rates, better terms of trade, increased export volumes and higher public revenues". And there is "little evidence that China is re-indebting the highly indebted poor countries (HIPC)" as claimed by the developed countries (Woods 2008, 1206). Furthermore, the claim that China allocates more aid to authoritarian countries in Africa also does not hold ground as China is found to be not solely driven by selfish motives and quest for natural resources (Dreher et al. 2015; Parks 2015). Instead, China is found to give maximum assistance to LDCs in Africa and sometimes based on

[12] China has been involved in large-scale economic infrastructure projects including Tanzania-Zambia Railway, railway projects in Botswana, the Lagdo Hydropower station in Cameroon and the Gotera interchange in Addis Ababa (White Paper 2011).

[13] China has several agricultural projects in several African countries including, Rwanda, Burkina Faso, Ghana and Niger. In order to share agricultural technology with its partners, China has opened several institutions in Africa like the Agricultural Demonstration Centre in Tanzania and Zimbabwe (Li et al. 2014).

[14] This includes water supply projects in Mauritania, Tanzania and Niger.

[15] For example, Hospitals were built in different countries in Africa including the Taizz Revolution Comprehensive Hospital in Yemen and hospitals in the Guinea-Bissau, Zimbabwe and Chad.

[16] Considering the shared history of anti-colonial struggles, China can build more friendly and symmetric relations with Africa.

socio-economic and humanitarian needs of its recipients (Parks 2015). Hence, it might be unfair to call Chinese aid as "rogue aid".[17] The AidData study on Chinese assistance to Africa finds that Chinese aid is not any more selfish than other donors in Africa and concludes that less concessional loans that are more commercial in nature tend to go to the countries with authoritarian regimes and resource-rich countries (Dreher et al. 2015). Even though these loans are a part of what China considers its development assistance, these could not be considered as ODA as defined by the OECD-DAC because of its lesser grant element (Parks 2015). Hence, if these loans are excluded from the Chinese ODA calculated by the West, then the motivations behind Chinese development assistance could not be counted as any different from traditional donors' foreign aid. Therefore, the motivations driving China's development assistance are multifaceted, like any other donor country.

Initially, ideological and political interests dominated China's development cooperation with other developing countries. In the twenty-first century, strategic economic considerations as well as strengthening its diplomatic ties have dominated China's development assistance flows. For proactive engagement with the African countries, China also initiated the Forum on China-Africa Cooperation (FOCAC), with the first summit organised in 2000 in Beijing. China has also established strong ties with the African Union (AU). One of the most prestigious infrastructure project in Africa has been the AU headquarters in Addis Ababa made with Chinese aid of USD 200 million (BBC 2015, April 20).

China has benefitted immensely from its relationship with the African governments, especially in multilateral forums where China has been getting diplomatic support from partner countries. For example, African countries have time and again voted in favour of China in the United Nations General Assembly. China has reciprocated it with generous development assistance (Dreher et al. 2015; Parks 2015). Since China's export-oriented economic reforms in the 1970s, the pursuit of strategic interests has been broadened to include the search for markets and access to energy and natural resources.

[17] Moises Naim (2009) calls countries like China, Saudi Arabia and Venezuela as "rogue aid providers" who don't care nothing more than their self-interest and give aid to authoritarian regimes.

Asia

For China, Asia is important in historical, political, cultural and strategic terms. However, its relations with Asia has been rather complex. While its economic ties with the continent is on an all-time high, its political and strategic interests in the region have led to several tensions including border disputes with its neighbours including India, Japan and Vietnam, and increasing tensions regarding the exploration of natural resources in the South China Sea. With increasing economic might, China has been able to push its bilateral ties with other Asian countries foregoing the historical discontent to a greater extend. China's improved relations with Russia, which had gone cold in the second half of the nineteenth century and its efforts in binding Asian countries through economic regionalism and multilateralism have borne fruit in recent times. China's push for BRI and AIIB is expected to bolster trade and investment, and infrastructure development in Asian countries. China's efforts have been in the direction of improving its prestige and goodwill in Asia, in order to be recognised as the leading economic powerhouse. Importantly, China wants to "persuade its neighbours that its rise is not a threat but an opportunity" (Schuller and John 2011).

China's foreign aid was earlier mostly concentrated in Asia. While the initial development assistance was focussed on the Communist countries, including DPRK and Vietnam, it slowly expanded to the rest of Asia. China's focus was mainly on the infrastructure projects, including several highways[18] and ports[19] in South and Central Asia. However, it was also involved in human resource development cooperation (like hosting training courses in Vietnam and DPRK), humanitarian development assistance like assistance to Pakistan during floods and earthquakes, and Myanmar during tropical storm. China also extends food aid to countries like DPRK, Bangladesh, Nepal and Afghanistan (White Paper 2011).

Asia received about 32.8% of Chinese assistance in 2009 which was further reduced to 30.5% in 2010–2012 (see, Fig. 4.4). Even though its focus has shifted to Africa, Beijing is careful not to drastically cut short development assistance to its region. Chinese development assistance has become an important source of funding for the developing

[18] For example, the Karakoram Highway in Pakistan, the Greater Mekong Sub-region Information Highway in Myanmar and the No. 7 Highway in Cambodia.

[19] For example, Gwadar Port in Pakistan and the Hambantota port in Sri Lanka.

countries in Asia, and some of these countries have been dependent on Chinese assistance. For example, Pakistan receives a huge amount of aid from China especially in the form of grants and loans. In 2015, China sanctioned USD 46 billion to Pakistan in development deals, which amounts to about 20% of Pakistan's annual GDP (Stevens 2015). However, the most lucrative deal has been the USD 62 billion China-Pakistan Economic Corridor (CPEC), which is the most important leg of the BRI, starting from China's restive province of Xinjiang to Gwadar in Pakistan. However, several hurdles, including economic, political and environmental, have hit CPEC which has made Pakistan government rethink several projects and be wary of debt issues that could lead to the loss of ownership of its strategic assets (Purushothaman 2018b). Also, most of the CPEC projects are funded through concessional loans that come with interest which Pakistan would have to repay. Furthermore, the lack of transparency and accountability of the CPEC projects has raised concerns in Pakistan, which is itself going through a bad balance of payment crisis.

China has also been keen to reach out to other South Asian countries in order to expand its economic and strategic influence in the region. China's trade volume with all the South Asian nations is increasing year to year. Apart from Pakistan, the largest beneficiaries of Chinese development assistance in the region are Sri Lanka, Bangladesh and Nepal. All of these countries affirm the "One-China" policy of PRC and have China as the largest trading partner. Some of these countries have facilitated the expansion of China's political and economic clout in the region thereby helping China curb India's supremacy in the region. For example, Nepal has been using China and India against each other to secure its interests and curb their influence in Nepal's domestic affairs. Both China and India compete to give assistance to Nepal, a country of great strategic significance to both. However, China's opaque deals have also left countries like Sri Lanka in what is called a debt-trap, where the recipient might have to give away the ownership of assets to the donor as a way to repay the loans. Sri Lanka's Hambantota Port that was built by Chinese loans had to be handed over to China on a 99-year lease as a part of the debt-reduction deal. This has raised alarm among the recipient countries about the debt-trap that might come with Chinese loans, placing serious questions on the legitimacy of BRI itself.

Apart from South and Southeast Asia, China's focus has also shifted to the energy-rich Central Asian region. Chinese aid for Central Asia has been mostly for funding projects on oil, natural gas and mining (Wolf et al. 2013). Energy and natural resources were the prime concerns for China for its enhanced engagement with the region. The fact that the Silk Road Economic Belt[20] runs through Central Asia also makes the region strategically important for China. It has been vigorously pursuing its aim of connecting its western regions—that are less developed and economically backward compared to the affluent east—to Central Asia and Europe through its infrastructure and connectivity projects. BRI with its roads, railways, highways, infrastructure and energy projects are all in sync with China's foreign policy priority of increasing its influence around the world through economic instruments.

Latin America and the Caribbean

Latin America and the Caribbean together received 12.5% of total Chinese aid flows, which declined to 8.4% in 2010–2012 period (White Paper 2011, 2014). The official documents underline the main tenets of China's policy towards the LAC countries,

> The Chinese government views its relations with Latin America and the Caribbean from a strategic plane and seeks to develop a comprehensive and cooperative partnership featuring equality, mutual benefit and common development with countries in the region. (Xinhuanet 2008)

China has expanded its bilateral and multilateral cooperation in Latin American in diverse sectors like trade and investment, infrastructure, agriculture, natural resources and energy (Ishmael 2009). Recently, China has emerged as an attractive partner in the Latin American region. Despite the colonial links with the Europe and its dependency on the US, Latin American countries have welcomed China as an alternative source of finance. Some countries also see China as a more benevolent partner as opposed to the Western donors. The West, especially the US, has also been considered as neglecting the region as its focus has shifted to Asia and Africa. The traditional donors' assistance to the Latin America and the Caribbean has also been dwindling. This has helped China make inroads into the American neighbourhood. The requirements of the region for

[20] It starts from Xinjiang region in the western part of China to Europe via Central Asia.

enhanced infrastructure development, better education and health facilities, and creating employment opportunities and technical know-how, have been ignored by the developed countries of the Global North. China is pumping a lot of money into the region and has taken up several large-scale infrastructure projects of strategic importance. One of the biggest Chinese projects in Latin America has been the proposed USD 50 billion Nicaragua Canal, called the Grand Inter-Oceanic Canal, which would rival the Panama Canal. This would help China get easy access to the Atlantic as this canal would link the Pacific to the Atlantic.

China's relations with the Latin American countries have focussed on trade, investments and its ever-increasing demand for energy and natural resources (Ishmael 2009; Ray and Gallagher 2015; Peters 2015). China-Latin America trade ties have grown exponentially in the last one and a half decades, from USD 12 billion in 2000 to USD 289 billion in 2013 (Elson 2014, 44). Recently, China became the second-largest bilateral trade partner with its trade reaching USD 307.4 billion (Elmer 2019). Since 2012, it has also become the third-largest source of FDI for Latin America, only after the US and Japan (Peters 2015). Brazil is China's largest trading partner in Latin America. Brazil gets more than half of the total FDI inflows from China to the region, followed by Argentina, Chile, Mexico and Peru. Beijing also pledged to increase the annual trade to over USD 500 billion and expanding China's FDI stock to USD 250 billion by 2025 (Peters 2015, 7; Saxena 2015).

Energy is also an important factor driving China's economic diplomacy with Latin America. The oil-rich Venezuela has been the most important partner for energy. Venezuela alone gets half of total loans from China to Latin America, apart from nearly 42% of the total infrastructure projects sanctioned to the region (Peters 2015). Despite US sanctions on Venezuela, China has been keen to keep relations with Venezuela intact by finding new ways to dodge secondary sanction that will keep the oil flowing. Even though Venezuela is of great importance for China in its quest for oil, China makes sure that it engages with even the smaller countries in Latin America and the Caribbean, especially for strengthening its diplomatic support for one-China policy. For instance, in order to cut its relations with Taiwan, Dominican Republic was offered USD 122 million in assistance (Ishmael 2009). Dominican government reciprocated by breaking its diplomatic relations with Taiwan to recognise PRC (Sanders 2011).

At the multilateral level, China cooperates with the important regional organisations including the Southern Common Market (MERCOSUR), the Andean Community[21] and the Caribbean Community (CARICOM). In 2004, China also got a permanent observer status in the Organization of American States (OAS) and became a member of the Inter-American Development Bank (IDB) in 2009. The first ministerial meeting of the Forum of China and the Community of Latin American and the Caribbean States (CELAC) was held in Beijing in 2015, in which a Political Declaration, a Plan of Action and the CELAC-China Cooperation Plan (2015–2019) that covers diverse areas was finalised and approved.

Multilateral Development Cooperation

Even though China's priority remains its bilateral assistance, it has its presence in multilateral development initiatives as well. Even though China has been unwilling to be a part of the OECD-DAC, it has showed its readiness to support development initiatives under the UN umbrella (White Paper 2011). Beijing had been active member in the UN Sustainable Development Summit, UN High-Level Meeting on Financing for Development, UN High-Level Meeting on the MDGs, UN Development Cooperation Forum and WTO Global Review on Aid for Trade. It has also been keen to cooperate and strengthen its relations with other development assistance providers of the Global South. As an ardent supporter of SSC that remains an inescapable component of its development assistance policy, China also created a South-South Cooperation Assistance Fund (SSCAF) to assist developing countries in achieving their Sustainable Development Goals (SDGs). In 2017, Chinese government pledged USD 17 million through SSCAF in partnership with the UNDP to support five countries—Bangladesh, Pakistan, Nepal, Antigua and Barbuda—and the Commonwealth of Dominica—for their recovery and reconstruction efforts (UNDP 2019).

In addition, China started its trilateral and regional cooperation activities in sectors including, capacity-building, technical training and infrastructure construction. In 1981, China began to support the UNDP in implementing TCDC programmes and it has been giving training to technicians from other developing countries since then. Even though China was involved in bilateral agricultural cooperation with several developing

[21] It is a customs union comprising of Colombia, Ecuador, Peru and Bolivia.

countries, especially in Africa, it was only in the 1990s that China began to cooperate with the UN on agricultural support to developing countries. Chinese agricultural experts were sent to developing countries in cooperation with the United Nations Food and Agriculture Organization (UNFAO). The official data suggests that more than 700 agricultural experts and technicians were sent to other developing countries, including Africa and Latin America by the end of 2009 (White paper 2011). China has also been keen to support technical cooperation efforts of multilateral organisations, including the World Bank, the UN Conference on Trade and Development (UNCTAD), and the UN Industrial Development Organization (UNIDO). Further, China has also been collaborating with regional organisations through its development assistance. For example, China cooperated with the Asian Development Bank (ADB) and Thailand within the framework of the Greater Mekong Sub-regional cooperation, for building the Laos section of the Kunming-Bangkok Highway that was completed in 2008 (White Paper 2011). While bilateral assistance remains a priority, China ensures its role in various multilateral forums and organisations. The following section explains the modalities by which Chinese assistance reaches its recipients.

Modalities

Chinese development assistance is comprised of grants, interest-free loans and concessional loans (see, Fig. 4.3). Concessional loans form the largest component of China's development assistance. These are usually given

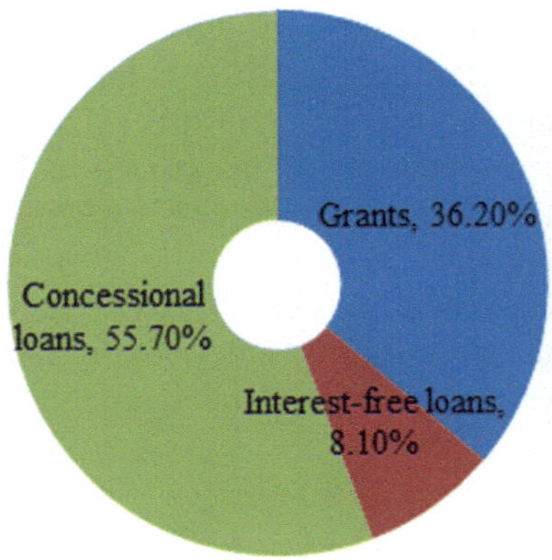

Fig. 4.3 Modalities of Chinese development assistance (*Source* White Paper [2014])

for completing infrastructure projects that are implemented by Chinese corporations, in partner countries. For China, two-thirds of its overall assistance is in the form of loans while the grant component is only one-third of its assistance. The finances for loans and interest-free loans are derived from the state budget while the concessional loans come from the China Exim Bank of the Chinese government (White Paper 2014).

The concessional loans given by China are tied to the goods and services from China, helping it promote trade and investments in its partner countries. Concessional loans are therefore an inevitable part of its development assistance strategy and are given preference over grants, which bring no financial returns to the country. The greater share of concessional loans in China's foreign aid demonstrates how China prioritises commercial gains through its foreign aid programme.

Chinese development assistance is comprised of eight forms of assistance: complete projects, goods and materials, technical cooperation, human resource development cooperation, medical teams sent abroad, emergency humanitarian aid, volunteer programs in foreign countries and debt relief (White Paper 2011).

The focus of Chinese development assistance is on infrastructure projects that form approximately 73% of China's overall assistance when economic infrastructure projects (44.8%) and social and public infrastructure projects (27.6%) are combined together (see, Fig. 4.4).

Complete projects form a major component of China's development assistance. These projects are usually financed by Chinese grants or interest-free loans. The complete projects were a part of Chinese assistance since its early days as a donor. Infrastructure projects were the main focus during those times. However, China expanded its scale and scope in the later years to cover varied sectors including agriculture, industry, health care, education, energy and transportation (White Paper 2011). Initially, complete projects, and goods and materials were the major components of Chinese aid. The materials and goods made in China were also used in complete projects which helped China benefit more out of its commitments abroad, helped the Chinese companies to prosper and reduced the cost of the project.

Technical cooperation is another sector where China has been excellent. It gives training to local people as a part of its capacity-building efforts in partner countries. China also sends its area experts to partner

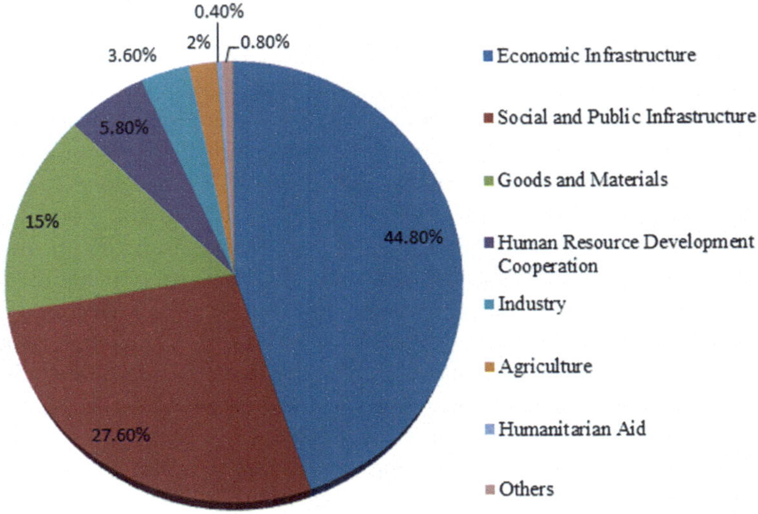

Fig. 4.4 Sectoral distribution of Chinese development assistance, 2010–2012 (*Source* White Paper [2014])

countries for guiding and supporting them in maintaining and operating the complete projects so as to support the partner country in being technically self-sufficient. China's technical cooperation projects are usually short-term projects that last no more than two years and are only extended upon request (White paper 2011). Another area of cooperation where China has a legacy is in human resource development, which started in 1953, and is carried out not only bilaterally but also through multilateral channels. This comprises "different kinds of research and training programs for government officials, education programs, technical training programs, and other personnel exchange programs for developing countries" (White Paper 2011). From 1953 to 1979, China had organised training programmes for people from countries like Vietnam, Cuba and Albania, mostly Communist countries, in sectors ranging from agriculture, forestry and water conservation to transportation and health care. Since the early 1980s, China started cooperating with the UNDP for technical cooperation and hosted training courses in practical techniques in various fields. China also started to give technical training and seminars for government officials of other developing countries since the late

1990s. By 2012, China has trained 49,148 people from its partner countries and conducted 1951 training sessions (White Paper 2014). These programmes garnered a lot of goodwill for China as these officials trained in China went back home and became bridges for strengthening China's political and economic ties with their home country.

Furthermore, China has been sending medical teams to its partner countries since early 1960s. The first medical team from China was sent to Algeria in 1963. Since then, China has been actively involved in providing medical teams and medical services to its recipients. They also give training to the local medical staff thereby helping the partner country to improve its local medical and health services. Furthermore, China has been actively involved in building infrastructure for medical assistance, especially in Africa. More than 100 hospitals and medical care centres have been constructed in different countries using Chinese aid, including Yemen, Guinea-Bissau, Zimbabwe and Chad.

China has also been an active partner to many countries during emergency humanitarian situation. In situations of natural calamity or disaster, it provides emergency relief either on its own accord or on request from the victim state. In December 2004, when Indian Ocean countries were hit by the Tsunami, China provided 700 million Yuan as emergency assistance. There have been several occasions when China has provided assistance during a humanitarian crisis. For example, China helped Nepal by providing emergency assistance of USD 500 million during the 2015 earthquake. Pakistan has also received assistance on several instances after earthquake and the floods. African countries, including Liberia, Sierra Leone and Guinea, got assistance from China to tackle the Ebola crisis (FOCAC 2016). Numerous medical teams were sent to these countries along with medicines and medical equipments. Medical assistance was given to Latin American countries in 2015 during the Zika spread. Furthermore, it also provided medical assistance to fight against dengue in Ecuador, influenza in Mexico and cholera in Guinea-Bissau. It also assisted Haiti and Chile after severe earthquakes. In addition, emergency food aid was given to several countries including Nepal, Afghanistan, Burundi, Zimbabwe and Mozambique (White Paper 2011).

Besides, volunteers from China take up assignments in different countries and work on medical support, health care, education and emergency relief operations. One of the important sectors in which a huge number of volunteers are sent from China is education. Many of them are posted as Chinese-language teachers in countries that have good diplomatic and trade relations with China. Initially, the language teachers were sent by China to its neighbourhood, the very first time to Laos in 2002. Subsequently, it sent volunteers to Indo-China, and then to far off countries in Africa and Latin America. China had sent around 7590 Chinese-language teachers to over 70 countries around the world by the end of 2009 (White Paper 2011). Promoting language has also been a way to enhance its cultural diplomacy and promoting its soft power around the world.

Assistance for agricultural development and poverty reduction in partner countries became an important mode of engagement with developing countries of the Global South. For example, China set up agricultural demonstration centres especially in Africa, which has more than 60% of world's arable land but still imports food (Sy 2015), to increase the agricultural productivity and to transfer agricultural technology to the local farmers (White Paper 2014). In Guinea-Bissau, eleven demonstration centres were opened by China to increase the production of rice. They also assisted in producing hybrid rice that increased the production up to three times than the normal. Furthermore, China helped Mali in increasing its sugarcane production and helped it in establishing sugarcane farms and sugar mills, thereby making Mali self-sufficient in growing sugarcane and processing sugar.

China maintains that debt relief[22] is one of the key components of its foreign aid. Many times, China has cancelled the debts incurred by mature interest-free loans owed to China by HIPCs in order to bail them out of the debt burden (White Paper 2011). Ordinarily, these recipient countries are those that maintain strong diplomatic ties with China. It is also claimed that debt relief is used by China as a reward for forging stronger relations with its partner countries (Pehnelt 2007, 3). China cancelled debts incurred by several countries including Tanzania, Mali, Sudan, Cameroon and others, and announced it during the FOCAC Ministerial Summits and the UN High-Level Meetings on the MDGs (White Paper 2014). However, today, the same China that was known for debt relief in developing countries is allegedly practising debt-trap diplomacy. Most countries are now increasingly looking at Chinese loans with suspicion after the Sri Lankan experience of Hambantota Port.

For China, funding economic infrastructure has always been a priority. It constitutes 44.8% of its total development assistance. China has

[22] The mature governmental debts of some developing countries that they owe China are cancelled as a part of its debt relief programme.

completed several infrastructure projects in transportation, power and energy supply as well as in communication sector. China channels its technical capacity, goods and materials and human resource into its projects that cuts the cost considerably and helps China complete the projects within short time periods. Some of the important projects include Sika Highway in Kenya, Mattala Rajapaksa International Airport in Sri Lanka and energy projects like the Bui Hydropower station in Ghana and the power grids in Senegal (White paper 2014).

The huge infrastructure projects that are also known as prestige projects are usually funded by China's public facilities financing. The most common of these are huge convention centres, sports stadiums, halls and theatres, including the National Stadium in Tanzania, Sports Centre in Kenya, Fiji's Multi-Functional Sports Stadium, the Stade d' Angondje stadium in Gabon, the Friendship Hall in Sudan, Convention centres in Egypt and Myanmar, the Bandaranaike Memorial International Conference Hall in Sri Lanka and the theatres in Senegal and Ghana.

In its early years as a development assistance provider, China's concerns were on infrastructure development and industrial aid that did not prove to be environment friendly in the later years. Industrial production and economic growth were given priority over environmental protection and sustainable development. It was only in the 1980s that conservation of the nature and safeguarding environment started to figure in China's development assistance policy. Since then, it started working with the UN on clean energy programmes and environmental protection. At a multilateral level, China started working with the UN on biogas technologies and later shared these technologies with partner countries through bilateral partnerships, like in Uganda, Tunisia and Guyana. It also started financing projects on clean energy in different countries, like the solar and wind energy projects in Morocco, Lebanon and Mongolia, and hydropower stations in Cameroon and Burundi. It also started training sessions on clean energy, environmental protection and sustainable development in its partner countries. With China's increasing concern for climate change and pollution, it decided to establish a "super ministry of Environmental Protection" in 2008 (Brautigam 2010, 29). Since then, the environment factor started figuring in while deciding different projects financed by Chinese assistance. However, there are growing concerns that several BRI projects ignore the environmental concerns of the communities in the partner countries. In Pakistan, the environmentalists have raised concerns over the large-scale deforestation that is happening to pave way for CPEC projects (Dadwal and Purushothaman 2017, 523).

China's development assistance grants and its zero-interest loans have helped it promote its broad diplomatic objectives. However, it is the concessional loans that have been highly beneficial for China in fulfilling its commercial and economic interests. The fact that it has been tied to goods and services from China, which has boosted its trade, investments and businesses, also makes it the most important aspect of china's development assistance. However, it is evident that some of the modalities of China's development assistance overlap with each other making it difficult to analyse which modality is altruistic and which one is focussed on self-interest. Moreover, it could be largely viewed as a combination of varied motivations that drive China in its aid policy, dealt in detail in the next section.

Motivations for Providing Development Cooperation

It is a common knowledge that the motivations driving donors to give foreign aid to less developed countries could range from self-interest to pure philanthropic pursuits. However, it is not one single motivation that is driving the donors but a multitude of them depending on their interests, the partner country and the nature of projects the donor choose to finance. The case of China is no different, making it important to analyse its foreign aid to develop a general understanding of the emerging powers' priorities and preferences, and the way foreign aid is used as an instrument of foreign policy.

China has not been able to strike a right balance between economic and social development, creating problems for its overall growth (Bijian 2005). China's growing population along with high industrial development to sustain the economic growth has resulted in a severe shortage of resources and daunting environmental issues. The increasing scarcity of its natural resources, especially energy and raw materials for its burgeoning industries, has forced it to look out for these in other energy-rich and resource-rich developing countries. China has been using development assistance to meet these demands at home so that it can continue to start rising in the global world order with its economic, political and diplomatic clout.

Hence, it is amply clear that the motivations behind china's development assistance are not purely altruistic or humanitarian. China's development assistance policy could be considered as a part of its broader foreign policy strategy that is referred to as the "Grand Strategy" (Goldstein 2005). Since the 1970s, China has been successful in coordinating its foreign and defence policies with its domestic priorities. China has been careful that its growing capabilities do not alarm or provoke others, which would create difficulties in its growth. This approach has been referred to as the strategy for propagating its "peaceful rise" (Goldstein 2005). Since the mid-1990s, China's efforts in this direction have been centred on two broad policies. China has tried to enhance its reputation as a more responsible and cooperative international actor as well as a friendly neighbour. Reassuring its neighbours has been the priority for China since the 1990s. Hence, China began pushing for regionalism since the last decade of the nineteenth century. China began playing a key role in the Shanghai Cooperation Organization (SCO), facilitated greater cooperation with ASEAN, and took constructive role in resolving the nuclear crisis that loomed on the Korean Peninsula, in a peaceful manner. Another policy priority for China, since 1996, has been to improve bilateral ties with the great powers, especially the US and its allies, so as to reduce the chances that they might come together to balance against China. Hence, China's "grand strategy" emerged as a reaction to the challenges faced by Beijing as a country whose growing power and influence has been a matter of concern for other countries who might later oppose China. The goal was to protect its key strategic interests that would help it endure its economic and strategic rise. The combination of policies that make up its "grand strategy" was designed to enhance China's standing as a responsible global power. The efforts to nurture partnerships with its neighbours and other major powers was to ensure that China continues to have the opportunity to carry on its decades-long process of modernisation, which was significant for it to become truly a great power (Goldstein 2005).

In the late 1980s, China was also concerned about escaping political isolation caused by the Tiananmen Square massacre in 1989. The gross human rights violations that occurred led to the Western countries[23] cutting off China from their diplomatic radar (NSARCHIVE 2016). However, it is notable that several Asian countries remained silent during this period and some countries, especially Communist countries, even went on to support China (NSARCHIVE 2016).[24] The support from these countries prompted China to further hike its development assistance and strategic investments that became instrumental in boosting China's bilateral ties with several countries.

China has therefore used its economic diplomacy to enhance its presence and visibility in the Global South. It became a major source of development assistance to the developing countries in Asia, Africa and Latin America. Initially, development assistance was provided to garner diplomatic support for a permanent seat in the UNSC. Today, its development assistance appears to be tied to its interests in energy, natural resources and raw materials, for its growing industrial sector as well as trade, investment and for supporting Chinese businesses. While economic interest is the driver for China to enhance its foreign aid, the political and strategic interests also come to occupy centre-stage with its rise as a formidable economic power in the twenty-first century. Gaining support for one-China policy and cutting out Taiwan's diplomatic support also governs China's foreign policy preferences. Since 2016, Taiwan lost six of its allies, the last being Solomon Islands. China has been successful in gaining diplomatic support using foreign aid and Taiwan is now left with only 16 allies (Lyons 2019). China aims to build strong ties with developing countries so that they provide support for Chinese domestic and foreign policies in the international fora (Lancaster 2007). In order to expand its political influence, China has also been keen to form alliances with small developing countries of the Global South and promotes SSC in order to expand its influence among the Third World countries (Pehnelt 2007, 5).

With the high economic growth achieved by China in the 1990s, economic and diplomatic considerations became priority for China. Efforts were made to advance the interests of Chinese businesses as well as to find new markets for Chinese goods and services. The involvement of MOFCOM in China's development assistance is a reminder of how

[23] It included the US, Canada, Western Europe, Australia, New Zealand, Japan, etc.

[24] This group includes East Germany, Cuba, North Korea and Czechoslovakia.

China strategically pursues its economic interests through foreign aid. It is on a continuous lookout for economic opportunities in its partner countries including trade and investment opportunities, search for new markets, supporting Chinese business interests in foreign countries as well as getting raw materials for its own industries (Brautigam 2009).

The recent posture of China has been of a more confident and aggressive power that is capable of acting against any threat that affects its interests. Under the leadership of President Xi, China's foreign policy has taken a more assertive and definitive turn in which it is clear of its priorities and preferences, and is ready to take bold steps or even confront when its interests are at risk. This has made it challenge countries in the South China Sea, waging a trade war against the US, and has been locked in border disputes with its neighbours, including India. After China introduced to the world its plans for global influence through BRI, nothing is holding it back from openly admitting its aspirations of rising in the world order. It has started several BRI projects, which are clearly in favour of China or help China again access to energy or natural resources in the partner country. While increasing connectivity and building infrastructure has been of supreme significance, China has not been hesitant to push its interests to the forefront, which also includes better trade and investments, helping Chinese companies take advantage of all the business opportunities by helping them win contracts, allowing them to get their own labour force from China and procuring materials from Chinese companies (Dadwal and Purushothaman 2017). This makes these projects highly in favour of China's growing global influence. Furthermore, through BRI, China is aiming to reorient most of the world economy towards China (China Power Team 2019), which will also give a major push to the Renminbi as an international currency by promoting its usage in international investment and finance (Kynge 2015). Like any regional and aspiring global power, China's policies and agendas are towards ensuring great power status, for which foreign aid has been an effective tool.

Chinese Development Assistance: Prospects and Challenges

China has ensured its position as the largest development assistance providers outside the OECD framework with an annual foreign aid volume of USD 4.8 billion or more (White Paper 2014). Even though

China has been giving development assistance since the 1950s, it has garnered a whole lot of attention in the last one decade with the massive increase in its foreign aid flows and its expanding geographical outreach. With BRI, China has initiated different projects in several countries, which would have definitely led to a rise in China's foreign aid from the 2012 official figure of USD 4.8 billion. Between 2000 and 2014, Chinese assistance was more than USD 354 billion, making it almost at par with the largest traditional donor, US, which gave USD 395 billion over the same period (Dreher et al. 2017). AidData also finds the average Chinese assistance during the 2000–2012 period to be USD 4.96 billion (Dreher et al. 2017). Another study of Chinese assistance for 2012 estimates it to be USD 5.2 billion (Kitano 2016).

China has been giving assistance according to its own rules and regulations and has distanced itself from the traditional donors' style of foreign aid-giving. China's development assistance is more or less governed by Beijing's principles on foreign policy and economic diplomacy. The OECD-DAC's foreign aid and China's development assistance differ mainly in terms of conditionalities, the donor-recipient relationship and the modalities of assistance (McCormick 2008, 84; Kjollesdal and Welle-Strand 2010, 3). China maintains that it gives assistance based on equal partnership between the countries involved. Chinese development assistance is based on the principles of SSC which opposes hierarchical relationship between the donor and the recipient. Instead, equality, mutual benefit and win-win situation are underlined by the partners involved in SSC.

Furthermore, China underscores that it provides aid without any conditionalities. This no-conditionalities policy, according to Li (2007), has its origin in China's domestic politics. China does not impose conditionalities like democracy and good governance, which are the most important tenets of OECD aid. It is no wonder that China, which has an authoritarian Communist government, shows no interest in promoting democracy or institutions for good governance. China is found to undermine democratic governance (Kersting and Kilby 2014).

China also observes a policy of non-interference in the domestic politics of the partner country which in turn helps Beijing escape the questions on its occupation in Tibet and its one-China policy. China's policy of non-interference in domestic affairs has led to several developing countries opt for China when compared to traditional donors. Moreover, China does not take into account the human rights records of the partner country. Having remained a human rights violator several times, China does not make any reservations against those countries involved in gross human rights violations. This has helped "rogue states" like Zimbabwe and Sudan get aid from China even when the Western countries have stopped giving aid to these countries. The Western countries have constantly criticised China for giving assistance to these states (Manning 2006). When the Western donors cut down aid to "pariah states", those projects left incomplete by the traditional donors are taken over and completed by China, thereby filling the gaps that the traditional donors have left behind (Pehnelt 2007, 9).

However, Chinese aid is not entirely devoid of any conditionalities. One of the political conditionalities imposed on the recipients is to adhere to one-China policy. Further, its concessional loans, which form 55.7% of its total assistance, are attached to goods and services from China. China also involves Chinese firms, to manage most of the projects, which in turn would use Chinese machinery and equipment, as well as bring labourers from China. The flow of labourers from China has also been criticised widely by the Western governments and also by the recipient countries. It has been claimed that China's development assistance has helped Chinese people to relocate to several parts of the world (Tso 2009, 3).

Even then, Chinese foreign aid is attractive to many developing countries which hope that China's own development experience and economic growth strategies could be replicated in their country to achieve high economic growth (Kjollesdal and Welle-Strand 2010, 4). Some of the recipient countries warmly welcome Chinese aid as relatively fewer conditionalities are imposed. Further, it also supports infrastructure projects that are greatly needed by the recipient countries and development assistance is complemented by closer trade and investment relations with China (Schuller et al. 2010, 15).

China traditionally funds high-profile and prestigious infrastructure projects like ministry buildings, state houses, dams, rails, roads and stadiums. Even though these projects are popular in many developing countries, the traditional donors do not prefer to finance these high-scale infrastructure projects. China is said to be following a "niche strategy, i.e., filling the gap other donors have left" (Pehnelt 2007, 10). Certain partner countries' governments, especially in Africa, demand such huge infrastructure projects from China that not only help China push its interests in the partner country but also help the recipient country governments to show off to their people the achievements of their government. China also projects itself as a development assistance provider that gives need-based and demand-driven assistance.

The changing aid scenario in the early 1990s, with the end of Cold War along that ended strategic aid and created aid fatigue among traditional donors, provided ample opportunity for China to rise as an important development assistance provider (Raposo and Potter 2010, 177). Even though China was giving development assistance since the 1950s, it began to be recognised as a prominent player outside the OECD-DAC only in the late 1990s. With the emerging powers playing a greater role in development assistance, the recipients got more options to choose from. With the mounting pressure from the traditional donors on the recipient countries to liberalise their economic and political system, many of them chose China over OECD-DAC to escape the tricky situation (Taylor 1998).

The traditional donors consider China's policy of helping "rogue states" and a lack of OECD-like conditionalities derailing their efforts to bring policy reforms in their recipient countries (Zafar 2007). Even though China's policies are popular in many countries, the traditional donors criticise Beijing for the lack of focus on democracy, human rights, good governance, sustainable development and lack of concern for environmental protection[25] (Zafar 2007, 106; Lum et al. 2009, 1). Furthermore, the West has blamed China for increasing corruption by giving aid without conditionalities and supporting corrupt elites in several recipient countries (Tso 2009, 1; Raposo and Potter 2010, 192). For example, World Bank's efforts to curb corruption in Nigeria were allegedly derailed by China by giving loans for constructing railways, without any conditionalities attached. Nigeria is an important partner for China in Africa because of its huge oil reserves, and its potential for trade and investments. Similarly, a new aqueduct was constructed in Manila, the Philippines, with Chinese assistance. This was supposed to be funded by the ADB, but was later taken over by China without imposing any conditionalities for financing.

However, there is growing international criticism that China is encouraging debt in partner countries to take away their strategic assets. After China took over Sri Lanka's Hambantota Port, several countries have either cancelled projects financed by Chinese loans or have reassessed

[25] China assisted Indonesia in expanding its electricity grid. However, China used highly polluting coal-based technology to build the power plants thereby increasing pollution in the country.

the terms. In several cases, the BRI has hit roadblock mainly because of the growing costs of the projects and the accumulating debt which has put countries in jeopardy (Ferchen and Perera 2019). For example, Malaysia renegotiated a major railway project under BRI and secured a one-third cut in the cost of construction and ensured greater level of local involvement in the project. Malaysian Prime Minister Mahathir Mohamad secured this deal after year-long negotiation with China.

Instead of generating legitimacy for China, the increasing criticisms can derail the kind of global influence that China is trying to create. BRI being a long-term project will take a few years to be fully functional. Hence, China cannot ignore the call for greater transparency and accountability in Chinese assistance that would not only help assess the nature of Chinese assistance but also its outcome. Disseminating aid data regularly could be the first step in this regard. Recently, President Xi clarified that China is recalibrating the BRI and open to policy adjustments. This was in the wake of growing fear among partner countries about the perils of debt-trap diplomacy and China's ambition of political influence through economic instruments. Xi clarified that "BRI is an economic cooperation initiative, not a military or geopolitical alliance" (Wong 2018).

Aid is never free from donor interests. Most donors use aid as per their priorities and preferences which are in line with their strategic self-interest. Hence, there might not be too many differences between China and traditional donors as far as development assistance motives are concerned. The traditional donors are also involved in trade facilitation and resource extraction through aid. Therefore, aid could be more of a bane than a boon for several recipient countries. Furthermore, the traditional donors who blame China for encouraging repressive regimes are themselves involved in giving foreign aid to those countries that are undemocratic and have a history of human right violations. For instance, the US is a major foreign aid donor to Israel and Pakistan.

The normative liberal discourse that has criticised China on several grounds fails to acknowledge that Chinese assistance could also have been beneficial for those countries, which are entirely dependent on foreign aid but fails to get it from the traditional donors or has been unsuccessful in bringing policy reforms and democratic institutions (Tan-Mullins et al. 2010, 857). Also, for some countries Chinese development assistance is an additional source of finance that can boost its economy. Despite all the drawbacks in Chinese assistance, it would be clearly unfair to "uncritically assume Western aid to be morally superior and more effective in terms of development outcomes" (Tan-Mullins et al. 2010, 857).

Conclusion

Two decades ago, Segal had claimed that China is a small market that matters little to the world and therefore is not a threat to the West economically, politically or culturally (Segal 1999). China was underestimated by many analysts and policy-makers even during last decade of the 20th century, which had to quickly change with China's rise in the international system as a country capable of turning international power dynamics in its favour.

Even though China has been providing development assistance to developing countries since the 1950s, its aid volume, recipients, motives and strategy behind aid-giving have changed considerably. Various reasons contribute to the changing geographical scope of Chinese development assistance ranging from political to economic to diplomatic. Interestingly, China has been quite clear about its interests while disbursing aid, may it be trade and investments, quest for natural resources and energy, or its assertion of its "One-China Policy". Despite the fact that China has not spelled out a clear development assistance policy, it is able to operate within a structured framework that made it efficiently use aid to its benefit.

Though Chinese aid cannot be said as very different from the traditional donors' aid, Chinese aid has its own characteristics. China is an emerging power that does not want to join the traditional donors club. China values its identity as a country of the Global South and distances itself from the developed donors' club of the OECD-DAC. Its aid is mostly centred on the SSC and it prefers its recipients to be considered as partners. This has been advantageous for China on several occasions, especially in international institutions where its development partners have come to its rescue. Thus, it considers its Third World identity as an inalienable part of its aid policy. At the same time, it cannot be ignored that China is an aspiring great power and it has been using development assistance as a tool of economic statecraft. Omuruyi argues that the Chinese "foreign aid behaviour indicates its aspirations to attain great power status" (Omuruyi 2001, 123). Kupchan (2001, 14) argues that "the rise of China will confront the United States and the West with economic and geopolitical dilemmas similar to those that America's rise posed to Britain". Despite criticisms from the West, China has been unapologetically pursuing its interests through foreign aid. The traditional donors find tough competition from China in several developing countries, mostly in Africa that is presently the priority area for Chinese aid. It is slowly trying to change the rules of the game that were made by the traditional donors.

China has been very keen to formulate its own rules, regulations and institutions in all aspects of development finance. The way China has expanded its development assistance volume and visibility demonstrates the importance of development assistance in its foreign policy and economic diplomacy. With BRI, it is expanding its economic and political influence to new levels that could change China's role and status in international politics. What we see now is a new China under Xi, which is confident and not scared of taking on even the great powers if its interests are at stake. This power shift in which China has evolved as a global power could be considered as one of the key developments in the twenty-first-century international politics. Moreover, development assistance has contributed to China's unmatched global reach and impact on the outside world.

References

Alden, Christopher. (2007), *China in Africa*, London and New York: Zed. Cited in Raposo, Pedro Amakasu and Potter, David M. (2010), "Chinese and Japanese Development Co-operation: South-South, North-South, or what?" *Journal of Contemporary African Studies*, 28(2): 177–202.

BBC. (2015: 20th April), "China's Prestige Projects Around the World" [Online: web]. Accessed on 27 June 2016, http://www.bbc.com/news/world-asia-china-32381190.

Bijian, Zhang. (2005), "China's 'Peaceful Rise' to Great Power Status", *Foreign Affairs*, 84(5): 18–24.

Brautigam, Deborah. (1998), *Chinese Aid and African development: Exporting Green Revolution*, New York: St. Martin's.

Brautigam, Deborah. (2009), *The Dragon's Gift: The Real Story of China in Africa*, New York: Oxford University Press.

Brautigam, Deborah. (2010), *China, Africa and the International Aid Architecture* [Online: web]. Accessed on 10 January 2011, Rev Working Paper, http://www.american.edu/sis/faculty/upload/Rev-working-paper-china-africa-aid-architecture-August-2010.pdf.

Brzezinski, Z. (2004), *The Choice: Global Domination or Global Leadership*, New York: Basic Books.

China Aid Blog. (2018), "CIDCA Issues Measures for the Administration of Foreign Aid Draft". Accessed on 16 August 2019, http://china-aid-blog.com/2018/11/20/cidca-issues-measures-for-the-administration-of-foreign-aid-draft/.

China Power Team. (2019). "How Will the Belt and Road Initiative Advance China's Interests?" China Power. May 8, 2017. Updated May 29, 2019. Accessed on 24 September 2019, https://chinapower.csis.org/china-belt-and-road-initiative/.

Cooper, John F. (1976), *China's Foreign Aid: An Instrument of Peking's Foreign Policy*, Lexington, MA: Lexington Books.

Dadwal, S.R. and Purushothaman, C. (2017). CPEC in Pakistan's Quest for Energy Security, *Strategic Analysis*, 41(5): 515–524.

Dreher, A. et al. (2015), "Apples and Dragon Fruits: The Determinants of Aid and Other Forms of State Financing from China to Africa", AidData, Working Paper 15 [Online: web]. Accessed on 18 June 2016, http://aiddata.org/sites/default/files/wps15_apples_and_dragon_fruits.pdf.

Dreher, A. et al. (2017), "Aid, China and Growth: Evidence from a New Global Development Finance Dataset". AidData, Working Paper 46. Accessed on 19 June 2019, http://docs.aiddata.org/ad4/pdfs/WPS46_Aid_China_and_Gro wth.pdf.

Elmer, K. (2019). "Latin America Trade Grows as China and US Tussle for Influence", *South China Morning Post*. Accessed on 5 August 2019. URL: https://www.scmp.com/news/china/diplomacy/article/302 0246/latin-america-trade-grows-china-and-us-tussle-influence.

Elson, Anthony. (2014), "Dragon Among the Iguanas", *Finance and Development*, 44–46, http://www.imf.org/external/pubs/ft/fandd/2014/12/pdf/elson.pdf.

Erikson, Daniel. (2009), "China in the Caribbean: The New Big Brother" [Online: web]. Accessed on 10 July 2011, http://www.jamestown.org/programs/chinabrief/single/?tx_ttnews%5Btt_news%5D=35848&tx_ttnews%5BbackPid%5D=25&cHash=83aaa0f966.

Ferchen, M. and Perera, A. (2019). "Why Unsustainable Chinese infrastructure Deals Are a Two-Way Street", *Carnegie-Tsinghua Center for Global Policy*. Accessed at https://carnegietsinghua.org/2019/07/23/why-unsustainable-chinese-infrastructure-deals-are-two-way-street-pub-79548.

FOCAC. (2016), "Forum on China-Africa Cooperation" [Online: web]. Accessed on 25 June 2016, http://www.focac.org/eng/zt/1_1_1/.

Goldstein, A. (2005), *Rising to the Challenge: China's Grand Strategy and International Security*, Stanford: Stanford University Press.

Gu, Jing et al. (2007), "Global Governance and Developing Countries: The Implications of the Rise of China", *World Development*, 36(2): 274–292.

Ishmael, Odeen. (2009), "China's Influence Growing in Latin America and the Caribbean", *Share Newspaper*, 1 July 2009 [Online: web]. Accessed on 10 July 2014, http://www.sharenews.com/opinion/2009/07/01/china%E2%80%99s-influence-growing-latin-america-caribbean.

Kersting, E. and Kilby, C. (2014). "Aid and Democracy Redux", *European Economic Review*, 67: 125–143.

Kitano, Naohiro and Harada, Yukinori. (2014), "Estimating China's Foreign Aid, 2001–2013", JICA-RI Working Paper, No. 78, Japan International Cooperation Agency Research Institute [Online: web]. Accessed on 28 October 2015, https://jica-ri.jica.go.jp/publication/assets/JICA-RI_WP_No.78_2014.pdf.

Kitano, N. (2016). "Estimating China's Foreign Aid II: 2014 Update", JICA-RI Working Paper No. 131.

Kjollesdal, Kristian and Welle-Strand, Anne. (2010), *Foreign Aid Strategies: China Taking Over?* Asian Social Science [Online: web]. Accessed on 10 January 2011, http://www.bi.no/OsloFiles/MICRO/2011/Foreign%20Aid%20Strategies%20China%20Taking%20Over.pdf.

Kupchan, C. (2001), "Explaining Peaceful Transitions" in C.A. Kupchan, E. Adler, Jean-MarcCoicaud, and Y.F. Khong (eds.), *Power in Transition: The Peaceful Change of International Order*, Tokyo, New York and Paris: United Nations University Press.

Kynge J. (2015), "'One Belt, One Road' Set to Turbocharge Renminbi Usage", *Financial Times*. Accessed on 13 September 2019, https://www.ft.com/content/6f105c2a-7f02–11e5-98fb-5a6d4728f74e.

Lancaster, Carol. (2007), *The Chinese Aid System*, Centre for Global Development Essay, [Online: web]. Accessed on 20 October 2014, www.cgdev.org/files/13953_file_Chinese_aid.pdf.

Li, A. (2007), "China and Africa: Policy and Challenges", *China Security*, 3: 69–93.

Li, Xiaoyun et al. (2014), "Difference or Indifference: China's Development Assistance Unpacked", *IDS Bulletin*, 45(4) [Online: web]. Accessed on 24 January 2016, http://folk.uio.no/danbanik/documents/Li_Banik_IDS_Bulletin.pdf.

Lin, R. (2001), "Complementary Measures to Foreign Aid: Taiwan and the PRC under Diplomatic Rivalry", *Contemporary Economic Policy*, 19(3): 360–368.

Lum, Thomas et al. (2009), *China's Foreign Aid Activities in Africa, Latin America and South-East Asia*, CRS Report, R40361 [Online: web]. Accessed on 22 October 2015, http://www.fas.org/sgp/crs/row/R40361.pdf.

Lyons, K. (2019), "China Extends Influence in Pacific as Soloman Islands Break With Taiwan", *The Guardian*. Accessed on 20 September 2019, https://www.theguardian.com/world/2019/sep/16/china-extends-influence-in-pac

ific-as-solomon-islands-break-with-taiwan?CMP=share_btn_fb&fbclid=IwAR1hH1FBN9gHpPVy6dBjtRm2lOhwhQNnUdjBdy8qKTO5wUXJielbCvARb5E.

Manning, Richard. (2006), *Will "Emerging Donors" Change the Face of International Cooperation?* ODI Lecture [Online: web]. Accessed on 1 December 2014, http://www.oecd.org/dataoecd/35/38/36417541.pdf.

McCormick, Dorothy. (2008), "China & India as Africa's New Donors: The Impact of Aid on Development", *Review of African Political Economy*, 35: 115, 73–92.

Medeiros, Evan S. and Fravel, M. Taylor. (2003), "China's New Diplomacy", *Foreign Affairs*, 82(6): 22–35.

Naim, Moises. (2009), "Rogue Aid", *Foreign Policy* [Online: web]. Accessed on 13 July 2015, http://foreignpolicy.com/2009/10/15/rogue-aid/.

NSARCHIVE. (2016), [Online: web]. Accessed on 28 June 2016, http://nsarchive.gwu.edu/NSAEBB/NSAEBB16/documents/36–04.htm.

Omuruyi, Leslie. (2001), *Contending Theories on Development Aid: Post-Cold War Evidence from Africa*, Farnham, UK: Ashgate.

Parks, Brad. (2015), "10 Essential Facts About Chinese Aid in Africa", *The National Interest* [Online: web]. Accessed on 23 April 2016, http://nationalinterest.org/feature/10-essential-facts-about-chinese-aid-africa-14456.

Pehnelt, Gernot. (2007), *The Political Economy of China's Aid Policy in Africa*, Jena Economic Research Paper No. 2007-051 [Online: web]. Accessed on 10 January 2014, http://papers.ssrn.com/sol3/papers.cfm?abstract_id=1022868.

People's Daily Online. (2018), "Wang Yong: Forming the National Development Cooperation Agency", *people.cn*. Accessed on 12 September 2019, http://lianghui.people.com.cn/2018npc/n1/2018/0313/c418468-29865075.html.

Peters, Enrique Dussel. (2015), "China's Evolving Role in Latin America: Can It Be a Win-Win?" *Atlantic Council*, Adrienne Arsht Latin America Center [Online: web]. Accessed on 5 April 2016, http://publications.atlanticcouncil.org/chinalatam//AC_CHINA090915DP.pdf.

Purushothaman, Chithra. (2018a), "Why Is China's Move to Institutionalise Foreign Aid Significant?" *Asia Dialogue*. Accessed on 22 August 2019, https://theasiadialogue.com/2018/04/20/why-is-chinas-move-to-institutionalise-foreign-aid-significant/.

Purushothaman, Chithra. (2018b), "As Financial Hurdles Hit CPEC, What's in Store for Pakistan?" *South Asian Voices*. Accessed on 20 August 2019, https://southasianvoices.org/as-financial-hurdles-hit-cpec-whats-in-store-for-pakistan/.

Radelet, Steve. (2006), *A Primer on Foreign Aid*, Working Paper 92 [Online: web]. Accessed on 12 October 2010, www.cgdev.org/files/8846_file_WP92.pdf.

Raposo, Pedro Amakasu and Potter, David M. (2010), "Chinese and Japanese Development Co-operation: South-South, North-South, or What?" *Journal of Contemporary African Studies*, 28(2): 177–202.

Ray, Rebecca and Gallagher, Kevin. (2015), *China-Latin America Economic Bulletin 2015 Edition*, Discussion Paper 2015-9, Working Group on Development and Environment in the Americas, Global Economic Governance Initiative [Online: web]. Accessed on 15 May 2016, https://www.bu.edu/pardeeschool/files/2015/02/Economic-Bulletin-2015.pdf.

Rudyak, M. (2019), "The Ins and Outs of China's International Development Agency. Carnegie Endowment for international Peace". Accessed on 8 September 2019, https://carnegieendowment.org/2019/09/02/ins-and-outs-of-china-s-international-development-agency-pub-79739.

SAIS-CARI. (2016a), "Data: Chinese Contracts and Workers in Africa" [Online: web]. Accessed on 29 May 2016, http://www.sais-cari.org/data-chinese-workers-in-africa.

SAIS-CARI. (2016b), "Data: Chinese Aid to Africa" [Online: web]. Accessed on 24 April 2016, www.sais-cari.org/data-chinese-aid-to-africa.

SAIS-CARI. (2016c), "Data: China-Africa Trade" [Online: web]. Accessed on 24 April 2016, http://www.sais-cari.org/data-china-africa-trade.

Sanders, Sir Ronald. (2011), "China's Presence in Dominica", *BBC Caribbean* [Online: web]. Accessed on 20 June 2015, http://www.caribbeannewsnow.com/topstory-Commentary%3A–China%27s-presence-in-Dominica-6189.html.

Saxena, Shobhan. (2015), "Doing the Tango, with Chinese Characteristics", *The Wire* [Online: web]. Accessed on 20 April 2016, http://thewire.in/2015/05/15/doing-the-tango-with-chinese-characteristics-1714/.

Schuller, Margot et al. (2010), *China's Emergence Within Southeast Asia's Aid Architecture: New Kid on the Block?* Working Paper, GIGA [Online: web]. Accessed on 14 January 2014, http://s3.amazonaws.com/aiddata/Schueller_aiddata.pdf.

Schuller, Margot and John, Jari. (2011), *China's Foreign Aid—Interests, Strategies and Instruments*, Digital Development Debates [Online: web]. Accessed on 10 July 2015, http://www.digital-development-debates.org/03-development-cooperation/new-donor-china/chinas-foreign-aid-interests-strategies-and-instruments.html#page-2.

Segal, Gerald. (1999), "Does China Matter?" *Foreign Affairs*, 78(5): 24–36.

Shambaugh, David L. (2004/2005), "China Engages Asia Reshaping the Regional Order", *International Security*, 29(3): 64–99.

Stevens, Andrew. (2015), "Pakistan Lands $46 billion Investment from china", *CNN Money*, [Online: web]. Accessed on 20 June 2016, http://money.cnn.com/2015/04/20/news/economy/pakistan-china-aid-infrastucture/.

Strange et al. (2013), "China's Development Finance to Africa: A Media-Based Approach to Data Collection", Working Paper 323 [Online: web]. Accessed on 25 July 2015, http://www.cgdev.org/sites/default/files/chinese-development-finance-africa_0.pdf.

Sun, Y. (2019), "One Year on, the Role of China International Development Cooperation Administration Remains Cloudy", *Brookings*. Accessed on 28 July 2019, https://www.brookings.edu/blog/africa-in-focus/2019/04/30/one-year-on-the-role-of-the-china-international-development-cooperation-administration-remains-cloudy/.

Sy, A. (2015), "What Do We Know About the Chinese Land Grab in Africa?" *Brookings*. Accessed on 17 June 2019, https://www.brookings.edu/blog/africa-in-focus/2015/11/05/what-do-we-know-about-the-chinese-land-grab-in-africa/.

Tan-Mullins, May et al. (2010), "Redefining 'Aid' in the China-Africa Context", *Development and Change*, 41(5): 857–881.

Taylor, Ian. (1998), "China's Foreign Policy Towards Africa in the 1990s", *Journal of Modern African Studies*, 36(3): 443–460.

Taylor, Ian. (2006), "China's Oil Diplomacy in Africa", *International Affairs*, 82(5): 937–959.

Tso, Chen-Dong. (2009), "Coming to Term with China's Foreign Aid" [Online: web]. Accessed on 30 January 2015, http://www.mac.gov.tw/public/Attachment/05271618499.pdf.

Tull, Denis M. (2006), "China's Engagement in Africa: Scope, Significance and Consequences", *Journal of Modern African Studies*, 44(3): 459–479.

UN (United Nations). (1958), "Treaties and International Agreements Registered or Filed and Recorded with the Secretariat of the United Nations, Volume 299", https://treaties.un.org/doc/publication/unts/volume%20299/v299.pdf.

UNDP. (2019), "South-South Cooperation Assistance Fund Brochure". UNDP China. Accessed on 15 September 2019, http://www.cn.undp.org/content/china/en/home/library/south-south-cooperation/south-south-cooperation-assistance-fund.html.

White Paper. (2011), *China's Foreign Aid*, Information Office of the State Council of the People's Republic of China [Online: web]. Accessed on 21 July 2015, http://www.china.org.cn/government/whitepaper/node_7116362.htm.

White Paper. (2014), *China's Foreign Aid*, Information Office of the State Council of the People's Republic of China [Online: web]. Accessed on 11 January 2016, http://ssc.undp.org/content/dam/ssc/dgspaces/China/files/China%202nd%20White%20Paper%20on%20Foreign%20Aid%202014.pdf.

Wolf Jr. Charles et al. (2013), "Chinese foreign Aid and Government-Sponsored Investment Activities: Scale, Content, Destinations and Implications", RAND Corporation. Accessed on 28 June 2016, http://www.rand.org/pubs/research_reports/RR118.html.

Wong, C. (2018), "Xi Jinping Says Belt and Road Plan Isn't About Creating a 'China Club'". *South China Morning Post*. Accessed at https://www.scmp.com/news/china/diplomacy-defence/article/2161580/xi-jinping-says-belt-and-road-plan-isnt-about-creating.

Woods, Ngaire. (2008), "Whose Aid? Whose Influence? China, Emerging Donors and the Silent Revolution in Development Assistance", *International Affairs*, 84(6):1205–1221.

World Bank. (2016a), "Gross Domestic Product, 2015" [Online: web]. Accessed on 8 July 2016, http://databank.worldbank.org/data/download/GDP.pdf.

World Bank. (2016b), "China Overview" [Online: web]. Accessed on 29 June 2016, http://www.worldbank.org/en/country/china/overview#1.

Xinhuanet. (2008), *China's Policy Paper on Latin America and the Caribbean*, Chinese Government White paper [Online: web]. Accessed on 28 June 2014, http://news.xinhuanet.com/english/2008-11/05/content_10308117.htm.

Zafar, Ali. (2007), "The Growing Relationship Between China and Sub-Saharan Africa: Macroeconomic, Trade, Investment and Aid Links", *World Bank Research Observer*, 22(1): 103–130.

Zhang, D. and Smith, G. (2017), "China's Foreign Aid System: Structure, Agencies and Identities", *Third World Quarterly*, 38(10): 2330–2346.

CHAPTER 5

Indian Development Cooperation: Aiming High, Falling Short

In 1947, when India gained independence, its position in international politics was that of an underdeveloped country struggling to preserve its hard gained freedom. The huge territory and population looked rather disadvantageous for a country suffering from poverty and illiteracy that could derail any newly independent country from the path of democracy, and might possibly slip away into the hands of dictators for the pathetic economic situation that existed in the country at that point of time. India, like other underdeveloped countries, started receiving foreign aid from developed countries of the world since the early days after independence. During the course of time, Indian economy survived the shocks, both domestic and international and its economic boom started in the last decade of the twentieth century.

India's status of being a recipient of foreign aid has given way to its repositioning in international aid architecture as that of a donor. Even though India received foreign aid from most of the traditional donors, what is commendable is that it has never been entirely dependent on foreign aid. Though foreign aid came as a relief for an impoverished India, the realisation that developing its own economy would bring it out of the aid-dependency cycle and poverty at large made India prioritise economic self-sufficiency as an important tenet of its foreign and economic policy since early days after independence. This confident

C. Purushothaman, *Emerging Powers, Development Cooperation and South-South Relations*, International Political Economy Series,
https://doi.org/10.1007/978-3-030-51537-9_5

approach of the Indian leadership led India to initiate its own programme for development that eventually achieved tremendous economic growth, pulling India out of the category of underdeveloped and impoverished country to an emerging power to reckon with.

What is more impressive is that even while India was struggling with its own development issues, it started giving development assistance as early as the 1950s. Though its development assistance was rather small, India was still a development assistance provider to its small neighbours who also were struggling with difficulties similar to that of its own. Gradually, India has expanded its development cooperation programme in volume, focus and strategy to become one of the biggest development cooperation providers from the Global South in the international aid architecture, which has been monopolised by the affluent countries of the Global North, the OECD-DAC. Indian development cooperation is nothing new, therefore. It has been in existence for as long as the traditional donors' aid programme if the time-span of aid-giving is considered. While many scholars have used the term "emerging donor" to denote India's role as a development assistance provider, India does not really belong to this group of countries whose development assistance programme is new. India but prefers to distance itself from the OECD-DAC because it considers its development cooperation as very different from the OECD-DAC's definition of foreign aid. Therefore, it becomes even more difficult to tag India as an "emerging donor" if the term means a new donor whose development assistance programme is rising. However, India might fit into this category of "emerging" if it refers to an emerging power that has its own development assistance programme. Then again, the official discourse of India's development cooperation totally discards the idea of emerging donor and calls itself a "partner". India identifies its assistance to the Global South as horizontal cooperation and detaches itself from traditional aid hierarchy.

Nehru had assumed that "India, along with the United States, the Soviet Union, China, and the British Commonwealth, would be among the world's major powers" (Nehru 1946). The consistency of India's economic growth has made India the third largest economy[1] in the world with enhanced capacity and means to contribute to international development efforts more systematically. India's economic boom and geopolitical

[1] In GDP (PPP) terms, India ranks third after China and the US. In GDP (nominal terms), India stands at fifth position. However, in GDP per capita terms, India stands much below the world average.

importance has raised expectations of the fellow developing countries from India, particularly with whom India had teamed up for various initiatives, especially on international forums for restructuring of global trade, finance and other developmental aspects (Chaturvedi 2008, 3). India's growing role as a leader of the developing world, as an active proponent of SSC and as a key player for regional stability in South Asia, seems to be important factors in garnering attention from the developed world (Jobelius 2007, 3). Global powers like the US and UK has taken note of India's economic and political revaluation and has been keen to boost economic, political and strategic ties with India.

This evolving interest in India's development cooperation has generated a curiosity amongst the academia and policy-makers to study India's position in the international aid architecture. India, which was considered as an aid recipient,[2] has redefined its role to that of a development assistance provider. However, India's dual position as that of a recipient and a provider continues even in the twenty-first century, 70 years after it first started its development assistance programme.

While India has maintained close contacts with the great powers and all the major powers in international politics, New Delhi has also been keen to establish lasting political and economic ties with other developing countries in Asia, Africa and Latin America. This is also reflected in the selection pattern of beneficiary countries, which India has diversified beyond South Asia to include most countries in the Global South.

Apart from bilateral engagements, India has been involved in forging stronger relations with other countries through active participation in multilateral organisations.[3] All these efforts from New Delhi point to India's aspiration to become a global power with system-shaping capabilities.

Foreign aid has been an important aspect of India's engagement with the Global South. With the setting up of a specialised agency for providing development assistance, the Development Partnership Administration (DPA) in 2012, institutionalisation of IDC has reached a new phase with greater emphasis on making its own rules and regulations

[2] Between 1951 and 1992, India received USD55 billion in foreign aid, becoming the world's largest recipient, although when translated into per capita terms, it appears much less reliant on aid (Bijoy 2010, 65).

[3] Like the G-20, BRICS, IBSA, G-77 and NAM.

without getting pulled down by the pressure of being drawn into the traditional donor club.

This chapter examines India's role as a development assistance provider with in-depth analysis on its development assistance policy, patterns of giving, modalities, agendas and motives behind its development assistance programme and the criteria for the selection of its partner countries. This chapter would also scrutinise how Indian development cooperation is different from the traditional foreign aid and whether India has been able to devise its own aid programme with its own rules. In addition, this chapter aims to analyse whether India could successfully use its development assistance programme to realise its national interest.

Historical Overview of IDC

India's development assistance programme started off since early years after independence. Therefore, the novelty regarding IDC exists only in the increased volume, geographical reach and its strategic dimension behind extending development support to developing countries of the Global South, and not in its time-span. Since IDC had been in existence since 1950, it becomes essential to look into the scope and dimension of IDC during its early years in order to sketch the growth, institutionalisation, geographical spread, policies and genesis of IDC. This would also help in bringing out the trajectory of IDC and plot the diversions in IDC over the last 70 years. The modest beginnings gave way to more ambitious projects, especially in the twenty-first century.

Initially, IDC budget was small and focussed on local capacity-building and manpower training. India's foreign policy was based on its support for Non-Aligned Movement (NAM) which stressed on partnership and solidarity between the developing countries. India's development cooperation framework was also guided by the Colombo Plan[4] and the Panchsheel agreement,[5] both signed in 1950. The Colombo Plan was

[4] Colombo plan was conceived by the seven developed and developing Commonwealth Countries—Australia, Britain, Canada, Ceylon, India, New Zealand and Pakistan—at the Commonwealth Conference of Foreign Affairs in Colombo, Ceylon (now Sri Lanka) in January 1950. It was instituted as a regional intergovernmental organization for the developing countries in Asia-Pacific region (The Colombo Plan 2016).

[5] Also known as the Five Principles of Peaceful Coexistence, signed between India and China, outlined the principles that govern the relationship between these two neighbours (UN 1958, 70).

"based on the partnership concept for self-help and mutual help in the development process" with a focus on technical cooperation, skill development, infrastructure development and south-south cooperation (The Colombo Plan 2016). With changing times, the focus has been on "providing advance skills and experience sharing aimed at arriving at the best practices in different fields of economic and social activities as a means of good policy making and governance". With the signing of the Panchsheel agreement, the principle of "mutual respect for each other's territorial integrity and sovereignty" became the guiding principle of Indian foreign policy (UN 1958, 70). Moreover, India incorporated these five principles—"mutual respect for each other's territorial integrity and sovereignty, mutual non-aggression, mutual non-interference in each other's internal affairs, equality and mutual benefit, and peaceful co-existence"—as the basis of its own development programme, which started off soon after (UN 1958, 70).

IDC started off with its assistance to Nepal[6] in the early 1950s. Nepal has always been a priority for Indian foreign policy since India's independence. Furthermore, the institutionalisation of IDC was first tried and tested in Nepal, where India felt the need to assess and evaluate its development cooperation programme. Consequently, India established an Indian Aid Mission (IAM), the first of its kind, in Kathmandu in 1954. The scope of the IAM was to coordinate and monitor implementation of various development cooperation projects. The IAM also participated in a major development exhibition organised by the Nepal government at Kathmandu in 1963, which was a major event attended by more than 75,000 people (MEA 1965, 37). In 1964, the two governments also announced an agreement for undertaking "a periodic review of the progress made on Indian-aided projects", the first of which was held in Kathmandu between 29 October 1964 and 2 November 1964 (MEA 1965, 35). Within a span of a decade, IDC projects in Nepal expanded in volume and got diversified in terms of modality. India started to focus extensively on infrastructure development and humanitarian assistance apart from technical cooperation. This was instrumental in re-designating the IAM into Indian Cooperation Mission (ICM), in 1966, to emphasise

[6] During the initial years, India's aid to Nepal constituted grants, especially towards developing agriculture, transportation infrastructure and power generation. Some of the important projects that India helped Nepal to build were the airport in Kathmandu and the Kosi Dam, followed by various irrigation projects.

India's position as a larger stakeholder in Nepal's social and economic development, as well as to underline India's readiness to cooperate in Nepal's overall development (MEA 1967, 7). Later, in 1980, the ICM was replaced by an Economic Cooperation Wing (ECW) which was established at the Indian Mission at Kathmandu to address several other important economic activities such as expanding trade and investments that went much beyond development cooperation projects (Chaturvedi 2012, 560).

Like in Nepal, India decided to take periodic review of IDC projects in other countries of strategic importance, like Afghanistan[7] (Chaturvedi 2012, 560). However, this time, India went on with establishing a new Joint Commission (JC) at the ministerial level in 1970 with a much wider mandate than earlier institutions set up for reviewing IDC. JC was set up mainly "to study and plan various projects for the mutual benefit of the two countries based on the coordination of the resources and capabilities of each country" (MEA 1970, 21). The first meeting of the Commission was held in New Delhi and the mandate of the Commission included undertaking immediate measures for the expansion of trade between India and Afghanistan. Later, JCs were established for several other countries, for example, Sri Lanka, Iran[8] and Czechoslovakia, with the idea of boosting India's economic cooperation and technical assistance with these countries (MEA 1970, 80).

At the central level, the institution-building mechanisms started off in the 1960s. In 1961, the Economic and Coordination Division (ECD) was established within the Ministry of External Affairs (MEA) exclusively to deal with India's development cooperation programmes. Until January 1961, the development cooperation programmes[9] were originally based at the Ministry of Finance (MoF), which was later transferred to the MEA and, six months later, to the ECD (MEA 1963, 54). ECD was

[7] Prime Minister Indira Gandhi visited Afghanistan in 1969, where both the countries discussed economic and technical cooperation, by identifying areas of mutual interest. The leaders from both the countries also agreed to work towards boosting economic cooperation and trade by ending the difficulties in land transit trade in the region on an urgent basis (MEA 1970, 21).

[8] India-Iran Joint Commission was established in 1969 and its first meeting was held in 1970 in New Delhi where a Protocol for economic, trade and technical cooperation was signed between both the countries which was expected to strengthen and diversify the cooperation between them (MEA 1970, 50).

[9] This mainly includes Indian development projects in Nepal.

also responsible for India's aid and trade relations with Nepal which were previously dealt with by the Eastern Division (MEA 1963, 54). ECD also played an advisory role in matters such as "trade agreements, credit and payments agreements, foreign aid negotiations and other technical agreements including air and shipping agreements" (MEA 1963, 54). It also assumed direct responsibility for all projects related to technical assistance with the exception of schemes and programmes within the scope of the Colombo Plan, which remained with the MoF. ECD also dealt with political and economic conferences other than the regular conferences of the UN which are the responsibility of the UN Division (MEA 1963, 54). This division also established inter-ministerial committees and study groups, in order to understand whether India's economic aspects had a bearing on its foreign policy (MEA 1964, 80).

Eventually, with the steady expansion of India's training programmes, New Delhi soon realised the need for a new programme dedicated for technical cooperation, named as the Indian Technical and Economic Cooperation (ITEC) which came into being in 1964. ECD was entrusted with the ITEC projects, particularly in Asia and Africa. The Indian Missions abroad were assigned the task of expanding India's exports and exploring markets in its partner countries so as "to utilise surplus capacities and talents to mutual advantage" (MEA 1970, 77). Moreover, India accumulated experience in skills development by being part of several multilateral programmes for skills development and capacity-building, such as the Colombo Plan, the Special Commonwealth Assistance for Africa Programme (SCAAP), the US Third Country Programme and the Technical Assistance Programme of the UN and its specialised agencies (MEA 1965, 84). What comprised the economic activities of MEA include "technical assistance, promotion of economic collaboration and analytical and advisory functions on matters related to aid and trade" (MEA 1970, 79). Under the ITEC programme, several techno-economic surveys for industrial development were carried out under the National Industrial Development Cooperation (NIDC) of India in several countries, including Afghanistan, Yemen, Fiji, Iran and Mauritius. The ITEC programmes also provided support for countries like Ghana, Nigeria, Tanzania and Uganda in developing small-scale industries (MEA 1970, 79).

In 1995, the Economic Division was restructured which resulted in the creation of a special administrative division within the MEA to deal with the ITEC programme. This new ITEC division had other related programmes like SCAAP[10] and Aid to Disaster Relief (ADR) added to its purview. However, within a year ITEC was merged with the Technical Cooperation Division. In 1994, India added a new dimension to its policy of SSC through the Special Volunteers Programme (SVP), to provide development assistance to the partner countries in Asia and Africa (MEA 1995, 113). The main aim of sending the special volunteers through the SVP was to assist its partner countries in their development programmes. Initially, only as few as ten countries were identified as "target countries". The target country list was revised periodically by the Committee on SVP based on the assessment of SVP undertaken by the Indian Missions in target countries. Based on the positive responses from the target countries in Asia and Africa, the list was expanded to include the countries in Central Asia. New Delhi also decided to send its volunteers based on the inputs received from the partner countries so that their development priorities and interests are very well taken into consideration (MEA 1995, 114). However, there is not much known about this programme after the initial years of its launch (Chaturvedi 2012, 563).

With the start of twenty-first century, there were major developments taking place in India's position as both a recipient and a development assistance provider. In the early 2000s, India decided to stop accepting tied aid and in 2003, India laid out its new policy on accepting foreign aid and also decided to bring changes in its own development assistance programme under the India Development Initiative (IDI). This initiative, with an allocation of Rs. 200 crores for 2003–2004, was supposed "to promote India as both a production centre and an investment destination" (GOI 2003, 20). Established under the MoF, the IDI was expected "to leverage and promote strategic economic interests abroad" (GOI 2003, 20). Under this initiative, India borrowed capital from the international capital markets so as to "lend on concessional terms to less creditworthy countries" (Bijoy 2010, 68). The Minister of Finance and Company Affairs, Jaswant Singh, while presenting the annual budget in 2003, announced:

> A stage has come in our development where we should now, firstly, review our dependence on external donors. Second, extend support to

[10]The SCAAP programme is aimed at providing technical assistance by India to 15 African countries which are the ex-colonies of UK. Activities under SCAAP are directed at extension of training to nominees from these countries in Indian institutes.

> the national efforts of other developing countries. And, thirdly, re-examine the line of credit route of international assistance to others. (GOI 2003, 21)

The decision to reorient its aid policies was followed by extensive meetings to establish the guidelines and operational strategies that were issued in 2003 (Chaturvedi 2012, 563).

The India Development and Economic Assistance Scheme (IDEAS) was also introduced to provide LOC through the EXIM Bank rather than from the government of India (GOI). The IDEAS was intended to provide professional support and technical guidance in managing loan portfolios for partner countries. It was designed to finance exports from India of project equipment, goods and services (Chaturvedi 2012, 567).

In 2003, India decided to accept bilateral aid only from five countries, namely the US, UK, Japan, Germany and Russia in addition to the European Union (EU). However, in 2004, a few donors including Canada, France, Italy and the Scandinavian countries were reinstated with a caveat that the bilateral cooperation with these donors would not be renewed after the completion of the on-going programmes. Yet, these donors could still direct their aid through either non-government organisations (NGOs) or any multilateral agency (Bijoy 2010, 67; Chaturvedi 2012, 559). In 2003, New Delhi also decided to pay back some of its bilateral debt to all but Germany, Japan, the US and France. The MoF announced that it would repay bilateral credit involving USD1.6 billion owed to 15 countries[11] (Bijoy 2010, 67). During this period, India's contribution to the UN also increased "from Rs.185.9 million in 2002 to Rs. 279.9 million in 2004" (Bijoy 2010, 68).

In 2007, the institutional structures were called for renewal with the announcement of a new agency called the India International Development Cooperation Agency (IIDCA) which was a step towards unified administration and management of the India's outgoing development assistance. IIDCA was supposed to be represented by the MEA, Ministry of Finance and Commerce and other stakeholders involved in Indian development Cooperation (GOI 2007). In the budget speech of 2007–2008, then Finance Minister P. Chidambaram announced that,

[11] This includes the Netherlands, Canada, the Russian Federation, Italy, Sweden, Belgium, Denmark, Kuwait, Austria, Switzerland, Spain, Australia, Saudi Arabia and the Czech and Slovak Republics.

> In keeping with India's growing stature in international affairs, we must willingly assume greater responsibility in promoting development in other developing countries. At present, India extends development cooperation through a number of Ministries and agencies and the total sum is about US$ 1 billion per annum. It is felt that all activities relating to development cooperation should be brought under one umbrella. (GOI 2007, para 107)

The guiding principle for India's decision to set up this new agency was New Delhi's position on its development assistance reaching those developing countries that were in greater need of external aid than India. Chaturvedi (2012, 65) notes that "all the announcements related to IIDCA were either in Parliament or in the media there was no mention of this in any of the MEA documents". In 2011, the name of IIDCA was changed to the Indian Agency for Partnership and Development (Chaturvedi 2012, 565).

In January 2012, a Development Partnership Administration (DPA) was setup within the MEA. The primary responsibilities of DPA include ensuring speedy and efficient implementation of India's external economic assistance programme, especially with developing countries for capacity-building; and overall responsibility for projects falling under grants or lines of credit through the "stages of concept, launch, execution and completion" (MEA 2012a, xviii). The setting up of DPA signifies the growing prominence of development cooperation in Indian foreign policy as well as the growing need for coordinating aid and aligning it to India's foreign policy priorities.

Indian Development Cooperation in the Twenty-First Century

As an emerging power that gives development assistance to the Global South, India has repositioned itself from a recipient to a donor thereby joining the club of the most powerful and influential countries in international politics. India is not a part of the OECD-DAC and does not align with the OECD definition and guidelines on foreign aid. India prefers not to call its development assistance as "foreign aid" and has been very articulate about its position on development assistance that it assumes to be way different from the OECD definition and principles. New Delhi has been very adamant about its position as "a partner" and discards the term donor which denotes a vertical relationship rather than a horizontal one.

In accordance with the philosophy of India's foreign policy, "an approach of friendship and cooperation with the aim of peaceful co-existence" became the founding principle of India's development cooperation policy (Chaturvedi 2012, 558). The framework of SSC and its associated values facilitate the overcoming of multitudes of problems, differences and conflicts that might have pulled down India's efforts for cooperation.

What Constitutes IDC?

Scholars have attempted to define IDC that has led to different ideas of what it constitutes. Bijoy (2010, 68) describes India's "overseas development assistance as a combo of project assistance, purchase subsidies, lines of credit, travel costs, and technical training costs and many more, incurred by the Indian government". The non-plan grant is inclusive of humanitarian assistance as well as technical and economic assistance (Bijoy 2010, 68). Chanana (2009, 11) defines India's "aid-related activities" as "grants, contributions to inter-national organisations (IOs) and inter-national financial institutions (IFIs), direct loans, and subsidies for preferential bilateral loans". These are more of a comparison of the IDC modalities with OECD's definition of the ODA.

However, the reality is that there exists no standard definition for IDC. Details of IDC are not easily available since India does not report its complete aid flows to any international aid agency nor does it publish any status paper on its development assistance. Even though several components constitute IDC, these components vary from time to time and whether some of the components are still added while calculating IDC in unknown. The MEA Annual Report 2018 describes IDC as a combination of "lines of credit, grant assistance, technical consultancy, small development projects, disaster relief and humanitarian aid, as well as a wide range of capacity-building programmes for civilian and military training courses under ITEC" (MEA 2018, 190).

Institutional Structures

The institutional structures for the implementation of the IDC have seen slow and steady development. Even though several institutional innovations have been attempted at various levels and at different points of time for improving delivery mechanisms and also for bringing the idea of impact evaluation and assessment into the IDC programmes, what is striking is the lack of consistency in these efforts. Nevertheless, the concerned divisions within the MEA dealing with planning and delivery (at the end of missions) have gone through several changes with more institutional innovations seen in the twenty-first century.

The three important institutions that are involved in India's development assistance are the MEA, MoF and MoCI. MEA has the coordinating role and enjoys a greater power over the others despite the fact that other ministries are equally important players in India's development cooperation. The other important player, the Department of Economic Affairs (DEA) in the MoF coordinates India's bilateral assistance with its partner countries. The MoCI also plays an important role due to the interweaving of trade and IDC flows. The EXIM Bank[12] is the topmost financial institution that is involved in financing, facilitating and promoting India's international trade relations with other countries (EXIM Bank 2015a, 21). Apart from financing LOCs, it also takes care of budget support and loans. Further, the payment and settlement of IDC is generally administered by Indian embassies and consulates located in the partner countries (Jobelius 2007, 7). Even though several efforts were made towards reforming and developing the institutional mechanisms for IDC, the major changes came about only in the twenty-first century.

There were speculations of a centralised agency for IDC being set up within the MEA since 2003, however, it was only in January 2012 that the DPA was set up within the MEA, for "efficient execution and monitoring of India's development projects through the stages of conceptualization, launch, implementation and commissioning" (MEA 2015a, xvi). Initially, DPA focussed on its key projects under the LOC to various partner countries as well as different development projects in Africa and its neighbourhood, including Afghanistan, Nepal, Myanmar, Sri Lanka and Bangladesh (MEA 2015a, 162). However, DPA was soon involved in streamlining and upgrading the processes involved in the delivery of the key components of IDC, including grants and ITEC. It also works in close coordination with different territorial divisions of the MEA. The

[12]The bank extends LOCs to overseas financial institutions, regional development banks, sovereign governments, etc. to enable buyers in those countries to import projects, goods and services from India on deferred credit terms and plays an important role in the implementation of needed foreign exchange and capacity provision for the implementation of the projects (EXIM Bank 2015a, 21; Chaturvedi 2008, 34, 2012, 567).

territorial divisions are "the main interlocutors with partner countries on the prioritization and selection of projects" covered under the IDC initiatives (MEA 2015a, 162), which makes it important for the DPA to closely coordinate with them. DPA is also entrusted with the responsibility of "developing the expertise required to handle projects in varied sectors and regions through the stages of project appraisal, implementation, monitoring and evaluation" (MEA 2018, 190).

The DPA has three divisions—DPA-I, DPA-II and DPA-III—each of which manages different aspects of IDC (MEA 2016). While DPA-I controls the project appraisal and LOC, DPA-II deals with capacity-building programmes, disaster-relief and ITEC; and DPA-III deals with project implementation. All the three divisions are led by Joint Secretary-level officers.

DPA-I handles all LOCs. DPA-II manages all training—including civilian and defence personnel training—under ITEC programme in Asia and the Pacific. It managed over 10,918 civilian training slots allocated to 161 partner countries during the year 2017–2018 (MEA 2018, 194). Furthermore, humanitarian assistance and disaster relief is also handled by this division. DPA-III deals with the implementation of grant assistance projects in neighbouring countries, including Afghanistan, Maldives, Myanmar, Nepal and Sri Lanka.

In 2003, New Delhi decided to channel its foreign loans through the EXIM Bank. From an organisational perspective, this implied that the MEA lost its monopoly on IDC, which indicated the growing influence of the MoCI in India's aid allocation. Such a change was even reflected in the allocation of bilateral loans from MEA that "fell from 32 to 6.7% of its total aid budget" (Chanana 2009, 12). Also, there was an increase in EXIM Bank loan approvals that "grew at a CAGR of 37.7% during the period" (Chanana 2009, 12).

The EXIM Bank works closely with the Investment and Technology Promotion Division (ITP), now part of DPA, the DEA and India's overseas diplomatic missions to ensure effective implementation of LOC. The government support is in terms of providing repayment guarantees and interest subsidy/equalisation to the EXIM Bank in order to compensate the Bank for the interest differential between the market rates and the amount it charges from its partners (Chaturvedi 2012, 567).

In several countries, LOCs have played an important role in providing industrial competitiveness and improved infrastructure. One of the facets of this programme is that the EXIM Bank suggests neither the nature of projects nor the individual entitlement of a country. It is left to the countries to decide, provided they come up with their own procurement laws as enunciated in their government documents. The EXIM Bank runs two separate programmes under the LOC scheme. One is on commercial terms and the other is on non-commercial concessional terms. The difference from the international market rate of interest is borne by the GOI (Chaturvedi 2012, 567).

The importance of evaluation and impact assessment was also one of the concerns that ran through the MEA at several points of time but no standing institutional arrangement was established for undertaking a periodic review of progress made on India's development assistance projects (Chaturvedi 2012, 560). However, there is no arrangement at the central level to coordinate and harmonise various policy decisions across countries and associated institutional changes. Immediate need, rather than long-term vision, seems to be the prime driver of India's approach in the area of development cooperation (Chaturvedi 2012, 562).

Policy Framework

Indian government has not published any White Paper or policy statement on IDC. Besides, India does not seem to have a clear-cut policy framework on its development cooperation. However, there are several factors that signify IDC, which also make it stand out from the traditional concepts of foreign aid as well as enabling it carve out a niche of its own.

Since India is not a part of the OECD-DAC, it does not follow the definition and the guidelines set by the traditional donors, which give it certain amount of discretion in its own policy and strategy for development cooperation. Most Indian government officials, during interviews conducted with them during March–May 2016, reiterated that IDC is horizontal cooperation which is given to the partner country for its development. India bats for an egalitarian relationship with its partner countries which is in sharp contrast to the vertical and hierarchical donor-recipient relationship maintained by the traditional donors. India has made its position clear in the international arena by refusing to be a signatory of the Paris Declaration, Accra Agenda for Action (AAA) and the Busan Partnership Agreement, which New Delhi considers as hierarchical and harsh on the country on the receiving end.

India's position on development cooperation has always been governed by the principles of SSC, including respect for sovereignty of the partners, ownership, no-conditionalities, and mutual benefit, which is of great prominence from the very beginning of IDC. India considers itself as a developing country partner to those countries which it provides development assistance. For India, IDC has also been an instrument to enhance its solidarity with the Global South.

Since the early days after independence, India has been following the principle of non-interference in other countries' domestic affairs as well as respect for sovereignty of partner countries (Mullen 2013, 5). With the signing of the Panchsheel agreement, Indian establishment upheld these ideals in its foreign policy, which can also be found in its development cooperation policy. Furthermore, India gives its partner country the choice to determine the kind of assistance it wants from India, which makes IDC need-based and largely demand-driven. In most cases, the partner country identifies the kind of development assistance projects it requires and then the aid-request is routed through the Indian embassy in their country for the consideration of the MEA. The MEA, upon receiving the request from the partner country, coordinates with different ministries and agencies for finalising the partnership. India's demand-driven approach differs significantly from the approach used by traditional donors. Furthermore, India's commitment to not impose any conditionalities on the partners gives them a greater voice in the whole process. For example, the African Union (AU) had full freedom to decide on the participants of the India-Africa Business Summit, with little or no interference from India. This allows the partner countries to set their priorities and action plans without any interference or pressure from the donor.

At the international level, even though India is not inclined to join the OECD-DAC, it has been really keen to be part of the UN umbrella. It was one of the countries that propelled the creation of DCF under the ECOSOC in 2007. For India, DCF has been an organisation with an egalitarian perspective on donors and recipients unlike the OECD-DAC that is biased towards developed country donors (Chanana 2009, 12). India has shown its continued belief and support for multilateralism. New Delhi's readiness to sidestep institutions created by the traditional donors implies that India is not simply a passive observer, but an active participant in the multilateral system (Chanana 2009, 12).

Furthermore, India's role as a development assistance provider has been based on its own experience as a recipient of foreign aid as well as a developing country that could successfully achieve enviable economic growth in the twenty-first century, despite having several domestic issues and limitations to deal with. India has been trying to create a new discourse on development assistance using its foreign policy considerations and development experiences. Even though it has little resources at its disposal for development assistance, it has been trying to use these resources to fulfil its own interests while also keeping in mind the welfare of its partners.

However, in order to make its development cooperation policies more acceptable and legitimate, it has to incorporate accountability into its development assistance. Being accountable to its citizens as well as the partner countries would enable its policymakers make more coherent development assistance policies based on a clear assessment of its strengths and weaknesses.

IDC Flows to Partner Countries

As per the OECD figures, the volume of IDC allotted to partner countries reached USD1.8 billion in 2015 as opposed to USD1.4 billion in the previous year (OECD 2019). As there are no consolidated estimates of IDC, the annual budgetary allocations by the government have been used to assess India's development assistance volume, geographical outreach and modalities. The data is dispersed and some data is not available. However, the available data has been used to comprehend the sectoral allocation and geographical patterns of Indian's development cooperation. It is noted that India's assistance to partner countries has seen a slow and steady rise over the years. This section would also give a fair idea of the factors that go into India's selection of the partner countries and the major tools used by India for its development assistance allocation and delivery.

Geographical Patterns of IDC

India's development assistance had been South Asia-centric since inception. However, in the past few years New Delhi has diversified and expanded its development cooperation to Africa and Latin America as well. Apart from growing geographical reach, there has also been a marked increase in the quantum of assistance, range of activities and nature of development assistance. This largely means greater emphasis on coherence in India's foreign policy and economic diplomacy that support development cooperation across partner countries. For instance, India announced granting unilateral market access to most exports from the least-developed countries (LDCs) in 2008. This scheme covers products that account for 92.5% of the LDCs' total global exports (and 94% of India's total tariff lines) (Chaturvedi 2012, 565). This section will elaborate on the expanding geographical footprint of India through its development cooperation programme.

Neighbourhood First

For New Delhi, the immediate neighbourhood continues to be the main focus of its development cooperation policy. The MEA Outcome Budgets for the years 2010–2011 to 2016–2017 suggest that there has been a steady increase in the development assistance to the neighbourhood. Within South Asia, Bhutan has received the largest amounts of development assistance, followed by Afghanistan, Sri Lanka, Nepal and Myanmar in the financial year 2015–2016 (MEA 2016, 11).

Bhutan has been India's most important development partner since the 1950s. India shares close historical, political and cultural ties with Bhutan and this was reaffirmed by the Treaty of Friendship and Cooperation signed between the two countries in 1949. Bhutan received more than 60% of India's overall grants and loans in 2016–2017 (MEA 2016). Initially, most of the grants for Bhutan were in the form of budgetary support that helped Bhutan develop its infrastructure and hydroelectric capacity. Further, India also started contributing towards Bhutan's five-year plans from 1961, to help Bhutan walk on the path of development and economic growth. With the beginning of India's ITEC programme in 1964, Bhutan also began to get a significant amount of assistance in the form of technical assistance and capacity-building. For example, there was a tremendous increase in the number of ITEC slots received by Bhutan from 20 slots in 2000 to 217 slots in 2014 (Mullen 2014, 13; IDCR 2015, 13). From the 1970s, India began to extensively finance Bhutan's hydroelectric power projects which later became a major boon for India as most of the power harnessed from these stations is exported to India once the local demands are met. The major hydroelectric power projects funded by India include Chhukha hydroelectric project, Kurichhu hydroelectric project and Tala hydroelectric project. Several other projects have been commissioned by India and are expected to be completed soon.

Nepal has been another important development cooperation partner and foreign policy priority for India. The historical and cultural links with Nepal has been a key reason behind India's political and economic cooperation with Nepal. However, when compared to Bhutan, Nepal gets lesser volume of development assistance from India. It has been giving development assistance to Nepal since the early days after independence. The most important sectors for development cooperation have been infrastructure, health, education and technical assistance and capacity-building (MEA 2013a). India initiated its development assistance with its assistance to Nepal to build the Kosi dam and the airport at Kathmandu. Similarly, it also started developing and upgrading its institutions for development cooperation from its experience in Nepal. Apart from being historically and culturally important, Nepal has geopolitical and strategic significance for India. New Delhi is also cautious of Nepal's growing proximity with China and wanted to ensure Nepal's continuous support and cooperation. For this, New Delhi has been providing generous assistance for Nepal's development and its transition to democracy. India has also been cooperating with Kathmandu in rehabilitation and reconstruction efforts after the earthquake in 2015. In this regard, India pledged USD 1 million as assistance (The Indian Express 2015, June 25). Furthermore, India is also the largest trading partner for Nepal and also a major source of FDI. India's development assistance has, since the beginning, been focussed on Bhutan and Nepal and continues to be so. However, the partner that has gained greater prominence in IDC is Afghanistan, which gets a heightened volume of IDC in the past one decade.

Despite having strong historical and cultural linkages, Afghanistan was not a major development cooperation partner for India until September 2001, after which it deepened its economic and political ties with its South Asian partner. Afghanistan was allocated Rs. 683 crore in loans and grants in the financial year 2015–2016 (MEA 2016, 11). The main areas of IDC in Afghanistan are infrastructure development, humanitarian assistance, health, education, and technical assistance and capacity-building (MEA 2012b, 2). The most prestigious project for India in Afghanistan has been the Parliament building, a Rs. 969 crore project, inaugurated by Prime Minister Modi in December 2015 (The Indian Express 2016, January 28). Other important projects include the Salma Dam in Herat, the Zaranj-Delaram Road, the Women's Vocational Training Centre in Kabul and Agricultural University ANASTU in Kandahar. Linked to this, India-Afghan trade relations have improved considerably since the early 2000s, standing at USD683.02 million in 2013–2014 (Embassy of India Kabul 2016). Even though economic, political and strategic motivations drive India's development assistance to Afghanistan, one of the most important considerations for India has also been bringing long-term stability and peace in the country.

Among its immediate neighbours, Bangladesh began to receive assistance from India soon after its birth in 1971. Since 2010, India extended three LOCs worth USD7.5 billion—USD1 billion, USD2 billion and USD4.5 billion in the years 2010, 2015 and 2017, respectively—making Bangladesh the largest recipient of India's LOC (MEA 2017). The major sectors of cooperation include energy, technical assistance and capacity-building, humanitarian assistance and infrastructure (MEA 2017). For India, better infrastructure facilities in Bangladesh meant increased connectivity with its north-eastern states. India has been pushing for greater political and economic engagement with Bangladesh through its development assistance efforts.

Another major South Asian partner with which India shares close historical and cultural ties is Sri Lanka. India's bilateral relationship has improved considerably after the end of the civil war in 2009. Indian assistance to Sri Lanka is focussed on infrastructure, humanitarian assistance, education, technical assistance and capacity-building. Some of the important projects include the Housing Project, Cultural Centre at Jaffna, Vocational Training Centres, upgrading the rail link between Colombo and Matara, and coal power plant at Sampur (MEA 2015b).

South Asia continues to be the priority for India. Even though economic and commercial interests are important for India, what drives India's engagement with South Asia are strategic considerations and its vision of regional stability, which New Delhi expects to fulfil through its growing development cooperation efforts in the region.

Africa

Even though there has been consistent increase in IDC to South Asia, the region that is gaining prominence in India's development cooperation efforts is Africa. The allocations to African countries have increased from Rs. 9 crores in 1990–1991 to Rs. 125.8 crores in 2009–2010 (Chaturvedi 2012, 570). There have been significant fluctuations during certain years, but the trends show that the focus on Africa is growing. In 2014–2015, Indian development assistance to Africa in the form of loans and grants were estimated as Rs. 350 crores, nearly six-fold increase in the volume from financial year 2005–2006 when it was Rs. 60 crores (MEA 2014, 12). Apart from loans and grants, India's LOCs to Africa has also been rising. It increased from USD 304 million in 2004–2005 to USD 5.1 billion in 2012–2013 (Mullen 2014, 5). Since 2004–2005, India has allocated LOC worth USD9.42 to Africa (MEA 2018, 192). In addition, India has offered a grant assistance worth USD600 million and LOCs worth USD10 billion for Africa during the India-Africa Forum Summit (IAFS)[13] in 2015 (MEA 2018). The development assistance to Africa has ranged across technical assistance and capacity-building, educational scholarships, medical support and infrastructure building and maintenance.

India's increasing development cooperation with Africa has been complimented by trade and commercial ties that has been growing. Apart from "Focus Africa" programme launched in 2002 aimed at improving India's trade and commercial ties with Africa, the IAFS launched in 2008 has been significant steps in strengthening political, economic and strategic ties with Africa (WTO 2013, 38). India's trade with Africa increased eight-fold between 2001 and 2017, from USD7.2 billion to USD59.9 billion (EXIM BANK 2018). India-Africa trade ties peaked in 2014 at USD78 billion, which plummeted largely due to the global economic slowdown and falling commodity prices (EXIM Bank 2018, 23). While India's relation with Africa was governed by historical ties and political considerations in the second-half of twentieth century, it is now overwhelmingly governed by economic and commercial interests in the region.

Latin America and the Caribbean

India's is looking forward to strengthen its engagement with LAC countries, which was earlier ignored because of the geographical distance and language barriers. With India's growing economic and political ambitions to be a great power, it has become a priority to engage with countries far and wide. Furthermore, without engaging with LAC countries, India's approach to SSC will not be complete.

[13] The IAFS was initiated for strengthening India-Africa relations. Until now, three summits have been held; two in New Delhi (2008 and 2015) and one in Addis Ababa (2011).

The volume of development assistance allocated for Latin America and Caribbean has been much less when compared to what India gives to Asia and Africa. It got a meagre sum of Rs. 15 crore as loans and grants in the year 2015–2016 as opposed to the Rs. 200 crore that was given to Africa (MEA 2016). However, this is a huge improvement when compared to 2009–2010 figures, which was Rs. 2 crore. The major sectors of assistance in the region include infrastructure, technical assistance and capacity-building and pharmaceuticals.

India has consciously been trying to push for a greater engagement with the region, especially in trade and commerce. There has been a 20-fold increase in India-Latin America trade from 2000 to 2012. What was just USD 2 billion in 2000 jumped to USD 46 billion in 2012 (MEA 2013b). However, the region accounts for only five per cent of India's total trade. Also, India's economic engagements are mostly with a few big countries in Latin America including, Brazil, Mexico, Venezuela, Colombia and Chile. Other countries, mostly smaller ones, did not figure in New Delhi's foreign policy considerations until recently, but is changing in a significant way with trade and investment being expanded to smaller countries in the region (Viswanathan 2019). India is keen to engage with Latin America and the Caribbean, seemingly more for economic and commercial interests, and less for political and strategic considerations. However, multilateral diplomacy is one of the important considerations for India to engage with this region. A permanent seat in the UNSC cannot materialise without the support of countries in the Global South.

Multilateral Development Assistance

In addition to its bilateral aid initiatives, India has made increasing contributions to support other developing countries in their social and economic development, and in the process enabling them to attend to their Millennium Development Goals (MDGs) and now, the Sustainable Development Goals (SDGs). With the rapid growth of India's economy, the government is also keen to expand India's role in various multilateral fora.

New Delhi's growing amount of humanitarian assistance through the UN's initiatives indicates India's increasing role in international aid architecture. India has also joined several global public-private partnership programmes which are dedicated to attracting and allocating additional resources to prevent and treat communicable diseases. One such example is the Global Fund,[14] which has focussed specifically on dealing globally with HIV/AIDS, tuberculosis and malaria (Chaturvedi 2012, 572). India has become the host country for two major Asian regional research centres for advance technologies, namely the International Center for Genetic Engineering and Biotechnology (ICGEB), and the International Crops Research Institute for the Semi-Arid Tropics (ICRISAT), both operating under the UN umbrella. These institutes coordinate and support research in medicine and agriculture in Asia. Furthermore, India also hosts the UN Educational, Scientific and Cultural Organization (UNESCO), Regional Centre for Biotechnology (RCB) and the Asian and Pacific Centre for Transfer of Technology (APCTT) of the UN Economic and Social Commission for Asia and the Pacific (UNESCAP).

Being the largest democracy, India has been actively involved in strengthening democratic institutions around the world through its support and contributions to the UN Democracy Fund (UNDEF). India is the second-largest contributor to this fund, having contributed US$ 31.56 million by 2014 (PMINEWYORK 2016). The Fund supports various projects for developing democratic institutions around the world. India has a strong history of sharing experiences in conducting and managing election processes; for example, in Nepal,[15] Burma[16] and Sudan.[17] However, these efforts are guided by India's policy of non-interference and respect for each other's territorial integrity and sovereignty, as envisaged in the Panchsheel principles. Unlike the West which tries to thrust democracy on other countries, India's efforts have been in the direction of supporting partner countries in smooth transition to democracy based on its own experience of transforming itself from a British colony into the largest democracy in the world.

[14] Global Fund, created in 2002, with approved funding of USD18.4 billion for more than 572 programmes in 140 countries, provides a quarter of all international financing for AIDS globally, two-thirds for tuberculosis and three-quarters for malaria. India has contributed USD11 million to this programme (Chaturvedi 2012, 573).

[15] India sent a team of experts for supporting the smooth conduct of an election in 1959.

[16] Burma Election Commission visited India to observe the conduct of general elections in India in 1962 with the support of the Indian government.

[17] India's Election Commissioner visited Sudan in 1953 in order to facilitate the implementation of the Anglo-Egyptian Agreement for self-government and self-determination in Sudan.

Under the IBSA initiative, India has contributed to the IBSA Fund, established in 2004. Its work has been managed and disbursed through the Special Unit for SSC of the UNDP, "thereby helping to 'de-nationalize' a portion of the countries' national aid flows" (Chaturvedi 2012, 574). Through the UN's special agencies, India has provided assistance to victims of the earthquake in Haiti as well as to the victims of floods in Pakistan.

India has been supportive of the development assistance efforts through the UN and its agencies because it considers UN as an egalitarian organisation. However, IDC is mostly bilateral assistance and little multilateral. India prefers giving assistance more through bilateral means as it would allow it to better influence its partner countries, and help mould its development assistance as per its priorities and interests.

Sectoral Distribution

IDC is composed mainly of three elements: LOCs, grants and ITEC (MEA 2015a, 162). This section would focus on each of these sectors in detail in order to capture IDC's priority areas (Fig. 5.1).

ITEC

India's ITEC programme was initiated in 1964 by a decision of the Indian Cabinet. The Cabinet observed that,

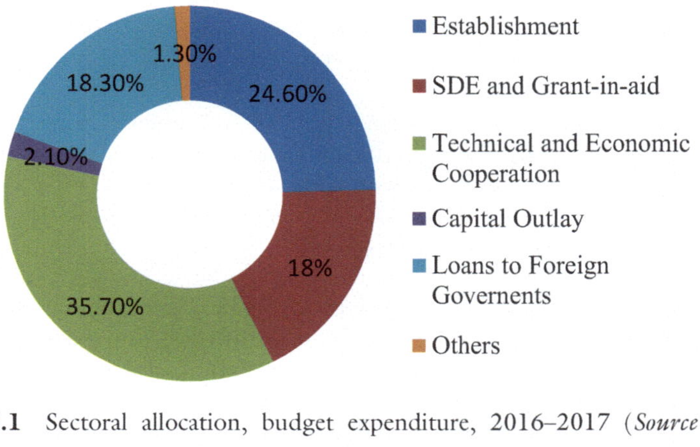

Fig. 5.1 Sectoral allocation, budget expenditure, 2016–2017 (*Source* MEA 2016)

> a programme of technical and economic cooperation is essential for the development of our relations with the other developing countries on the basis of partnership and cooperation for mutual benefit. (ITEC 2014, 1)

Since then, ITEC programme has emerged as a flagship programme of the MEA. All the capacity-building programmes of the Indian government, including the ITEC, SCAAP and TCS of Colombo Plan, are managed by the DPA-II (ITEC 2016a).

India's own experience as a receiver of capacity-building assistance that proved to be tremendously beneficial for India's development inspired and paved the way for the ITEC programme that aimed at sharing the lessons in development imbibed by India in the early years after independence. More than 160 countries were invited during a span of five decades, under the ITEC, SCAAP and TCS of Colombo Plan programmes, to share India's developmental experience after independence (ITEC 2014, 1).

Conceived initially as a bilateral programme, ITEC has grown tremendously to become a multilateral one with slots being allotted to multilateral groupings like the G-77, ASEAN, AU, CARICOM, IOR-ARC, IAFS and WTO (ITEC 2016b). With the expansion of the ITEC programme, the competence of India as a provider of technical know-how and expertise is accepted and appreciated by several countries. India aims to show its solidarity with other developing countries of the Global South which would also generate immense goodwill for India. India also grants assistance under ITEC based on the needs and demands of its partners, which make it one of the important modes of cooperation for partner countries.

The ITEC programme has several components:

> organising training (civil and defence) in India of nominees from ITEC partner countries, deputation of Indian experts abroad, aid for disaster relief, gifts/donations of equipment at the request of the ITEC partner countries, study tours and project and project related activities such as feasibility studies/consultancy services. (ITEC 2014, 4)

One of the most important components of ITEC programme is giving training to government officials and professionals from partner countries. This includes both civilian and defence training courses. The civilian training courses are fully funded by GOI. The courses have been divided into seven broad categories: "Accounts, Audit, Banking and Finance

Courses; IT, Telecommunication and English Courses; Management Courses; SME/Rural Development Courses; Specialized Courses; Technical Courses; and Environment and Renewable Energy Courses" (ITEC 2016b). These courses are considered as important platform for skill development and capacity-building as these are the areas in which India has excelled over the years and is ready to pass on these skills to its partners. Hence, these courses are in great demand from partner countries that also send their senior level officials for training in India (ITEC 2016b).

India also gives defence training to those nominated by the partner countries and it covers all the three wings of the Defence Services, i.e., Army, Navy and Air Force. The areas of training include security and strategic studies, defence management, and aeronautical and marine engineering. Trainings are given in India's most prestigious institutions like National Defence College, Defence Services Staff College and Indian Military Academy. India's defence training facilities is not just available for the developing countries of the Global South. Developed countries can also request for India's defence training services on self-financing basis.

New Delhi also provides its partner countries with assistance in technical activities by sending experts who could analyse the issues and suggest solutions based on the socio-economic and political situation of the partner countries. Indian experts are sent only on the request of the partner country for assistance on technical matters. Some important areas covered under this project include military training, IT, medicine, English teaching, telecommunications and agricultural research. Furthermore, other developing countries find India's experience and expertise as matching to their stages of development and technological advancement. The success achieved by India in the areas of small- and medium-scale industries, agriculture and financial management are of great interest and curiosity to other developing countries (ITEC 2016b).

Further, India has also been providing study tours to its partners as a part of its ITEC programme. These tours are completely demand-driven. Upon the request of its partner countries, New Delhi sends invitations to their delegates to visit and stay in India for study programme of two to three weeks duration in which they are taken to different institutions and training centres in various parts of India.

Apart from assistance to other developing countries in the form of gift or donations, India under its aid for disaster-relief programme of the ITEC supplies humanitarian assistance in the form of food grains, medicines and other important items to those countries struck by natural disasters.

The increasing number of participants coming for ITEC programme signifies its utility and relevance to other developing countries. With the increasing number of participants, India has also increased its budgetary allocation for ITEC. It rose from Rs. 4.46 lakhs in 1964–1965 to more than Rs. 1 crore in 1971–1972, and to Rs. 200 crores in 2013–2014 (ITEC 2014, 3).

For India, technology transfer is an important mode of assistance to the Global South. In 2007, India created a Pan-African e-Network to foster digital connectivity between India and Africa. Through this initiative, it became possible to connect schools and hospitals in Africa with top institutions in India using advanced satellite technology. Usually large public sector enterprises under the ITEC umbrella are entrusted to implement these kinds of projects (Chanana 2009, 12). Pan-African e-Network project was implemented by Telecommunications Consultants India Limited (IDCR 2015, 5). Under ITEC, India has been successful in expanding its relations with other developing countries of the Global South.

One of the advantages that India has over other developed countries that give development assistance is the significantly lower overhead costs. The fact that most of the ITEC courses were conducted in India ensured that the overall cost of training given per head was a fraction of similar kinds of training conducted in developed countries. Also, the impact of an ITEC course for bureaucrats was much greater than the rupee value of the development cooperation provided by India. Because of this, IDC could train more people for the assistance given through ITEC provided to each of its partner country (Mullen 2013, 7).

Furthermore, ITEC programme has been instrumental in creating goodwill for India through the huge network of ITEC alumni who develop a “powerful cultural bridge between India and the country concerned” (ITEC 2014, 6). With most of the ITEC alumni holding important positions at home, in different fields like ministry, academia, policy-making and business, India has the support of a powerful group of people in its partner country that would help in facilitating the bilateral ties between the two countries (ITEC 2014, 6).

The ITEC programme could also be considered as a symbol of India’s role and contribution to SSC, a partnership based on a shared sense of solidarity, the idea of national ownership and no-conditionalities approach. Furthermore, India's respect for sovereignty of its partners, lack of conditionalities and demand-driven approach is markedly different from the aid given by most of the traditional donors. Henceforth, India's competence in providing technical assistance and capacity-building has been recognised around the world through the ITEC programme. As a result, India is being increasingly recognised and branded as a "provider of technical know-how and expertise" (ITEC 2014, 6).

Lines of Credit (LOCs)

EXIM Bank defines "a line of credit as a financing mechanism through which EXIM Bank of India extends support for export of projects, equipment, goods and services from India" (EXIM Bank 2013, 2). In 2003–2004, New Delhi formulated the Indian Development Initiative (IDI), now known as Indian Development and Economic Assistance Scheme (IDEAS) to extend concessional LOCs routed through EXIM Bank. The main idea was to share India's development experience through capacity-building and skills transfer. Through LOCs, trade and infrastructure development also became a part IDC. LOCs, therefore, are essentially concessional loans with a certain grant element which are administered by the EXIM Bank of India on its own and coordinated by DPA-I.

EXIM Bank extends LOCs to

> the foreign governments or their nominated agencies such as central banks, state owned commercial banks and para-statal organizations; national or regional development banks; overseas financial institutions; commercial banks abroad and other suitable overseas entities. (EXIM Bank 2013, 2)

In 2014–2015, seventeen LOCs worth USD1.67 billion were provided by the EXIM Bank in order to support Indian exports including goods, projects and services. The countries that received maximum LOCs from India include Nigeria, Vietnam, Democratic Republic of Congo, Fiji Islands, Gambia, Mauritius, Nepal, Nicaragua, Djibouti and Senegal. Most of the LOCs were provided for projects like "cement plants, electrification expansion, transmission lines and substation, rice self-sufficiency programme, fertilizer plant and upgradation of the sugar industry" (EXIM Bank 2015a, 21).

In 2012, more than 50% of total LOCs went to sub-Saharan Africa, followed by South Asia with 39% (Chaturvedi 2012, 568). As per the

MEA Annual Report 2017–2018, a total of 246 LOCs were allocated since 2005–2006 which amounted to USD24.33 billion (MEA 2018).

LOCs are extended to developing countries on concessional terms with the condition imposed on the recipients that they "import Indian equipment, technology, projects, goods and services on deferred credit terms for a minimum of 75% of the contract value" (EXIM Bank 2013, 8, 2015b, 2). Therefore, LOCs provide "a safe mode of non-recourse financing option to Indian exporters", especially the Small and Medium Enterprises (SMEs). This helped the Indian businesses to easily enter the new export markets as well as in expanding their business in existing export markets "without any payment risk from the overseas importers" (EXIM Bank 2013, 2). These, therefore, function as instruments for facilitating trade and less of development assistance (Roychoudhury 2013, 23; Chaturvedi et al. 2014, 2).

Grants/Loans

India's grants were mainly focussed on the neighbourhood. However, grant component of IDC is relatively small compared to ITEC and LOCs despite an overall increase in grant element in IDC since 1990. From Rs. 2.6 billion grant in 1990–1991, it increased to about Rs. 28.5 billion in 2009–2010 and reached Rs. 48 billion in 2012–2013. The key sectors in which grants got allocated were infrastructure development, agriculture, power generation, education and health sector (MEA 2018).

It appears that LOCs have occupied a major place in India's development cooperation landscape compared to other components of IDC like grants and the ITEC programme. This has similarities with India's own experience as a recipient of aid over the last 60 years. Since 1981–1982, the share of loans and grants in the overall inflow of aid did not change much in the Indian context. In 1981, India was receiving external assistance of USD 2079 million, out of which USD 1694 million was loans while USD 385 million was grants (Ministry of Finance 2012). In 2010–2011, India received overall assistance of USD 8287 million, out of which loans constituted USD 7679 million while grants totalled USD 608 million. According to Chaturvedi (2012, 566), the analysis for the period (1981–1982 to 2010–2011) shows that the share of loans in the total assistance moved from 81% in 1981–1982 to 93% in 2010–2011. India's top bilateral donors during the year 2010–2011 included Japan (17%), the UK (4%) and Germany (4%). India also received aid from multilateral donors like the International Bank for Reconstruction and Development

(IBRD) (38%), Asian Development Bank (ADB) (20%) and International Development Association (IDA) (13%).

The reduced grant element and the surge in LOCs in IDC significantly demonstrate New Delhi's growing trade and commercial interests that accompany its development assistance. LOCs have been greatly beneficial in facilitating trade and pushing India's economic diplomacy abroad as it has always been tied to Indian goods and services. This aligns with what is termed as "development compact" (Chaturvedi 2016, 53), which includes five elements—capacity-building, trade and investments, development finance, grants and technology—that are all part of SSC and have been incorporated into India's development cooperation framework. The primary emphasis of this concept is on policy coherence and overall development of the partner country (Chaturvedi 2016).Even though India's development cooperation aims at playing a role in the development story of the partner country, the inclusion of trade and investments as a component brings in the aspect of donor interest into it.

Like most donors, India's development cooperation caters to varied interests and motivations driving New Delhi's foreign policy. The following section would elaborate on the motivations and agendas driving India's development cooperation to its partners in the Global South.

Motivations Driving India's Development Cooperation Programme

India's growing visibility in the international aid architecture has raised questions about the motivations and agendas driving its development cooperation programme. Can IDC be only guided by self-interest or are there any altruistic elements in it?

In the early days after independence when India started giving assistance, IDC was focussed more on helping the newly independent countries of the Global South—especially those in Asia and Africa—by focussing on their common history of colonial subjugation. India forged a sense of shared history and culture, especially in South Asia, which acted as the driving force behind India's development assistance programme. This sense of shared history with other newly independent states is said to have created a perception of equality among many developing countries (Mullen 2013, 3). Furthermore, the Cold War and India's leadership in the NAM provided a greater impetus for New Delhi to focus on SSC and provide assistance to developing countries in Asia and Africa.

Since the beginning of the twenty-first century, IDC gained greater importance in India's foreign policy. With increasing volume, introduction of different modalities and expanding geographical spread, IDC began to mould itself to compliment India's foreign policy priorities and preferences, and the country's changing role in international politics. Two important factors that has ensured the strategic value of IDC within Indian foreign policy: first, the country's dynamic economic growth that contributed to new economic motives in its SSC, and second, New Delhi's increasing prominence in international politics and its greater claim to status of a "South Asian hegemonic power and global spokesperson of other developing countries" (Jobelius 2007, 3). Even though these factors are relevant to India's changing development assistance policy, a multitude of factors play a role in India's growing development assistance and its increasing scope. This section delves into these motivations.

Regional Stability and Leadership

India shares close historical, cultural, political and economic ties with the countries in its neighbourhood. South Asia remains a foreign policy priority for India. The volume of IDC allocated to its closest neighbours has been steadily increasing over the years since independence. Bhutan is the largest recipient of IDC and received more than 60% of its grants and loans in 2016–2017 (MEA 2014). This trend continues in the 2018-2019 budget as well (GOI Budget 2019). Even as volume of IDC allocated to Bhutan has increased, the share of Bhutan in the overall aid budget has gone down to 30 per cent (Mitra 2019). Other important partners include Maldives, Nepal, Afghanistan, Bangladesh and Sri Lanka. All these countries are of great strategic significance for India.

For New Delhi, maintaining influence in the region has always been a priority and a concern. India faces tough competition from China in the region. China has wooed all the countries in the region with its increasing soft power capabilities and economic might. China's growing foreign aid and investments in the region has always been a concern for India that wants to restrict Chinese influence in the region. Furthermore, India is also concerned about Pakistan's growing proximity with China. One of the ways in which India is trying to tackle the China-Pakistan problem in the region is through development assistance to its small neighbours. However, China has also been using its economic instruments, including aid, to maintain its influence in the region as well as to balance India. Moreover, one of the primary concerns for India is maintaining stability in the region. In 2017, India-China standoff in the Doklam region of Bhutan, had it not been tackled maturely, would have escalated into a war between India and China for influence. India, through its development assistance, has also been supporting its neighbours to maintain political stability and economic growth, which is in turn important for maintaining stability and peace in the region. Hence, trade, investments, energy and natural resources, though important for India, take a backseat when it comes to its immediate neighbourhood.

Trade, Markets and Business

With the liberalisation of the Indian economy in the early 1990s, IDC has been moulded to incorporate India's growing economic interests into its external development assistance. Even when India continues to be one of the most dynamically growing markets in the world, to sustain its economic growth, it has become imperative to get access to new markets; to improve deficits in the trade balance; secure the supply of raw materials for its growing industries, and obtain energy resources (Jobelius 2007, 3). This has had a significant effect on India's foreign policy towards other developing countries thereby making Indian development cooperation invariably linked to trade and search for new markets.

Indian business has had a favourable time since the 1990s and the IDC was also seen in a favourable light as these businesses have benefited enormously from New Delhi's emphasis on economic diplomacy (Chenoy and Joshi 2016). Chaturvedi et al. (2014) argues that it is India's partner countries that receive most of India's foreign direct investment (FDI) and capital as well. Slowly, Indian businesses and trading interests have diversified to meet these ends. There is widespread support for the increasing role of businesses in development, both among the political classes and the bureaucracy.

The institution that has played the most important role in merging the interests of the business in IDC has been the EXIM Bank, which has been supporting "the Indian industries in their globalisation efforts through a comprehensive range of financing and advisory support programmes encompassing all stages of the export business cycle" (EXIM Bank 2013, 1). The Bank's vision is "to go beyond traditional financing and facilitate exports of a variety of products and services which have the potential to go overseas, by creating a niche for them in the international market" (EXIM Bank 2013, 1). With the Bank's support, many Indian companies operate as either Engineering Procurement Construction (EPC) contractors or consortium members in export markets. Companies like Tata Motors,[18] the state-owned RITES[19] and oil companies such as ONGC Videsh and Indian Oil Corporation Ltd. (IOC) have got lucrative deals in Asia, Africa and Latin America (Bijoy 2010, 71). EXIM Bank has been supporting and encouraging Indian companies to venture out to different countries and to seek project opportunities thereby facilitating project exports from India.

The fact that Indian LOCs has been tied to goods and services from India also demonstrates how India has made trade and investments an integral part of its development cooperation. This has given a boost to India's trade and investments, especially in Africa and Latin America and the Caribbean. Furthermore, with the increasing geographical outreach of IDC, Indian firms have also expanded their businesses to several countries that were not earlier in their agenda. Hence, Indian government and businesses began to coordinate their functions for mutual benefit. However, India should avoid getting tagged in as being involved in land grab in Africa, like in case of Ethiopia, which can go against the very principles on which it is trying to build its aid programme (Purushothaman 2017).

Clearly, LOCs have helped India in facilitating trade and investments in far-off countries in Africa and Latin America. India's trade with its neighbouring countries, except Pakistan, has been growing steadily. India's largest beneficiary, Bhutan, is also one of the important trading partners for India in the region (see, Fig. 5.2). It should also be noted that India's trade and investments with Africa has grown exponentially (EXIM Bank 2018). Apart from trade and investments, India has been on a look out for energy and natural resources to support its growing industrial sector as well as fulfilling the energy needs of its growing population.

Despite India's expanding economic diplomacy and outreach, New Delhi is adamant about its foreign policy principles based on SSC. Even though it is encouraging the Indian businesses to expand their circle, it has given clear guidelines for the businesses to respect and follow the

[18] Tata Motors got a USD 19 million World Bank tender to provide 500 buses to Senbus, a transport company in Senegal.

[19] RITES has been involved in the sale of locomotives to Sudan Railways and other involvements in Tanzania, Ethiopia and Uganda.

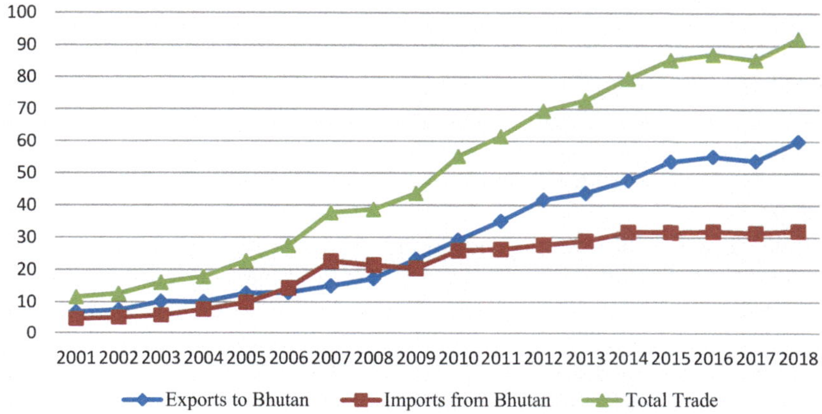

Fig. 5.2 India-Bhutan Trade, 2001–2018 (in billion Rs.) (*Source* Compiled by author [Embassy of India Thimphu 2019; MEA 2012c, 4])

rules of the country where they have invested in projects (Chaturvedi et al. 2014, 2). For the Indian businesses, India's expanding development cooperation activities and its enhanced economic diplomacy with the Global South has proved to be highly beneficial in expanding their business interests in far-away countries where they have ample opportunity to grow and make profits.

Henceforth, India has been relatively successful in complementing its development assistance with trade and investments. Also, its increasing development cooperation programme has given a much needed push to the Indian businesses.

Diplomatic Support/Permanent Seat in the United Nations Security Council (UNSC)

Apart from India's interests in regional stability, expanding its trade and investments and its quest for energy and natural resources, another important dimension of its development cooperation is gaining diplomatic support from the developing countries of the Global South in international platforms.

India, since independence, has been a supporter of the Global South and adheres to the principle of SSC in its foreign policy and economic diplomacy. It has also helped many colonies in Asia and Africa in their struggle for independence. Furthermore, India was an important figure in NAM and worked for solidarity and self-determination of the Global South. Apart from bringing solidarity and goodwill, India considers its development cooperation as a way to gain diplomatic support from its partner countries in global governance institutions like the UN, IMF or WTO.

Like several other developing countries, India has also been aspiring for a permanent seat in the reformed UNSC and has been pushing for an early reform in the present system to incorporate more emerging powers into the high table. The current set-up of the Security Council represent the power equations of the Second World War that has failed to address the changing power dynamics in the international system. India is also perturbed by the unequal representation and are questioning the hegemony and over-representation of the West in the UNSC.

India considers itself as a major contender for the permanent membership which has made it important for New Delhi to garner support from other developing countries of the Global South. One of the reasons why India has been expanding its development cooperation from its neighbourhood to other countries in Africa and Latin America has been its desire to mobilise support for its candidacy from the Global South. While the reforms might take several years, New Delhi has been engaged in gathering diplomatic support for this distant dream.

Even though multiple interests drive IDC, these are not entirely focussed on fulfilling India's self-interests. India also gives assistance for helping countries to achieve economic growth and development. India has especially been forthcoming in time of need, for example, New Delhi has always responded to any call for humanitarian assistance from any country affected by natural disasters or humanitarian crisis. India's development assistance to Nepal, Mozambique, Sri Lanka and Afghanistan has humanitarian elements as well. Through development cooperation, India also hopes to present itself as a powerful and self-reliant country that has the capacity to help others as well as readiness to take responsibilities in the international system.

India, the Development Partner: Prospects and Challenges

Even when India has transformed itself into a development partner with its own principles and approach towards development cooperation, there are several challenges that needs to be addressed in order to create its own distinct development assistance programme. For this, India needs to build on its strengths and do away with its weaknesses to be able to be a reliable and responsible partner to the Global South.

The future of India's role as a development assistance provider will depend on whether it can overcome some of the main institutional and policy constraints. The lack of coordination among different ministries responsible for executing and implementing India's development assistance is a major challenge that needs immediate solutions. The lack of a central authority for implementation and management of development cooperation is restricting India from utilising its full potential. Even though the DPA was created for this purpose; from the interviews conducted by the author with the officials in DPA-I, II and III between April–June 2016, it was clear that there is a lack of coordination among these three wings of the agency and that they pursued their own individual agendas without any consultation with each other. A central agency which can align IDC would also help in reducing administrative costs, overlaps and duplication of assistance, and would bring more transparency into the horizon with all data in one place. This could also make way for project evaluation and impact assessment, which is important, but totally absent from India's development cooperation for now. With the increasing scale and scope of development cooperation, India will have to address this issue on an urgent basis for optimum results from its development cooperation programme.

India has to recognise its strength in development cooperation and improve and build on its successes. India's technical assistance and capacity-building has helped in local capacity-building in the partner countries. This has been a huge success for India and has set India apart from other donors in the eyes of its partners. This has helped build India's goodwill and strengthen its bilateral ties with its partner countries. Being less intrusive and cooperative has also served Indian interests rather well as building lasting social and cultural links would usually bring better political and economic outcomes (Chanana 2009, 14).

Another issue that India needs to sort out is its lack of commitment to multilateral and trilateral development cooperation. Even though India has shown its readiness to cooperate under the UN umbrella, it has been hesitant to make use of the prospects of multilateral and trilateral cooperation. For example, it has not fully tapped the potential of cooperation with other countries of BRICS or IBSA. Teaming up with these countries, especially in Africa, and Latin America and the Caribbean would have better outcomes for all the partners.

Discussions on India's challenges for advancing its economic diplomacy would lead us to the domestic challenge. India's domestic situations have not been highly encouraging for New Delhi to go generous abroad. India is still strangled by issues like poverty, illiteracy, unemployment, population explosion, economic inequalities, and lack of infrastructure to support its growing population. There are increasing concerns as to whether India should be using its resources for development cooperation or for its own internal development considering the problems at home (Chanana 2009, 11). While domestic issues would definitely need to be managed and resolved, India is not left with a choice to not undertake its economic diplomacy efforts abroad as increasing trade and investments, ensuring access to energy resources, and strengthening diplomatic ties are all necessary to ensure India's unhindered rise, predominantly for maintaining high economic growth rate. India has to sustain high economic growth to be able to expand its aid programme.

Hence, IDC should focus on India's strengths and address the issues hampering its development cooperation and economic diplomacy. India's forays into economic diplomacy need to be expanded if it has to rise from its emerging power status and fulfil its great power ambitions.

Conclusion

Indian development cooperation has seven decade long history, which is a story of slow and steady development of an underdeveloped country into an emerging power aspiring to have system-shaping capabilities. The marked shift in the volume, scope and geographic reach of India's development cooperation signifies political, economic and strategic significance of development cooperation in advancing its economic diplomacy abroad.

While multiple factors drive India's development cooperation, including trade, investment, quest for energy and resources, regional stability and a seat in the UNSC, what is important for India is also to be recognised as a leader to the countries in the Global South. India's footprint in the developing countries of Asia, Africa and Latin America has been increasing with its growing development assistance programme. However, India has been criticised for resource-extraction, land acquisition, mining activities and its search for new markets in Africa and Latin America. Although trade, investments, search for markets and energy resources comprise India's interests in these continents, India has been keen to build solidarity across the Global South. India, being a developing country that has played a major role in NAM, and its continuing role as a staunch supporter of SSC, it has not shed its Third World identity and speaks on behalf of the developing South in most multilateral forums. In reality, IDC has not brought India desired returns at least in the short term. This is mainly because of the inability to streamline aid and align it with its foreign policy priorities and preferences. For this, New Delhi has to work on a concrete framework on India's development cooperation by bringing together all the stakeholders. However, what India has been successful in creating is goodwill among countries of the Global South.

The successive governments have contributed to India's rise as a development cooperation provider. However, India's development cooperation has been more or less stable despite the change in governments and there has not been any dramatic increase or decrease in the quantum of development cooperation. However, the government under Prime Minister Modi is known for proactive foreign policy and economic diplomacy. During his last tenure (2014–2019), there was substantial increase in India's foreign aid budget. The budget allocation for the year 2019–2020 saw a spike in IDC from the previous years (Mitra 2019). Furthermore, Modi government has been keen to support India's economic diplomacy abroad and has been pushing for greater engagement with both the Global North and the South. However, it is for time to tell if these policies would yield positive results in the long-term. India is keen to ensure a place for itself in the global high table, where it can have a say. However, it considers itself as a developing country of the Global South and does not want to be identified as belonging to the developed countries club by joining OECD. What makes India's assistance different from the traditional donors' aid is that it is anchored on principles of SSC, making IDC more egalitarian, non-conditional and based on mutual gains and win-win situation. India attaches great importance to its developing country identity despite its aspirations to climb up in the international world order. With its long nurtured and cherished Third World identity, it hopes to earn legitimacy both at home and abroad and build a long-lasting relation with its partners based on hope and trust. New Delhi is making clear that it is ready to take more responsibilities in the international system. However, India's rise from an emerging power to a global leader would depend on several domestic and international factors that will all have to be aligned.

References

Bijoy, C.R. (2010), "India: Transiting to a Global Donor, Special Report on South-South Cooperation 2010" [Online: web]. Accessed on 28 October 2010, http://www.realityofaid.org/userfiles/roareports/roareport_3ce2522270.pdf.

Chanana, Dweep. (2009), "India as an Emerging Donor", *Economic and Political Weekly*, 44(12): 11–14.

Chaturvedi, Sachin. (2008), "Emerging Patterns in Architecture for Management of Economic Assistance and Development Cooperation: Implications and Challenges for India" [Online: web]. Accessed on 20 January 2014, saber.eaber.org/intranet/documents/109/1177/RIS_Chaturvedi_2008.pdf.

Chaturvedi, Sachin. (2012), "India's Development Partnership: Key Policy Shifts and Institutional Evolution", *Cambridge Review of International Affairs*, 25(4): 557–577.

Chaturvedi, Sachin. (2016), *The Logic of Sharing: Indian Approaches to South-South Cooperation*, New Delhi: Cambridge University Press.

Chaturvedi, Sachin et al. (2014), "Learning from India's Development Cooperation", IDS Policy Brief, Issue 70 [Online: web]. Accessed on 20 July 2015, http://opendocs.ids.ac.uk/opendocs/bitstream/handle/123456789/4198/AD_ID148_PB;jsessionid=C253823DB526627895C7AF0740404DA9?sequence=1#70_India_Web.pdf.

Chenoy, A. and Joshi, A. (2016), "India: From Technical Cooperation to Trade and Investment", In Gu J. et al. (eds.), *The BRICS in International Development*, London: Palgrave Macmillan.

Embassy of India Kabul. (2016), "India-Afghanistan Relations" [Online: web]. Accessed on 18 May 2016, http://eoi.gov.in/kabul/?0354?000.

Embassy of India Thimphu. (2019), "India-Bhutan Trade Relation". Accessed at https://www.indembthimphu.gov.in/pages.php?id=42.

EXIM Bank. (2013), "Export Lines of Credit: A Safe and Convenient Export Financing Option, Export-Import Bank of India Brochure" [Online: web]. Accessed on 21 April 2016, http://www.eximbankindia.in/sites/default/files/loc-english.pdf.

EXIM Bank. (2015a), "Annual Report 2014–2015" [Online: web]. Accessed on 12 March 2016, http://www.eximbankindia.in/sites/default/files/English%20Annual%20Report_0.pdf.

EXIM Bank. (2015b), "Guidelines on Lines of Credit extended by the Government of India to various countries under the Indian Development and Economic Assistance Scheme (IDEAS), No. 21/3/2015-IDEAS, Ministry of Finance, Department of Economic Affairs, Bilateral Cooperation Division" [Online: web]. Accessed on 20 May 2016, http://www.eximbankindia.in/sites/default/files/C.pdf.

EXIM Bank. (2018), "Deepening South-South Collaboration: An Analysis of Africa and India's Trade and Investment". Accessed at https://www.eximbankindia.in/Assets/Dynamic/PDF/Publication-Resources/SpecialPublications/Deepening-South-South-Collaboration_An-Analysis-of-Africa-and-Indias-Trade-and-Investment.pdf.

GOI. (2003), "Budget 2003–2004 Speech of Jaswant Singh, Minister of Finance and Company Affairs, Government of India" [Online: web]. Accessed on 25 March 2016, http://indiabudget.nic.in/bspeech/bs200304.pdf.

GOI. (2007), "Budget 2007–2008 Speech of P. Chidambaram, Minister of Finance, Government of India" [Online: web]. Accessed on 25 January 2016, http://indiabudget.nic.in/ub2007-08/bs/speecha.htm.

GOI Budget. (2019), "Grants and Loans to Foreign Governments, Expenditure Profile 2019–2020". Accessed at https://www.indiabudget.gov.in/doc/eb/stat20.pdf.

IDCR. (2015), "50 Years of Indian Technical and Economic Cooperation, Indian Development Cooperation Research Report" [Online: web]. Accessed on 20 January 2016, http://www.cprindia.org/sites/default/files/working_papers/IDCR%20Report%20-%2050%20years%20of%20ITEC.pdf.

ITEC. (2014), "50 years of ITEC" [Online: web]. Accessed on 18 May 2016, http://www.mea.gov.in/Uploads/PublicationDocs/24148_REVISED_50_yrs_of_ITEC_brochure.pdf.

ITEC. (2016a), [Online: web]. Accessed on 9 March 2016, http://itec.mea.gov.in/.

ITEC. (2016b), "About ITEC" [Online: web]. Accessed on 9 March 2016, http://itec.mea.gov.in/?1320?000.

Jobelius, Matthias. (2007), *New Powers for Global Change? Challenges for the International Development Cooperation: The Case of India*, Berlin: Friedrich Ebert Stiftung Briefing Paper 5 [Online: web]. Accessed on 10 April 2011, http://www.basas.org.uk/projects/Jobelius.pdf.

MEA. (1963), "Annual Report 1962–1963, Ministry of External Affairs, Government of India" [Online: web]. Accessed on 28 May 2016, http://mealib.nic.in/?pdf2489?000.

MEA. (1964), "Annual Report 1963–1964, Ministry of External Affairs, Government of India". Accessed at https://mealib.nic.in/?pdf2491?000.
MEA. (1965), "Annual Report 1964–1965, Ministry of External Affairs, Government of India" [Online: web]. Accessed on 19 February 2016, http://mealib.nic.in/?pdf2491?000.
MEA. (1967), "Annual Report 1966–1967, Ministry of External Affairs, Government of India" [Online: web]. Accessed on 23 May 2016, http://mealib.nic.in/?pdf2493?000.
MEA. (1970), "Annual Report 1969–1970, Ministry of External Affairs, Government of India" [Online: web]. Accessed on 23 May 2016, http://mealib.nic.in/?pdf2496?000.
MEA. (1995), "Annual Report 1994-1995, Ministry of External Affairs, Government of India" [Online: web]. Accessed on 20 February 2016, https://mealib.nic.in/?2523?000.
MEA. (2012a), "Annual Report 2011–2012, Ministry of External Affairs, Government of India" [Online: web]. Accessed on 18 May 2016, http://www.mea.gov.in/Uploads/PublicationDocs/19337_annual-report-2011-2012.pdf.
MEA. (2012b), "India-Afghanistan Relations, Ministry of External Affairs, Government of India" [Online: web]. Accessed on 18 March 2016, https://www.mea.gov.in/Portal/ForeignRelation/afghanistan-aug-2012.pdf.
MEA. (2012c), "India-Bhutan Relations, Ministry of External Affairs, Government of India" [Online: web]. Accessed on 29 March 2016, https://mea.gov.in/Portal/ForeignRelation/Bhutan-February-2012.pdf.
MEA. (2013a), "Factsheet: India-Nepal Partnership, Ministry of External Affairs, Government of India" [Online: web]. Accessed on 11 May 2016, http://www.mea.gov.in/press-releases.htm?dtl/21920/Fact+Sheet+IndiaNepal+Partnership.
MEA. (2013b), "External Affairs Minister's Speech on "India-Latin America & Caribbean: The Way Forward" at the CII India-LAC Conclave Valedictory Session, Ministry of External Affairs, Government of India" [Online: web]. Accessed on 03 May 2016, http://www.mea.gov.in/Speeches-Statements.htm?dtl/22605/External+Affairs+Ministers+Speech+on+IndiaLatin+America+amp+Caribbean+The+Way+Forward+at+the+CII+IndiaLAC+Conclave+Valedictory+Session.
MEA. (2014), "MEA Outcome Budget 2014–2015, Ministry of External Affairs, Government of India" [Online: web]. Accessed on 11 May 2016, http://www.mea.gov.in/Uploads/PublicationDocs/23954_MEA_Outcome_Budget_ENG_2014-15.pdf.
MEA. (2015a), "Annual Report 2014–2015, Ministry of External Affairs, Government of India" [Online: web]. Accessed on 1 May 2016, http://

www.mea.gov.in/Uploads/PublicationDocs/25009_External_Affairs_2014-2015__English_.pdf.

MEA. (2015b), "India-Sri Lanka Relations, Ministry of External Affairs, Government of India" [Online: web]. Accessed on 29 April 2016, http://www.mea.gov.in/Portal/ForeignRelation/SrilankaBrief_August2015.pdf.

MEA. (2016), "MEA Outcome Budget 2016–2017". Accessed at http://mea.gov.in/Uploads/PublicationDocs/26823_1-MEA_Outcome_2016-17_English_1.pdf.

MEA. (2017), "India-Bangladesh Relations". Accessed at https://mea.gov.in/Portal/ForeignRelation/Bangladesh_September_2017_en.pdf.

MEA. (2018), "Annual Report 2017–2018, Ministry of External Affairs, Government of India". Accessed at http://www.mea.gov.in/Uploads/PublicationDocs/29788_MEA-AR-2017-18-03-02-2018.pdf.

Ministry of Finance. (2012), *Economic Survey 2011–2012*, New Delhi: Oxford University Press.

Mitra, D. (2019), "Six Charts to Make Sense of India's Overall Budget for Foreign Policy", *The Wire*. Accessed at https://thewire.in/diplomacy/budget-mea-foreign-policy-charts.

Mullen, Rani. (2013), "India's Development Assistance: Will it Change the Global Development Finance Paradigm?, Paper presented in the Workshop on Innovation in Governance of Development Finance: Causes, Consequences & the Role of Law Conference, April 8–9, 2013 at Gießen & New York University School of Law" [Online: web]. Accessed on 15 July 2015, http://www.iilj.org/newsandevents/documents/mullen.pdf.

Mullen, Rani. (2014), "IDCR Report: The State of Indian Development Cooperation" [Online: web]. Accessed on 25 August 2015, http://www.cprindia.org/sites/default/files/policy-briefs/Spring_2014_IDCR_Report_the_State_of_Indian_Development_Cooperation.pdf.

Nehru, Jawaharlal. (1946), *The Discovery of India,* New York: John Day Company.

OECD. (2019), "India's Development Co-operation". Accessed at https://www.oecd.org/dac/dac-global-relations/indias-development-co-operation.htm.

PMINEWYORK. (2016), "India and United Nations" [Online: web] Accessed on 22 March 2016, https://www.pminewyork.org/pages.php?id=1989.

Purushothaman, Chithra. (2017), "India's Economic Diplomacy with Ethiopia", *Africa Trends*, 6(2): 8–12. Accessed at https://idsa.in/system/files/page/2015/africatrend_6_2.pdf.

Roychoudhury, Supriya. (2013), "India's External Aid: Lessons and Opportunities", *Economic and Political Weekly*, XLVIII(36): 22–26.

The Colombo Plan. (2016), "History" [Online: web]. Accessed on 2 January 2016, http://www.colombo-plan.org/index.php/about-cps/history/.

The Indian Express. (2015: June 25), "India Pledges USD1 billion Aid for Nepal's Reconstruction Programme" [Online: web]. Accessed on 10 January 2016, http://indianexpress.com/article/india/india-others/india-pledges-usd-1-billion-aid-for-nepals-reconstruction-programme/.

The Indian Express. (2016: January 28), "Project Cost of Afghan Parliament Building" [Online: web]. Accessed on 13 July 2016, http://indianexpress.com/article/india/india-news-india/project-cost-of-afghan-parliament-building/.

UN (United Nations). (1958), "Treaties and International Agreements Registered or Filed and Recorded with the Secretariat of the United Nations", Volume 299, https://treaties.un.org/doc/publication/unts/volume%20299/v299.pdf.

Viswanathan, R. (2019), "Latin America More Vital for Indian Exports Than Many Other Traditional Trading Partners", *The Wire*. Accessed at https://thewire.in/trade/latin-america-india-exports-trading-partners.

WTO. (2013), "India-Africa: South-South Trade and Investment for Development" [Online: web]. Accessed on 22 March 2016, https://www.wto.org/english/tratop_e/devel_e/a4t_e/global_review13prog_e/india_africa_report.pdf.

CHAPTER 6

Comparisons: Brazil, China and India as Development Assistance Providers

Foreign aid evolved as a dominant paradigm under the traditional donors. However, the current state of international development is very different from what it was in the twentieth century. The increasing presence and visibility of the emerging powers as development assistance providers have changed the international development landscape forever. What was generally considered as an exclusively North-South flow of money and resources is now slowly getting accustomed to the idea of South-South Cooperation (SSC) in development. The exclusive competence of the West in development assistance has been challenged by the emerging powers. These emerging powers of the Global South have emerged as an indelible force in international development with growing impact and influence.

In the previous chapters, the three largest development assistance providers of the Global South, Brazil, China and India's development assistance was evaluated and explained in order to understand the emerging powers' development assistance policies, geographical scope, modalities and motivations behind their development assistance. This chapter would analyse these three countries' development cooperation in a comparative perspective to arrive at conclusions on the trajectory of development cooperation of the Global South.

C. Purushothaman, *Emerging Powers, Development Cooperation and South-South Relations*, International Political Economy Series,
https://doi.org/10.1007/978-3-030-51537-9_6

The development assistance policies and patterns of these three countries—Brazil, China and India—show several convergences and divergences. They consider their development cooperation different from that of the OECD-DAC aid and are not part of the Western donors' club. The cornerstone of emerging powers' foreign policy as well as development cooperation policy has been SSC, that made them stand out in the international development landscape.

While it is important to compare these emerging powers and their international development cooperation, the lack of comprehensive and reliable data on each of their development assistance programmes makes it difficult to make useful comparisons in terms of the amount or volume of development assistance provided by them. Even though the exact numbers are not available, the broader patterns and values have been used to compare these three countries' development assistance.

Emerging Powers' Development Cooperation: Definitions

There is no single definition for emerging powers' development assistance. Each country has its own definition for development assistance, which is mostly defined in terms of the modalities of their assistance. Hence, arriving at common definitions will not be feasible until the countries of the Global South decide to institutionalise their development cooperation, where they agree upon a common framework.

Among the three countries, it is only Brazil that has a clearer definition for its development cooperation. It was only in 2011 that Brazil initiated its efforts towards bringing more clarity towards its development cooperation. Until then, there were no official reports on Cobradi, and Brazil had not defined as what constitutes development assistance. Both China and India do not give any specific definition for their development assistance. Their development cooperation is based on the modalities they offer.

The concept of "100% non-repayable grants" offered by Brazil differentiates Cobradi from Indian and Chinese development cooperation. For both China and India, their development assistance need not be 100% grants as it could be any percentage of the grant element. Moreover, debt relief and LOC/concessional loans are included in their development cooperation. Debt relief is not considered as a component of development cooperation by Brazil.

Both the Indian LOCs and Chinese concessional loans are tied to the goods and services from these countries. The EXIM Bank under the Ministry of Finance manages Indian LOCs. Indian LOCs are 75% tied with goods and services from India (EXIM Bank 2015a, 2). China also gives concessional loans, managed by China Exim Bank, and is tied to goods and services from China. For China and India, these loans constitute the majority of their development cooperation to their partners. These are primarily aimed at facilitating their trade and investment opportunities with their partner countries as well as in supporting their domestic firms in expanding their businesses in those countries. This however would not be classified as development cooperation for Brazil, as for them development cooperation is "non-profit" and will not include loans of any kind. China and India are more similar in what constitutes their development assistance. The fact that Brazil does not include its loans to foreign governments as development cooperation might make its development cooperation volume much lesser than what it actually is. However, if its loans are taken into account, the actual volume might increase considerably.

Emerging Powers and Their Institutions for Development Cooperation

The institutionalisation of development cooperation is still an ongoing process. The emerging powers are considering greater institutionalisation as their development cooperation is expanding, making it important to have an agency to administer it. An exclusive agency to manage aid is now in place for all the three countries. Even then, several ministries and actors manage their development cooperation. This is mainly because these institutions have grown incrementally and these countries pull in resources, both material and human resources, from various ministries, which make it feasible to implement projects at lesser budgets.

The institutional set-up of Brazil, China and India shows more similarities than dissimilarities. For all the three countries, there are several institutions managing their development assistance. There is no single development cooperation agency, for any three of them, to manage, coordinate and implement their development assistance. For Brazil, China and India there are specialised agencies, ABC, CIDCA and DPA, respectively, devoted to take care of their development cooperation activities in partner countries. However, these agencies are just one of those several institutions involved in the business. The creation of these agencies has done little towards coordinating their development assistance.

For Brazil, more than 100 government agencies and many more federated states and municipalities take care of Cobradi (IPEA 2014). There is little or no data exchanged by these ministries and there is no centralised record keeping of Cobradi projects and its volume. Despite the existence of ABC as a central agency for exclusively managing Brazil's incoming and outgoing assistance, there is no rule that requires development assistance to be diverted through ABC. Instead, most ministries directly manage their development assistance funds without channelling it through the ABC. Mostly, ABC is entrusted with the responsibility to handle the assistance through the MRE while other ministries deal with their development assistance partners on their own. Hence, the role of ABC is not more than an agent of the MRE.

For India, three ministries, MEA, MoF and MoCI, manage IDC and there is a lack of coordination among all three of these ministries. All the institutions involved in development cooperation of Brazil and India mostly work in silos. Furthermore, it was alarming to see that even the three divisions of the DPA—DPA-I, DPA-II and DPA-III—do not work in coordination. During author's interview with the officials of these three divisions, it was evident that there is a lack of coordination between these divisions and at times one division is not aware of the workings of the other. This brings less coherence into IDC. Further, the lack of a concrete development assistance policy for India also stems from India's inability to bring all its institutions together to develop a pragmatic development cooperation policy.

China established CIDCA in 2018 and hence it is too early to judge whether all the development cooperation decisions will eventually rest with the agency. The main institutions that used to manage Chinese development assistance are the Ministry of Commerce (MOFCOM), Ministry of Finance, Ministry of Foreign Affairs and the China Exim Bank. All the related departments of the Chinese government communicate and cooperate with each other regularly. Despite the involvement of several institutions in the disbursal of Chinese development assistance, China was able to bring coherence into its development assistance programme mainly because of its disciplined institutional framework for development assistance and the interconnectedness of these institutions involved.

For all the three countries, the institutionalisation process has been rather too slow. Brazil has the oldest development cooperation agency among the three countries. Brazil set up ABC in 1987. However, it took India more than 60 years, after it started its development assistance, to set up DPA in 2012. And, CIDCA is just a year old. Despite all these institutional constraints, Brazil, China and India continue to give development cooperation to other developing countries. The volume of their assistance and their visibility as development assistance provider has been on the rise, especially in the twenty-first century.

Development Assistance Policies

None of the three countries have any concrete development cooperation policies or frameworks. There is no official statement released by any of these countries regarding their development cooperation policies leaving enough space for ambiguity and confusion. The policies that are said to be the principles driving emerging powers' development assistance came out gradually into the public domain through meticulous research on the patterns of their development cooperation, their choice of recipients and from the speeches of the leadership.

The most common feature of Brazil, China and India's development cooperation is that they emphasise on SSC, based on respect for sovereignty of partners, non-interference in their domestic affairs, no-conditionalities attached, equality, mutual benefit, demand-driven approach and win-win situation. They emphasise that they consider their partners as equals and vouch for horizontal development cooperation with them. It is because of their support for SSC that they refuse to consider themselves as donors and their development cooperation as foreign aid.

For Brazil, multilateral cooperation and trilateral cooperation form important vehicles for allocating its development cooperation. Even though bilateral SSC is important for Brazil, triangular partnerships are considered as "valuable mechanisms to strengthen the impact of development initiatives" (Corrêa 2009, 3). Most of Brazil's development cooperation is given through multilateral organisations. Brazil gives about 81.4% in multilateral assistance especially to the institutions under the UN umbrella. Brazil also cooperates with the OECD countries for triangular cooperation in other developing countries of the Global South. However, both India and China prefer bilateral development cooperation to multilateral assistance. Unlike Brazil, they do not prefer to engage in triangular cooperation involving the OECD countries.

However, Brazil, China and India are keen to cooperate under the UN umbrella. They consider UN as more egalitarian organisation when compared to OECD-DAC. For them, UN is a platform that gives them adequate space for discussions and debates on development, and is considered to be unbiased. For this reason, they have been active members of the DCF.

Because these countries do not belong to the OECD-DAC, they have no obligations to provide development assistance based on any set rules and regulations. Therefore, each of them has their own approach to development and their development assistance policy is based on their own preferences and interests. None of them publicly disseminate comprehensive data on their development cooperation. The lack of transparency and absence of impact evaluation or measurement of their development cooperation could be considered as major challenge in analysing their development assistance.

All the three countries achieved considerable economic growth in the twenty-first century and are important global economic powers. They are keen to share their own experiences of economic growth and development and their policy successes. These countries focus on their strengths, especially technology and knowledge sharing that could be considered as a good match for their partner countries. Existence of several features that are common to the development cooperation policies of the three countries emphasise on the priorities of emerging powers as development assistance providers.

All the three countries were keen not to be part of the developed donors' club and wanted to be considered as a part of the Global South. However, the policies of Brazil has shifted since 2016 in favour of OECD, in which it is currently seeking membership, thereby going in the path of Latin American neighbours including Mexico, Colombia and Chile. This is in sharp contrast with what China and India's preferences are. Until recently, Brazil was also clear about preserving is status as a Southern development assistance provider. However, the change in leadership has had an effect on the policies of the country. With the right-wing government under Bolsonaro in power, Brazil is increasingly moving into the OECD-fold, which would completely change how Brazil has traditionally perceived its development cooperation.

Geographical Patterns

Brazil, China and India have expanded their geographical reach to far-off countries and regions. Their increased presence in most continents has raised curiosity and interest in their development cooperation activities. The geographical patterns of the development assistance flows signify the prioritising of certain countries over others and the factors behind the selection of their beneficiaries.

While India and Brazil focus on their region, Chinese development assistance is focussed on Africa. The trends suggest that more than 80% of Indian grants and loans were given to South Asia, 68% of Cobradi goes to Latin America and the Caribbean and 51.8% of Chinese development cooperation flows to Africa.

Both Brazil and India give maximum assistance to their neighbours. This clearly demonstrates the importance of neighbourhood for these countries and their aim to maintain their influence in the region through their development cooperation. However, China gives maximum assistance to Africa, which clarifies that its priorities have in recent years shifted from its neighbourhood to other economically and strategically important areas around the world. China has expanded its footprint around the world, much more than Brazil or India. Even though Brazil and India have expanded their development cooperation to Africa, their own region continues to be their priority.

Being the largest economic and political entity in Latin America and the Caribbean, Brazil's foreign policy has been focussed on exerting political and economic influence in its region. Brazil's development cooperation also aligns with its foreign policy priorities. Apart from Haiti, other major partners include its close neighbours, Chile, Argentina, Peru, Paraguay and Colombia. Brazil's forays into Africa are driven by linguistic ties followed by quest for energy and natural resources as well as trade and investments. More than 75% of Cobradi going to African continent is for the PALOPs (IPEA 2014, 21). The driving factor has been strengthening its linguistic, historical and cultural ties with these countries. Most of the assistance to these countries is in the areas of education, technical assistance, agriculture and humanitarian assistance. Furthermore, Brazil is also trying to expand its development cooperation to other parts of Africa, including Francophone and Anglophone Africa.

Initially, Chinese development assistance was based on ideological and political considerations, and was therefore mostly given to its close neighbours in its region and the Communist countries. Presently, China gives at least half of its total assistance to Africa (White Paper 2014). For China, Africa has become a priority region with its increasing trade and investments, quest for energy and natural resources and search for new markets. Apart from the strategic economic ties, diplomatic considerations have also dominated China's increasing development assistance to Africa. The focus areas of China's development assistance in Africa are large infrastructure projects, agriculture, health and technical assistance. Asia received 30.5% of Chinese development assistance from 2010 to 2012. Its neighbourhood has been of great political and strategic significance to China. However, its development assistance to its neighbourhood has slowly declined. This is attributed to what China aims to achieve through its foreign assistance. China's focus has been to achieve economic benefits through its development assistance and economic diplomacy, which it has been doing in Africa. Furthermore, China has become more assertive in its region with its increasing political and economic weight, no more relying entirely on soft power and economic diplomacy. Regarding political and strategic interests in its region, China does not hesitate to use hard power to achieve its interests as well as to reinforce its position as a dominant power in East, South and Southeast Asia. Economic interests in Asia were taken care of through its large-scale infrastructure and connectivity projects. China's development cooperation in Latin America and the Caribbean is focussed on trade and investment opportunities, energy and natural resources as well as exploring and capturing new markets. Further, China is strengthening its ties with Africa and Latin America for diplomatic support at various international forums. It also has expanded its ties with even the smallest countries in these regions in order to garner support for its one-China policy.

For India, South Asia continues to be the topmost priority. More than 80% of all grants and loans from India are allocated to this region. The important concerns for India are maintaining regional stability and increasing its goodwill in its region. India is also expanding its development assistance allocation from Asia to Africa and Latin America and the Caribbean. What drives IDC to the countries in Africa and Asia has been trade and investments, energy and natural resources, and search for new markets. Even though the IDC volume is much lesser to these regions when compared to the volume of IDC given to its neighbours, it is still important to note that India has been keen to strengthen its ties with the Global South through its development assistance.

While all these countries started their development cooperation with providing assistance to their neighbourhood, there has been a strategic shift in China's geographical outreach through development assistance. While India and Brazil continue to give maximum development assistance to their neighbours, China gives maximum assistance to Africa. Both India and Brazil's regional focus has remained the same since the beginning of their development cooperation activities in the mid-twentieth century. But China has moved on confidently to pursue its changing interests through its development assistance programme to the Global South.

Modalities

Brazil, China and India started their development assistance in the form of technical cooperation and capacity-building which was later expanded to varied sectors including infrastructure, agriculture, health and humanitarian assistance. Infrastructure development became a key component of their development assistance from the very beginning.

In case of Brazil, maximum Cobradi goes into multilateral assistance (70%) (IPEA 2014). This includes assistance for UN peace-keeping (36%) and expenditures with international organisations (34%). For India, technical and economic cooperation is of topmost priority as this has proved to be helpful in creating a lot of goodwill and solidarity for India as its technical cooperation has been a huge success in many countries and there is growing demand for cooperation from the partner countries. In China's case, maximum focus has been on economic infrastructure (44.8%), and social and public infrastructure (27.6%) which amounts to a total of 72.4% for infrastructure projects. Infrastructure development has been a priority area since the initial days of China's development assistance and it continues to remain so.

For Brazil, the only modality is grants as the loans it give are not considered as part of Cobradi. However, for China and India, loans with varied rates of interests also form an important modality. These loans are usually tied to the goods and services from China and India.

Apart from grants, China gives interest-free loans and concessional loans, which are tied to Chinese goods and services, making it the most preferred modality. Even though China's grants and interest-free loans have helped fulfilling its broad diplomatic objectives, concessional loans have proved to be of greater benefit as they facilitate Chinese trade, investments and businesses in its partner countries.

For India, grants, ITEC and LOCs form the three main modalities of its development assistance. India provides more assistance in the form of ITEC and LOCs as opposed to grants. The surge in LOCs points to India's growing trade and commercial interests that are attached to its development assistance. Furthermore, ITEC programmes have also been India's key development cooperation modality that focus on India's strength as a competent entity in providing technical assistance and capacity-building that has generated immense goodwill for India.

While India and China have directly incorporated their economic interests into their development assistance programmes, LOCs for India and concessional loans for China, Brazil has not directly incorporated any economic interests into Cobradi. While tied assistance from China and India could be considered as a form of conditionality, Brazil has kept itself out of this by making grants as the only component of Cobradi.

Motivations Behind Emerging Powers' Development Assistance

The official position of most of the emerging powers is that their development cooperation is driven by altruism. However, the previous chapters on Brazil, China and India's development cooperation clearly demonstrate that these countries are driven by varied motivations to provide development assistance to their peers. This could range from altruism to political, economic and strategic interests. Their development cooperation inevitably entails a degree of national interest and is not completely divorced from their broader foreign policy objectives.

Based on the geographical coverage of their development assistance, we can conclude that for India and Brazil, the priority is their region. India gives maximum assistance to South Asia and Brazil to Latin America and the Caribbean. Regional stability, building solidarity and goodwill, expanding trade and investments, and building historical and cultural ties remain the important agendas. Within this, regional stability and building solidarity and goodwill seem to take primacy over economic interests. China, however, cuts a different picture with economic and strategic interests playing most vital role in deciding its recipients. It gives maximum assistance to Africa followed by Asia, and Latin America and the Caribbean.

Furthermore, both Brazil and India give maximum assistance to Africa after their respective regions. In Africa, PALOPs get maximum assistance from Brazil. This is based on the linguistic, cultural and historical ties with the region. India also has close historical ties with Africa because of its role in their anti-colonial struggle as well as its role in NAM. Moreover, a common thread in Brazil, China and India's development assistance to Africa is strengthening their trade, investment and businesses in Africa. They also have interest in Africa's energy and natural resources. Another reason for pushing stronger ties with far-off countries has been garnering diplomatic support from these countries through stronger bilateral ties. Brazil, China and India seek diplomatic support in international fora and consider development assistance as an important tool for fulfilling their interests. While China seeks support for its one-China policy, both Brazil and India are seeking support for a permanent seat in the reformed UNSC. For all the three countries, diplomatic support is crucial in deciding the flow of their development assistance.

Another aspect that drives development assistance is trade and investments. These countries are on a constant look out for new markets. For China and India, Africa and Latin America are important trade and investment destinations and have been expanding their footprint in these regions. Even though Brazil is pushing for greater ties with Africa, it is not eager to expand its presence into Asia.

Regarding the modalities, Brazil gives Cobradi as full grants which could be considered as more of philanthropic in nature. However, China and India give loans with varying rates of interest. Chinese concessional loans and Indian LOCs are tied to goods and services from China and India, respectively. This is targeted to facilitate their trade and investments with their partners. Furthermore, both China and India prefer bilateral assistance over multilateral assistance, which gives them greater grip over their partner's choices. On the other hand, Brazil gives maximum assistance through multilateral and triangular cooperation. Bilateral assistance is useful in influencing partners because of the scope of direct engagement with partners. Multilateral assistance brings lesser leverage to the development assistance provider because of the lack of direct ties between the partners. Hence, Brazil could be said as slightly less strategically inclined than China or India as far as its development cooperation is concerned. This could be linked to the fact that Brazil is lagging behind in terms of economic growth and after Lula, the domestic turmoil has left very little space for foreign policy as a priority for the leadership.

The motivations behind Brazil, China and India's development assistance show more similarities than dissimilarities. The main agendas include trade and investment, quest for energy and natural resources; search for new markets; establishing diplomatic ties; and building historical, cultural and linguistic ties. For Brazil and India, a permanent seat in a reformed UNSC is also high on the list. Since China is already a P-5 member state, China's prioritises other factors to serve its interests. All three of them have set priorities as to suit their foreign policy requirements and interests. The only difference among these emerging powers would be the level of importance they attach to each of these motivations.

There are criticisms against the emerging powers' development assistance, both from the traditional donors and from their development cooperation partners. The traditional donors blame emerging powers for supporting rogue governments and giving aid without prescribing conditionalities like democratisation and good governance. Further, there are concerns among partner countries that the emerging powers, especially China, is exploiting their resources. There was backlash from several countries in Africa against China. For example, Ghana deported several Chinese workers from its gold mines where they were involved in illegal mining work (*The Guardian* 2013, July 15). Similarly, India and Brazil have been blamed for allegedly influencing the domestic politics of Nepal and Haiti, respectively. India and China are also accused of acquisition of large areas of land in Africa.

While national interest and strategic motivations might drive emerging powers' development cooperation, they are not devoid of altruistic motivations. Their technical cooperation and capacity-building efforts are all considered to be of great benefit to their partner countries. Also, emerging powers are quick to respond to humanitarian crisis and give humanitarian assistance to countries in distress. Further, they also provide need-based and demand-driven assistance to partners. For these countries, building solidarity and promoting goodwill are also of great importance which will in turn help establishing friendly relations with partners and gaining legitimacy. Also, these countries being regional powers are entrusted with the responsibility of building regional stability and solidarity. Moreover, these countries are also aiming to build lasting political and economic solidarity with the Global South.

For all the three countries, development cooperation is an instrument of economic statecraft. However, there is no single motivation that is driving their development cooperation, but a multitude of them. Emerging powers are able to use foreign aid for concrete political and economic gains without using any coercive strategies.

Effectiveness of Development Cooperation

Brazil, China and India do not adhere to the international standards of aid effectiveness that has been developed by the traditional donors. While this could be attributed to their absence in the traditional donors club, they have categorically stated that they do not give "aid" but "development cooperation". The argument is that because they do not give "aid" there comes no reason to join the aid effectiveness debates initiated and conducted by the traditional donors.

What is interesting here is that even though they do not want to join the traditional donors' aid effectiveness platforms, they could have initiated their own mechanisms to understand their development cooperation, its implementation in the partner country and its effectiveness. However, the emerging powers who give development assistance, including Brazil, China and India, have neither constituted any agency nor entrusted any organisation to undertake such measures nor are there any initiatives to set up any agency for impact evaluation and assessment of their development cooperation. One of the reasons why they are not initiating impact evaluation mechanisms is that it could be too expensive for both the partners and that money could be invested for other development activities.

However, the lack of transparency has brought little benefits for these countries. The regular dissemination of data could have been beneficial for their own assessment of the effectiveness of their assistance on their partner countries. Furthermore, it would also have enabled them and their partners in rectifying the flaws in their assistance and adopting more efficient mechanisms to provide support.

These countries need to progressively develop structures for monitoring and evaluation of development cooperation to create more legitimacy of its assistance programme. Apart from individual donor countries, multilateral donor agencies and civil society and private sector need to be engaged to ensure the legitimacy and effectiveness of the reforms (Burall et al. 2006, 13). The recipient countries need to be engaged into understand their needs and concerns which could help make aid more effective.

This will also give the recipients assurance and a feeling of security as they begin to understand the nuances of assistance from emerging powers, thereby bringing in more support for their projects.

Competition and Cooperation Among Brazil, China and India

The similarities and dissimilarities among these countries also give rise to enough scope for cooperation as well as competition.

Scope for Cooperation

Even though the scope for cooperation between emerging powers is plentiful, these countries have not utilised their full potential for development cooperation. Even though they are part of important groupings like BRICS or IBSA, they have not been using the full potential of these platforms to cooperate with each other for development assistance. BRICS being one of the most important groupings consisting of all three of these countries could be an important platform for working on development cooperation. Though BRICS is in its formative phase, there is ample scope for cooperation that these three countries should explore. Other groupings like IBSA and BASIC are all important groupings of the emerging powers that could be used for enhancing development cooperation to the Global South. Despite the fact that these institutions lack much-needed political and economic muscle, these institutions remain important considering the fact that these emerging powers could benefit immensely by cooperating with each other.

Apart from cooperating in multilateral forums, these countries could advance trilateral development cooperation in the Global South which could be to their advantage. The fact that these countries can contribute to different aspects of development of other developing countries makes it even more crucial for them to work together. There are prospects for trilateral cooperation, especially in Africa, where all three of them have high stakes. While these countries might compete with each other in their own region, prospects of cooperation in Africa are high.

Also, these countries could think of coming to an acceptable common definition of development assistance which could be a useful first step in the direction of bringing the perspectives of the Global South to the international aid architecture. This would also bring more coherence in their development assistance and take out the ambiguity surrounding their assistance because of the lack of proper transparency and accountability.

Further, these countries could also use the best practices from other emerging powers in their own region to enhance their development efforts in Global South. Even though, China and India are making forays into Latin America and the Caribbean, Brazil has not been looking East of Africa for its development cooperation. Brazil could cooperate with China and India, especially in agriculture and technical assistance in Asia. Brazil has not been in competition with China or India. However, China and India are competing in different countries for greater influence, especially in South Asia and Africa. China has an edge over other countries because they lack the economic weight and the political muscle that China has and they cannot match China's deep pockets. However, with whatever little resources they have, Brazil and India are pushing for greater influence in the Global South.

Areas of Competition

While there is ample scope for cooperation, there also exists cut-throat competition between emerging powers. This is especially true for China and India, which are close neighbours and competitors in their region. China and India have fought one war and have border disputes which have hampered any prospect of enhanced cooperation. Also, China's assistance to Pakistan has been a disturbing factor for New Delhi since long. China is also unhappy with India's support to Tibetan refugees and its involvement in giving refuge to Dalai-Lama. Another important factor has been China's efforts in distancing its close neighbours from India. Despite India's efforts in undoing the damage done by China, it has not been successful in taking its neighbours into confidence. There are also instances when their neighbours have played one against the other escalating tension in the region and hampering their bilateral relations. For example, Nepal has been using one against the other so that none of them could have an upper hand in deciding Nepal's domestic matters through development cooperation. Furthermore, India has been clear not to join BRI as the CPEC passes through the disputed territory of Kashmir, and China has not paid heed to India's reservations, which has prompted India not to respond to China's calls to join BRI. However, India is a partner in China-led AIIB, where India is also the largest borrower (Iwanek 2019), with 10 projects already approved and three under consideration (AIIB 2019). Despite political tussle between the two countries, they have been keen to continue with their economic ties.

However, Brazil seems to be less in competition with India or China. Geographic distance has helped in maintaining this cordiality in relationships with these countries. Yet, the increasing footprint of China and India in Africa and Latin America has led to some uneasiness and discomfort in its relationship with both China and India. The external interference in its turf has not gone down well with Brazil and has been trying to regain its influence in its region. Nevertheless, Brazil has also welcomed investments from China especially for infrastructure building and transport. Apart from the extra source of money, the realisation that the presence of China in the region could dilute the influence of the US has also prompted Brazil as well as other countries in the region to welcome China.

Conclusion

Despite the fact that Brazil, China and India are emerging powers that provide development assistance, there are several similarities and dissimilarities existing in their development assistance policies and patterns. Emerging powers as development assistance providers are not a homogeneous community.

Historically, these three emerging powers, Brazil, China and India, started their development cooperation by giving assistance to their neighbouring countries in the mid-twentieth century. All three countries were former colonies that could achieve high economic growth rates. They transformed themselves from recipients to development assistance providers despite being developing countries with severe domestic challenges, and limited money and resources at their disposal. They continue to receive aid and provide development assistance, a dual role that they have been playing for more than six decades.

Brazil, China and India prefer to be considered as developing countries of the Global South and vouch for SSC both in their foreign policy and economic diplomacy. Even though their development assistance is small in volume when compared to the traditional donors, they began to practice a development assistance design that is different from the traditional donor's foreign aid. Their own experiences of being a recipient resulted in bringing new ideas into the international aid architecture that is more in sync with the development concerns of the South and is based on equality and solidarity among the partners.

In the twenty-first century, the emerging powers' development assistance has gained greater momentum. They have increased their volume and are making their presence felt. Currently, the emerging powers are a heterogeneous group with their own development assistance programme that share similarities as well as dissimilarities, considering the diverse group they are.

In the case of definition for development cooperation, there is no single definition as what it means for emerging powers. It keeps changing from country to country. For Brazil, it is entirely comprised of grants; but for China and India, apart from grants, it also constitutes concessional loans that are tied to goods and services from their country. This has been helping China and India facilitate trade and investments with their partners.

Regarding institutions, all the three countries have several institutions managing their development cooperation. There is no central agency that coordinates, facilitates and implements their development assistance, despite having separate institutions set up for exclusively taking care of their development cooperation. These countries have created institutions for development cooperation according to their interests and preferences. The evolution of their institutions for international development has been rather slow, ad hoc but steady. However, these institutions were not made with the vision and mandate as it should have ideally been.

The development cooperation policies of Brazil, China and India are based on SSC. They push for horizontal development cooperation that is based on equality and goodwill. By giving assistance based on SSC, these countries hope to gain legitimacy and support from the countries of the Global South. Hence, they distance themselves from the traditional donors' club, OECD-DAC, and hence do not have the obligation to follow the rules and guidelines made by the developed countries. Therefore, each country has its own policy for development cooperation based on their interests and preferences. However, none of these countries publicly disseminate the data on their development cooperation. Lack of transparency, accountability and the absence of impact evaluation are the major roadblocks in measuring the precise volume of their development assistance.

Furthermore, the geographical outreach of their development cooperation demonstrates that emerging powers are continuously expanding their footprint in the Global South through their development cooperation. For Brazil and India, their immediate neighbourhood continues to be the priority and maximum assistance is allocated to these countries. But for China, the focus has been Africa. This signifies the changing foreign policy priorities of China and its evolving global power ambitions. Further, the trends of development assistance flows also demonstrate the primary motivations driving these countries. While Brazil and India gives more priority to regional solidarity and strategic considerations, China is more inclined to fulfilling its economic and commercial interests through its development assistance. All the three countries also focus on trade and investments, energy and natural resources, and diplomatic support at international platforms. The motivations behind emerging powers' development assistance are more or less similar. The difference is only in the levels of importance attached to their interests that they hope to achieve through development assistance. Yet, their development assistance is not just driven by strategic motivations, they are also involved in humanitarian cooperation, and technical cooperation and capacity-building that are considered to be mostly altruistic and intended to promote solidarity and goodwill among their partners.

Regarding modalities of assistance, China and India are more similar. They facilitate trade and investments through their concessional loans and LOCs. However, Brazil gives assistance as grants and hence does not explicitly promote its economic and commercial interests in the partner countries. Furthermore, Brazil prefers multilateral assistance to bilateral assistance. China and India give maximum assistance through bilateral means which gives them more leverage over their recipients.

The presence of the emerging powers has transformed the international development architecture, dominated by the Western countries. These countries have bought their own rules into development assistance and have been trying to carve out a niche of their own. Their efforts in the field of development cooperation have been commendable albeit their limitations in terms of financial resources and domestic constraints. Most of them are regional powers and development cooperation has helped in internationalisation of their political, economic, commercial and diplomatic interests.

References

AIIB. (2019), Approved Projects. *Asia Infrastructure Investment Bank* [Online: web]. Accessed on 8 September 2019, https://www.aiib.org/en/projects/approved/.

Burall, Simon et al. (2006), *Reforming the International Aid Architecture: Options and Ways Forward*, Working Paper 278. London: Overseas Development Institute [Online: web]. Accessed at http://www.odi.org.uk/resources/download/616.pdf.

Corrêa, M. L. (2009), Policy Dialogue on Development Co-operation Mexico City, 28–29 September 2009 [Online: web]. Accessed on 25 December 2015, http://www.oecd.org/dac/dac-global-relations/43876987.pdf.

EXIM Bank. (2015a), *Guidelines on Lines of Credit Extended by the Government of India to Various Countries Under the Indian Development and Economic Assistance Scheme (IDEAS)*, No. 21/3/2015-IDEAS, Ministry of Finance, Department of Economic Affairs, Bilateral Cooperation Division [Online: web]. Accessed at http://www.eximbankindia.in/sites/default/files/C.pdf.

IPEA. (2014), *Brazilian Cooperation for International Development 2010*. Brasilia: Institute for Applied Economic research.

Iwanek K. (2019), Fully Invested: India Remains the China-led AIIBs Biggest Borrower. *The Diplomat* [Online: web]. Accessed at https://thediplomat.com/2019/09/fully-invested-india-remains-the-china-led-aiibs-biggest-borrower/.

The Guardian. (2013: 15th July), "Ghana Deports Thousands in Crackdown on Illegal Chinese Goldminers" [Online: web]. Accessed at https://www.theguardian.com/world/2013/jul/15/ghana-deports-chinese-goldminers.

White Paper. (2014), *China's Foreign Aid*, Information Office of the State Council of the People's Republic of China [Online: web]. Accessed at http://ssc.undp.org/content/dam/ssc/dgspaces/China/files/China%202nd%20White%20Paper%20on%20Foreign%20Aid%202014.pdf.

CHAPTER 7

Conclusion

Foreign aid has since long occupied a prominent place in debates on international development. However, perceptions of its role and significance have changed dramatically over the years. Foreign aid, as a foreign policy tool, initiated by the Western countries had mixed motivations, strategic as also symbolic, which is expected to be met through the aid-giving. With the Marshall Plan in 1948, the US set an example of how foreign aid can be used as a mode to fulfil the national interest of the donor. With the passing of time, the West has used foreign aid as a leverage to affect the policies of the recipient countries and to gain access to markets and natural resources. However, the motives behind aid-giving have never been straight and simple. The donor motivations are highly complicated and vary from donor to donor. Although strategic self-interest remains the single strongest influence on the allocation of aid; the quest for natural resources, markets and the ambition to wield power has been some of the variables that have been motivating the donors to give aid.

For recipient countries, foreign aid has mostly proved to be a bane rather than a boon in many cases. They are forced to comply with donor's interests and strict conditionalities, ranging from privatisation to democratisation and institutional reforms for good governance. All this is known to adversely impact their domestic policies because of the top-down approach of foreign aid. Notwithstanding this, equally notable is the fact that foreign aid still continues to hold despite having its inherent

C. Purushothaman, *Emerging Powers, Development Cooperation and South-South Relations*, International Political Economy Series,
https://doi.org/10.1007/978-3-030-51537-9_7

flaws and limitations for both the donors and the recipients, and it has been invariably used as an instrument of economic statecraft.

Keeping in mind the demands of the developing countries to mitigate the inequalities inherent in the global economy, the UN set an aid target for the developed countries in the year 1970. Under this, the developed countries were expected to meet the UN target of 0.7% of GNI as official development assistance. Only a few countries have reached this target and a very few manage to cross this which shows that the West is quite reluctant and disinterested in bridging these gaps.

Earlier, aid used to be largely a unidirectional flow of money and resources, i.e. from the richer industrialised countries to the poorer developing or underdeveloped countries. It was largely a flow of resources from the Global North to the Global South. However, this has been changing with the increasing presence of emerging powers as development assistance providers that are pushing for increased SSC in international aid architecture. The increasing development assistance from these countries has transformed the international aid architecture established by the traditional donors' club of the OECD-DAC.

Attendant to the changing face of the global order, many developing countries that were net recipients of aid till recently have started to give development assistance to other fellow developing countries. Propelled by the high economic growth achieved by the emerging powers of the Global South in the late 20th century, South-South development cooperation started gaining momentum in the international aid architecture. However, SSC in development assistance is not new as these emerging powers have been involved in giving development assistance to their peers since the mid-twentieth century. Counting years, their assistance is as old as the traditional donors' foreign aid. The major difference is that they are playing a dual role, both as a recipient of traditional donors' aid and as a provider of assistance to other developing countries. This made their development assistance unique in approach and perspective.

The emerging powers' development assistance is based on the principles of SSC, including equality, respect for sovereignty, non-interference in domestic affairs of the partners, no-conditionalities, demand-driven approach and mutual benefit (Mawdsley 2012; Chenoy et al. 2016; Bergamaschi and Duran 2017). By bringing up the idea of horizontal cooperation in development assistance, the emerging powers put the recipient countries at par with themselves, whereby they are partners in discussing and debating their needs and concerns on development assistance that flows into their country. This novel approach from emerging powers put the hierarchical donor-recipient relationship employed by the traditional donors under the scanner. Further, by calling the recipient countries as partners, they try to build their relationship on the basis of friendship, trust and solidarity with the developing country. These instances were completely new to the international aid system that was dominated by the ideas of the developed countries of the West.

Therefore, the emerging powers' development cooperation became increasingly appealing to their partners. Apart from the principles of SSC, the emerging powers' development cooperation had more features that could help their partner countries to walk on the path of development. For the partner countries, the emerging powers' own policy experiences of achieving high economic growth and development could be of great relevance in building similar development strategies in their countries. Further, the technology and expertise offered by the emerging powers are found to be of very good match for the level of economic and institutional development of the partner countries. Furthermore, the emerging countries' experience as a colony and their development trajectory are considered as a successful model of development for countries that have historically been through colonial subjugation (ODI 2010, 2). Moreover, their experience as a recipient of traditional donors' aid gives them a better understanding of the needs and constraints faced by developing countries as aid recipients as well as the limitations and flaws of traditional aid.

The increasing prominence of the emerging powers as development assistance providers has challenged the role of the Global North as the only group of donors in the international aid architecture. They have been critical of not only the role of emerging powers as development assistance providers but also of their development cooperation policies. They criticise the emerging powers on several grounds. Firstly, they are criticised for limited availability of data regarding their development assistance volumes (O'Keefe 2007, 6; Manning 2006; Gu et al. 2016; Bergamaschi and Tickner 2017; Mthembu 2018). The lack of transparency and accountability has been one of the important points raised against the emerging powers. Further, emerging powers are blamed for their economic, political, commercial and strategic motivations behind their development cooperation. It is understood that the emerging powers' aid-giving is governed by several motivations, depending on their priorities (Mthembu 2018). They are also targeted for providing assistance to corrupt and undemocratic regimes, which could undermine efforts of the OECD-DAC, which claims to give aid according to the merit of the recipients.

On the other hand, the traditional donors consider themselves as superior to the emerging powers as they follow strict guidelines and rules set by the OECD-DAC and they regularly publicise their data on foreign aid. However, traditional donors have long been criticised for imposing harsh conditionalities on the recipients, for using their aid to fulfil their strategic interests as well as for supporting the donor-recipient hierarchy where the recipients are considered inferior. Hence, the change in approach from an unequal and conditionality-based aid of the traditional donors to a balanced and egalitarian engagement of the emerging powers is rather novel and helps in garnering more support than criticisms from the partners.

However, emerging powers are not a homogenous group. There are many convergences and divergences in their approaches to development cooperation. They share similarities and dissimilarities among themselves, and with the traditional donors. The three emerging powers—Brazil, China and India—are the key development assistance providers of the Global South. As regional powers and emerging global powers, their contribution to international aid architecture is increasingly important.

Brazil, China and India do not belong to the OECD-DAC and give assistance based on the principles of SSC. They have been trying to create a new discourse on development assistance based on SSC. These countries have been aiming at making their own definitions, institutions, development cooperation policies and agendas. Even while these countries continue to assert their status as a developing country of the Global South, they are also trying to reposition themselves into a more influential and legitimate status in international politics. Despite the varied constraints and challenges confronting these emerging powers, they are showing their readiness to play the leadership role not only in their respective regions but also in the developing Global South.

While several similarities define Brazil, China and India as development assistance providers, there are several dissimilarities that make them equally distinct. All three countries have different definitions for what they consider as development assistance. Unlike the traditional donors, there is no single definition that defines emerging powers' development assistance. Their modalities of aid delivery also differ considerably. Further, they have different institutional set-up for managing their development assistance. This is also in sharp contrast to the OECD-DAC aid that is guided by established rules and regulations.

Further, emerging powers' development assistance is based on their foreign policy interests and preferences. For both Brazil and India, the geographical patterns of development assistance indicate the importance they attach to their respective regions. Brazil has been involved in developing closer relationship with countries in Latin America and the Caribbean and has been a torch-bearer of regional solidarity because it is the largest economy in the region and other countries look up to it for taking regional initiatives as well as in implementing those. For India, regional stability and support from its smaller neighbouring countries has been a priority. Being the largest country in the region and the largest democracy in the world, India, to a large extend, assumes the responsibility of maintaining peace and stability in the South Asian region. Furthermore, it has been facing challenges from its rivals in the region, China and Pakistan, which makes it important for India to maintain its influence in the region and use its development cooperation as an instrument of economic statecraft. However, for China, the African continent has become a priority, especially to ensure its trade and investments, energy and natural resources, and diplomatic support at international forums. In recent years, China's neighbourhood is not the highest priority when its development assistance patterns are taken into consideration. However, China makes sure to retain hegemony in its region through the use of its economic, political, military and diplomatic clout.

Emerging powers are also expanding their footprint into far-off continents which were earlier not included in their development cooperation map. Initially, all these countries focussed on allocating their development assistance in their region and slowly expanded it to other parts of the world. Brazil expanded its development cooperation to PALOPs, the main reason being strengthening its linguistic, cultural and historical ties with these countries as well as to gain their diplomatic support in international organisations. Brazil's trade and investments in Africa have increased considerably with the increase in its development assistance to the region. Further, it has been slowly expanding its base from PALOPs to other countries in Africa. Similarly, India has also extending its development cooperation to countries in Africa and Latin America and the Caribbean. The key motivations behind India's assistance to these regions have been trade and investments, energy and natural resources and diplomatic support in international forums. Both India and Brazil are also eyeing for a permanent membership in an expanded UNSC. The main motivations behind Chinese development assistance in Africa and Latin America and the Caribbean have been trade and investments, energy and natural resources, and to gain diplomatic support for its one-China policy. The increasing geographical spread has exposed these countries to several external challenges and are, sometimes, overstretched in terms of their actual capacity vis-à-vis their commitments to their partners.

However, development cooperation has become an inevitable component of the emerging powers' economic diplomacy. These countries have been enhancing their economic diplomacy efforts in order to rise in the international system. Though the way they use aid is different from the traditional donors, the motivations behind their assistance have been quite similar. For all these countries that give development assistance, their national interest and foreign policy priorities have been driving their assistance. However, it is yet to be seen whether emerging powers could translate their development assistance into tangible outcomes. There is ample scope for future studies to explore the recipient perspectives and compare recipient data for greater understanding of the emerging powers' development assistance as well as the changing nature of SSC.

In SSC, the economic power of the states involved is more equally matched than what we see in asymmetric North-South relationships. The increased SSC is a welcome change. However, SSC is perceived to be "at best a complement, and not a replacement", for North-South cooperation (Nel 2010, 958). Moreover, the developing South has not yet attained a position where it can replace traditional aid. To replace traditional donors' foreign aid, the emerging powers have to go a long way in terms of increasing the volume and scope, setting up institutions, formulating clear-cut definitions and policies, and address the issue of effectiveness, impact assessment and evaluation. Even then, it is not about replacing the West, rather it is about expanding their development assistance to create their own unique place in the international system.

Brazil, China and India are showing their readiness to play the "leadership" role not only in their respective regions but also in the entire Global South. However, the binaries of Global North and Global South are increasingly getting blurred with the movement of actors in international aid architecture from Global South to North. For instance, Brazil's decision to join the OECD would place it in the club of the developed countries in the West. Therefore, the aggregate concept of Global North and Global South in international development is increasingly getting eroded. However, it is clear that they do not want to be branded in similar ways as the Western donors. It is very much evident from these three cases that these "emerging" powers very much harp on their existing identities even as they make a bid for great power status and systemic shifts.

Undoubtedly, emerging powers are carving out a niche for themselves in the international aid architecture. By emphasising on SSC, they are giving clear indications that the Global South is capable of creating enduring and equitable partnerships without the support of or interference from the Global North. An increasingly inward-looking North has given space for Global South to explore opportunities but it is also an indication that the South can no longer rely on North and have to ensure economic independence and self-sufficiency. The twenty-first century is for the emerging powers to discover their potential to change the system and institutions made by the Global North. And this could just be the beginning.

References

Bergamaschi, I. and Duran, Jimena. (2017), "Conclusion: South-South Cooperation Experiences Compared and the Way Forward" in Bergamaschi, I., Phoebe Moore and Arlene B. Tickner (eds.), *South-South Cooperation Beyond the Myths: Rising Donors, New Aid Practices?*, London: Palgrave Macmillan.

Bergamaschi, I. and Tickner, Arlene B. (2017), "Introduction: South-South Cooperation Beyond the Myths—A Critical Analysis" in Bergamaschi, I., Phoebe Moore and Arlene B. Tickner (eds.), *South-South Cooperation Beyond the Myths: Rising Donors, New Aid Practices?*, London: Palgrave Macmillan.

Chenoy A. et al. (2016), "Looking Across BRICS: An Emerging International Development Agenda?" in Gu, J., Alex Shankland and Anuradha Chenoy (eds.), *The BRICS in International Development*, London: Palgrave Macmillan.

Gu, J. et al. (2016), "Introduction: International Development, South-South Cooperation and the Rising Powers" in Gu, J., Alex Shankland and Anuradha Chenoy (eds.), *The BRICS in International Development*, London: Palgrave Macmillan.

ODI (2010), *Brazil: an Emerging Aid Player*, Briefing paper 64, Accessed at http://www.odi.org.uk/resources/download/5120.pdf.

O'Keefe, Joseph (2007), "Aid—From Consensus To Competition?", The Brookings Blum Roundtable, Accessed at http://www.brookings.edu/global/aspen/2007o%27keefe.pdf.

Manning, Richard. (2006), *Will "Emerging Donors" Change the Face of International Cooperation?*, ODI Lecture, Accessed at http://www.oecd.org/dataoecd/35/38/36417541.pdf.

Mawdsley, Emma. (2012), *From Recipients to Donors: Emerging Powers and the Changing Development Landscape*, London: Zed Books.
Modi, Renu (ed.). (2011), *South-South Cooperation: Africa on the Centre Stage*, London: Palgrave Macmillan.
Mthembu, P.M.S. (2018), *China and India's Development Cooperation in Africa: The Rise of Southern Powers*, London: Palgrave Macmillan.
Nel, Philip (2010), "Redistribution and Recognition: What Emerging Regional Powers Want?", *Review of International Studies*, 36(4): 951–974.

Index

C. Purushothaman, *Emerging Powers, Development Cooperation and South-South Relations*, International Political Economy Series, https://doi.org/10.1007/978-3-030-51537-9

The manufacturer's authorised representative in the EU is Springer Nature Customer Service Centre GmbH, Europaplatz 3, 69115 Heidelberg, Germany. If you have any concerns regarding our products, please contact ProductSafety@springernature.com

Printed and bound by CPI Group (UK) Ltd, Croydon, CR0 4YY
30/09/2026
02225456-0004